The Jane Gray

The Italian Prince and the Shipwreck That Forever Changed the History of Seattle

By Michelle Merritt

Cover image by Erminio Sella (1898) - courtesy of the Sella Foundation, Biella, Italy.

ISBN-10: 1482641712
ISBN-13: 978-1482641714
Discover other titles by this author at
www.michellemerritt.com

DEDICATION

This story is dedicated to all of the families and communities whose lives and histories were irreparably altered by the Jane Gray disaster:

The Lindsay Family

The City of Everett, Washington

The City of Seattle, Washington

The University of Washington

The Communities of Wapello, Iowa and Gambell, Alaska

San Francisco and S. P. Taylor State Park, California

Haller Lake Community, Washington

Long Island, New York

The Sella family and the community of Biella, Italy

And all of the others

Enormous gratitude is extended to the grandson of Edoardo Gaia and the entire Sella Family for their generous contribution of photographs and letters.

May this narrative offer some answers to the descendents of those who were impacted by the events surrounding the Jane Gray disaster.

TABLE OF CONTENTS

~~~
~~~

PROLOGUE

While researching family history, several documents referencing the sinking of the schooner Jane Gray captured my interest. Three members of the University of Washington football team were lost at sea, one of whom was a two-time team captain - and my great uncle. Within reading a few paragraphs of the various newspaper articles, I was hooked and went on the prowl for books that might detail the night of the fateful wreck. Although several made mention of the sinking of the Jane Gray, no complete account had ever been written.

The famous people packed on the decks of this ship made her sinking a significant event, not only in the history of Seattle, but in cities across the United States and in Italy. Major Edward S. Ingraham, the educator and mountaineer, was leading a team of sixteen prospectors funded by Prince Luigi, the Duke of Aosta. Clayton Packard, editor and publisher of the *Snohomish Eye* joined the Major's team as a mining expert. In addition to the three University of Washington students, Dr. Luther Lessey, of Seattle, five members of a prominent Italian family, one Austrian mountaineer, and four San Francisco paper company agents boarded the schooner that fateful day. James Blackwell, civil engineer, architect, and a former mayor of Bremerton, headed his own prospecting team of seven men. The rest were equally as well known in their respective hometowns.

By the spring of 1898, the Klondike Gold Rush had been in full swing for nearly a year. Swarms of ships were leaving Puget Sound for the Yukon and Alaska Territories daily. Because of the sheer number of vessels heading north, rarely a day passed without the report of a ship that was overdue, missing or wrecked.

As the tug Queen pulled the Jane Gray away from the dock at the end of Columbia Street in Seattle, the passengers and crew waved farewell to throngs of family, friends and admirers. The crowd cheered while the boys on deck yelled promises that they would return wealthy men.

Three days later, at two o'clock in the morning on Sunday, May 22, 1898, the eighty-two foot schooner sank outside of the Straits of Juan de Fuca, approximately ninety miles northwest of Cape Flattery. Twenty-seven survived. The remainder perished on that cold, moonless spring night. And to this day, the exact number and identities of some of lost remains in question.

The day that news of the tragedy reached Seattle, the entire city held its breath, awaiting word on who had survived.

Headlines spread across all of the major newspapers in the country, often eclipsing news of the Spanish-American War. From New York to San Francisco, conflicting accounts of the tragedy, as well as conflicting lists of those missing, dominated front pages. The passenger manifest went down with the ship. All that remained was an itemization of provisions that named the leaders of each party and the number of persons accompanying them, as well as the ticket stubs retained by the outfitting firm, and the words of those who lived to tell the tale.

In the aftermath of the wreck, some of the survivors and widows resorted to legal action in an attempt to gain compensation for their losses. The MacDougall and Southwick Company, along with their secretary, John Pacey, went to great lengths in order to limit their liability in the event that such a disaster might occur. A contentious battle ensued. Eighteen months after the sinking of the Jane Gray, the case came to a questionable conclusion.

Much of the court testimony and evidence remains on file in the National Archives at Seattle, Washington, and is printed, verbatim, in this narrative. Some quotes came from personal family records, some from the Sella Foundation in Biella, Italy, while others were taken from old newspaper accounts and the interviews with the survivors. (Spelling and grammar errors, as well as variations in the name of the schooner, have been retained in most quotes.) From these documents, a tale of hope, deceit and corruption emerges. It is left to the reader to decide whether or not justice prevailed.

As to the cause of the sinking, perhaps the words of Judge Cornelius H. Hanford remain the most accurate: "...probably the truth as to the cause of the disaster will never be known until the great ocean shall reveal the secrets buried in its depths."

MAPS

Images courtesy of the United States Geological Survey.

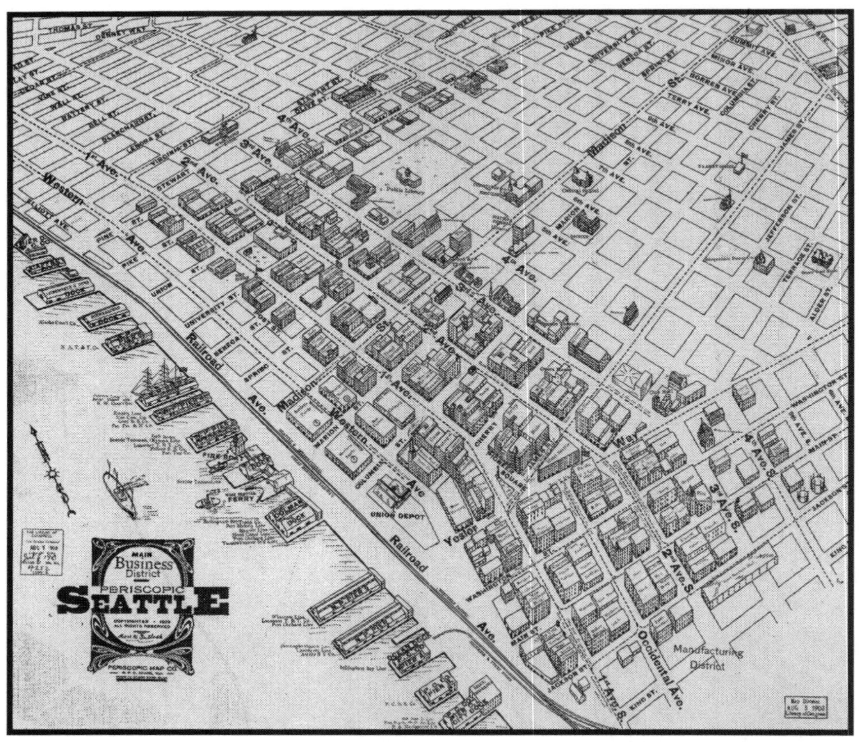

The City of Seattle, circa 1902.

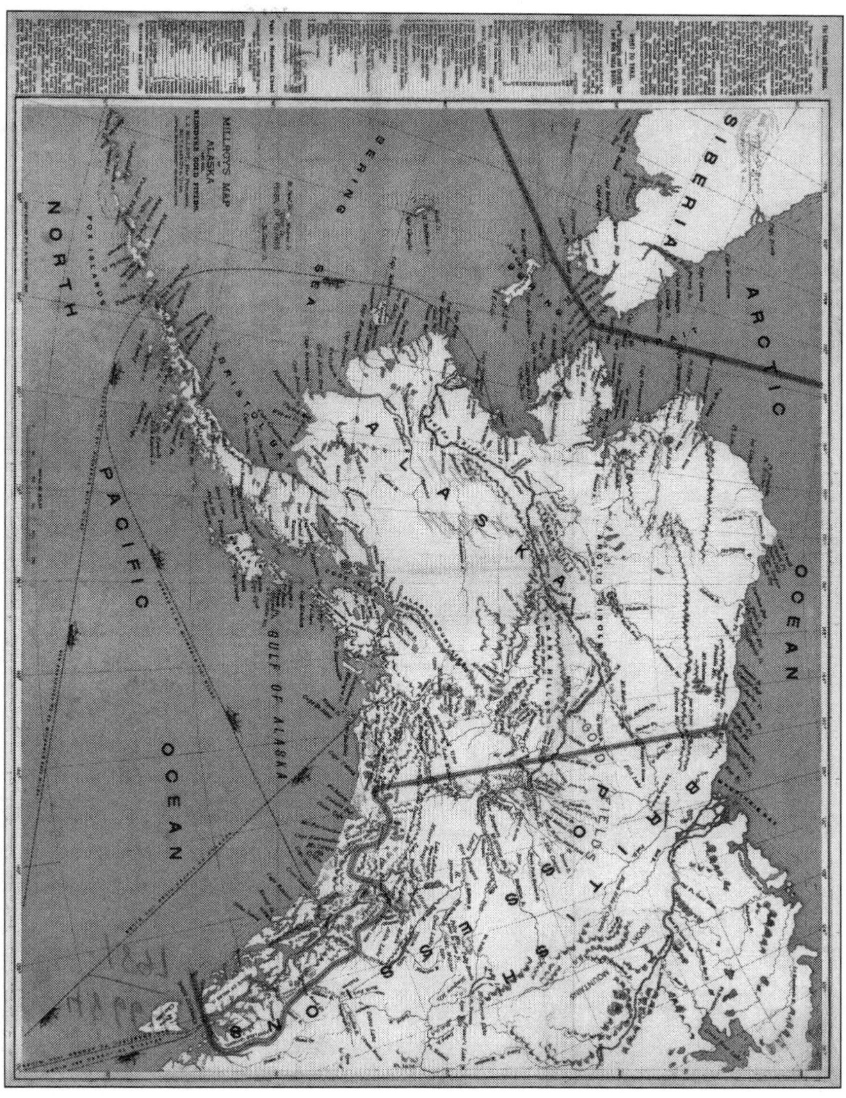

The Klondike run, complete with a recommended packing list for every argonaut.

CHAPTER 1 - THE PRINCE OF ADVENTURE

As the year 1896 was coming to a close, Prince Luigi of Italy, the Duke of Abruzzi, returned home from a nearly three-year voyage around the world and immediately began planning his next adventure. Prior to this lengthy maritime expedition, the young prince had developed a reputation as a skilled alpinist, climbing Mont Blanc and Monte Rosa, as well as other peaks in the Alps. The next mountains that he wished to conquer were in the Himalayan Range.

By early spring of 1897, events unfolded that caused a radical alteration in the plans of His Royal Highness. The plague broke out in the western provinces of India, directly in the path of the expedition's intended route to the Himalayan Mountains. In addition, severe famine was reported in the interior regions of the country. These combined crises heightened the risk that the prince's company would encounter thieves, marauders and the deathly ill in pursuit of this goal.

So, instead of a Himalayan ascent, the twenty-four year old prince made the decision to return to the North Pacific. Although he had read a great deal about Alaska, he had not had the opportunity to see or explore it. Once there, he and his chosen group of fellow mountaineers, photographers, and scientists would scale Mount St. Elias. With its summit only ten miles from the head of Icy Bay, this mountain is situated on the Alaska-Klondike border and is noted as the highest peak in the world in such close proximity to tidewater. The mountain is visible from over one hundred eighty miles at sea on a clear day. Although many had tried, no person was known to have made its summit before.

The expedition team's window of opportunity lay in the months when the waters of Icy Bay thawed. With this knowledge, Prince Luigi feverishly set about making plans to arrive at the headwaters by May of that year. In addition to other members of the Italian Alpine Club, the group included famed photographer Vittorio Sella and the mountaineering scientist, Fillipo de Fillipi. From Italy, the group of mountaineers would travel to England and assemble most of their gear before crossing the Atlantic to New York, then travel by train to San Francisco and on to Seattle.

Through mutually acquainted alpine enthusiasts in the United States, Major Edward S. Ingraham of Seattle was chosen to aid in the ascent. Charged with assembling hearty men to carry the Royal party's gear up the Arctic mountainside, the Major brought together a unique group who could hardly have been found in any other country. Four were University of Washington students; four were sailors, one of whom was a Swede, another an Italian, one a prospector, and one a poet born in Germany who had earned his living by teaching the classics and becoming a sailor. In addition to the Major, these other men were C. L. Andrews, Alexander Beno, F. Fiorini, Carl E. Morford, Ralph E. Nichols, Elin Ostberg, Victor Schmid, Conrad Schmid, W. Steele, and C. W. Thornton.

Carl Morford, Ralph Nichols, and Victor and Conrad Schmid were all members of the University of Washington football team. Clarence Andrews worked as a secretary at Ingraham's printing business in downtown Seattle and would later become a relatively famous photographer in his own right.

Under the Major's efficient guidance, these porters repeatedly traversed the route up Mount St. Elias, bringing supplies to the Royal expedition in relay fashion. For the entire month of July 1897, the men worked up and down the steep, icy slopes, alternately pushing laden sledges from camp to camp, often packing goods on their backs. At night they pitched canvas tents and fell into sleeping bags on the snow-covered ground. Their final camp was at 12,000 feet. By the time they heard the call from Fillipi that the prince had reached the summit at 18,000 feet, cheerful shouts rang across the melting snowfields. Their mission had been accomplished.

The ten-day trip off the mountain seemed anything but work. It was a gleeful descent, resembling a sledding party as the boys merrily ran over the ice fields. Sledges crashed into newly formed cracks in the ice as the porters half-heartedly attempted to slow the speed of their wooden barges. Righting the tipped cargo back onto the runners, the crew led the Prince's party down a path that the summer thaw had rendered barely recognizable except to the porters who had witnessed the change.

Prince Luigi's successful expedition made him the first documented person to summit Mount St. Elias. Nearly fifty years would pass before it was done again.

When the mountaineers made sight of the sails of their ship off of Manby Point, Alaska on August 10, 1897, the Italians and Major Ingraham's group had been out of communication with the world for nearly six weeks.

The following day, the royal party returned to the ship. The porters and all of their gear remained on shore where

Ingraham's team spent the last two nights in tents. By the morning of their departure from Manby Point, the bloodthirsty mosquitoes had rendered the porters' faces nearly unrecognizable. Sailing from Yakutat to Sitka, the group enjoyed a welcome four-day respite in spite of being "packed like herrings" in their tiny berths on board the schooner Aggie. After the spartan existence of their arduous trek, even the wealthy Italians didn't mind the close quarters.

On August 27, 1897, the *Los Angeles Daily Herald* reported on the successful expedition:

"LUIGI IS SUCCESSFUL

The Italian Party Reached the Summit of Mount St. Elias.

Seattle, Aug. 27.—A special to the Post-Intelligencer from Nanaimo, B. C., says: Prince Luigi, of Savoy, and party of Italians reached the summit of Mount St. Elias, July 31, at 12 o'clock noon. The altitude indicated by the mercurial barometer is 18,100 feet. It was the most successful expedition ever undertaken. The party was 51 days on the snow and ice without sickness or accident. The Italians are returning on the Topeka.

The Aggie left Sitka with the Seattle packers aboard August 20.

The Bryant party abandoned the trip at the foot of Newton glacier on account of the sickness of Packer Hix. Major E. S. Ingraham, of Seattle, is on the Topeka. The Luigi party was 41 days ascending the mountain and 10 days descending it.

Benefits of the Expedition.

Seattle, Aug. 27.—A Victoria special to the Post-Intelligencer says: The expedition has determined two facts of prime importance to the scientific world. It has fixed once for all the altitude of Mount St. Elias at 18,100 feet. The figures are subject only to such slight correction as may change the total 30 or 40 feet either way.

The expedition has also answered definitely and in the negative the question so long asked by scientists as to whether or not St. Elias was not at one time a great volcano. There is not the slightest indication of volcanic action anywhere. The mountain, like its neighbors, appears to have been raised in the ocean, tangible evidence of its cradling in the deep being found in many fossil shells, sandstone and beds of pebbles.

A new glacier was discovered on the eminence of the mountain between the August mountains and Great Logan. It takes its course apparently to the sea, and was named after Prince Columbo. This was the only geographical christening during the trip.

The Russell expedition landed at the head of Yucat bay, quite a distance from the point at which Luigi made his debarkation. The route was absolutely unknown. Advancing up the glaciers and moraines took 39 days, or until July 4, which day the prince declared a general holiday. They had then risen no more than 8,000 feet, in covering a tramp of 50 miles, but so difficult and rough had been the journey that all were quite ready for 24 hours' rest. The Americans in the party raised the Stars and Stripes over the camp in the great hills, and Prince Luigi and his party cheered again and again in honor of the flag.

At Pinnacle pass was found the first evidence of Mr. Russell's expedition in 1891, in the shape of a tent bottom and a single fork. Finally, the foot of the divide connecting

Mount St. Elias and Mount Newton was reached, with a supply of provisions to last 12 days.

At 1 o'clock on the morning of July 31 they commenced the ascent of the great mountain. For 11 hours the upward climb was made, and exactly five minutes before 12 o'clock the summit of St. Elias was beneath the feet of the explorers. The hour upon the summit was employed in planting the flagstaff, from which the Italian flag was given to the wind."

After returning from the expedition, Carl W. Thornton, one of the American porters, would write for *Overland Monthly* and *Out West Magazine*, telling of his experiences on the mountain "which so many had declared could not be scaled." He expressed admiration for Professor Israel C. Russell, "that indefatigable explorer and scientist," who had made two unsuccessful attempts, at the expense of six lives, while attributing the success of their own expedition to the fact that they had a "greater number of men to do the extremely fatiguing work, which at length wore out" a smaller party.

Interestingly, Professor Russell, of the University of Michigan, was also one of the men who recommended Major Ingraham to Prince Luigi.

While Ingraham and the Prince's party were still ascending the icy slopes of Mount St. Elias, the steamship Portland arrived in Seattle. She carried sixty-two prospectors and an estimated ton of gold from the banks of the Klondike River. Word announcing the ship's arrival at Schwabacher Warf on July 17, 1897, brought more than five thousand people to the waterfront where the newly rich passengers were greeted by enormous fanfare. Until they stepped onto the decks of the Aggie, the mountaineering team was oblivious to the fact that the Alaska gold rush had become a raging inferno.

Once the royal party passed through the Straits of Juan de Fuca and into Puget Sound, the scene of less than three months prior was vastly different. Placid waters were now churning with steamships and sailing vessels leaving for Alaska. Almost any wreck that could be patched together was resurrected for the voyage to the land of gold. New shops catering to prospectors had sprung up all over the waterfront. Fifteen hundred people had departed Seattle for the gold fields within ten days of the arrival of the Portland at the Schwabacher dock.

On August 28, 1897, Prince Luigi, Vittorio Sella, and Filipo di Fillipi bade farewell to Seattle and returned to Italy in the midst of the chaos, leaving behind a group of new friends. Ingraham respected the young Prince's intelligence and spirit of adventure, while the entire royal party had come to view their American team of porters as family. Fillipi wrote of the group "Major Ingraham, a tall, lean man, about forty years of age, of robust constitution, and great force of character, who was in charge of them—proved of the utmost service to the expedition. Indeed, his active and intelligent efforts, together with the hearty cooperation of his band, had no small share in its success." The feeling of brotherhood between the Italians and Americans was mutual. From this day forward, their lives would become intertwined.

CHAPTER 2 - MAJOR INGRAHAM

Photo courtesy of the Tacoma Public Library.

Well before Prince Luigi's expedition to Mount St. Elias, Edward Ingraham had achieved a life of legendary proportions. Ten years prior, in 1887, Ingraham was one of a party of mountaineers who climbed the northeast side of Mount Rainier, reaching the 13,800-foot level. The following year, in 1888, he climbed the mountain again, this time making the summit with John Muir, Daniel Bass, Norman Booth, N. Loomis, Charles Vancouver Piper, Philemon B. Van Trump, and Arthur Churchill Warner. In 1894, another ascent included three women, the first females to attempt the summit since Fay Fuller's historic 1890 climb. That same year, when a dispute arose between Tacoma and her rival city to the north as to whether Mount Rainier had actually erupted, Ingraham made a winter ascent with reporters and photographers from the *Seattle Post-Intelligencer*. On Christmas day, the party sent homing pigeons to the home of Fred Meeker in Puyallup, confirming that Tacoma residents had indeed experienced an earthquake - and yes, the mountain had erupted. By the time he was recommended for the Royal expedition to St. Elias, Major Ingraham had already scaled Mount Rainer on over a half a dozen occasions.

Although mountaineering was undeniably one of Ingraham's great passions, it did not define him. The son of an East Coast ship captain, his love of the mountains, the sea, adventure, and learning were formed at a very young age. He was raised in a home that believed in equality for all. His father was an early abolitionist who fought for the end of slavery before the onset of the Civil War. With the strong work ethic instilled by his family, Edward apprenticed in the printing trade while attending college in Maine. He rapidly became a well-regarded teacher after completing his studies. In August of 1875, the twenty-three year old Ingraham came west to visit the older half-brother whom he had never met. Within ten days of his arrival in Seattle, he was hired as principal at the Central School on Third and Madison. Ingraham was named the first superintendent of Seattle schools in 1881, presiding over the city's first high school graduation of a class of twelve in 1886.

In 1887, certain events caused Ingraham to resign as superintendent and return to his first vocation, publishing. He eventually incorporated with James Calvert and formed the Calvert Company, doing business in the Bailey Building at 2109 Second Avenue. The company published the *Seattle Guide* (a monthly directory), printed books and stationary, while at the same time vending school supplies from the front of the store.

During the 1886 anti-Chinese riots in Seattle, Ingraham became part of the Home Guards, an organization of loyal citizens that avowed "to uphold the Constitution, laws, and treaties of the United States at all hazards." While serving in the unit, he was promoted from private to corporal and rapidly rose to the rank of major, then lieutenant colonel. Because of the number of men using the title of colonel, Ingraham preferred to retain the title of major, and from that time forward, "Major" was the name that he was most often known by.

Edward's friends were many, his ties to the University of Washington and education deep. Edmond Meany, simultaneously school registrar, professor, and secretary to the board of regents at the University, shared Ingraham's passion for the mountains, education and history. The two of them also had mutual interests within the publishing world, Edmond being a former editor of the *Seattle Post-Intelligencer*.

Mr. and Mrs. Dexter Horton, owners of the first bank in the city of Seattle (the predecessor to SeaFirst National Bank and the Bank of America), were witnesses at Edward's marriage to Myra Carr.

On three occasions Ingraham had scaled Mount Rainier with Dr. Luther Lessey, the prominent Seattle dentist.

And he could always count on Clayton Packard, owner and editor of the *Snohomish Eye*, whether in a street brawl, a mining camp, or on the battlefields of newsprint.

The ascent of Mount St. Elias had been an international success that left Edward Ingraham anxious to begin another venture in Alaska. So, in the fall of 1897, his plan solidified. He would not only try his hand at gold mining, with the backing of Prince Luigi, he would strike it rich.

CHAPTER 3 - THE MISSIONARIES OF ST. LAWRENCE ISLAND

Recruited by Professor Sheldon Jackson, Vene Gambell and his young wife, Nellie, came to St. Lawrence Island in the summer of 1894. Hired as a teacher under the federal program established to educate the natives of Alaska, Reverend Gambell, upon accepting the post, promised Dr. Jackson that he would also fulfill the role of Presbyterian Minister, teaching Christian values to the people of the villages.

Drawn by the prospect of running a school free from the strict bureaucracy that was often found in the States, the couple left their home and families in Wapello, Iowa to board the brig Meyer in Seattle. The two thousand mile journey across the northern waters of the Pacific Ocean brought them to the village of Chibuchack, at the northernmost point of St. Lawrence Island, where Dr. Jackson had acquired a one-room structure that had been built years before for use as a church. Vene and Nellie were able to quickly ready their new home, adding sleeping quarters onto the church before the onslaught of the Arctic winter. They opened the doors to their school in November of 1894.

Life on St. Lawrence Island was not easy. However, Vene viewed his new situation as an opportunity to do things his own way. Writing home in August of 1895, he shared his thoughts on the advantages of educating in the remote outpost: "I could teach just as I wanted to or as I thought was right without fear of some patron under the influence of alcohol making complaints about the way some room was conducted, or how his child was ill treated. I have no fear of riff-raff being worked to vote some discontented man into the schoolboard, etc., etc. You see every 'cloud' has a silver lining."

During their years in the village, the Gambell home and school became a gathering place for the natives - as many as a hundred adults and children sometimes crowded the main room of the cabin.

Captain Healy of the revenue cutter Bear was often the only visitor outside of villagers that the Gambells would have in a year. Charged with patrolling the Alaskan waters, the captain and his crew served as supply ship, hospital, and the sole law enforcement agency in the Arctic. Vene and Nellie looked forward to the thaw that would allow the ship through the icepack, not only for fresh vegetables and flour, but also for the company of the crew, mail, and news from the outside world.

1896 was a particularly harsh year for the indigenous people of St. Lawrence Island. Although Captain Healy, with the financial support of Sheldon Jackson and the women of the Presbyterian Church, had begun introducing a Siberian reindeer population to Alaska, the benefit had not yet reached Vene's community. The climate and rocky landscape of the island made the cultivation of crops impossible. Traditional food supplies had been significantly diminished by the white whalers and seal hunters, forcing the Yupik population to subsist on less than half of their normal rations. In an effort to help his neighbors, Vene found himself trading for things he had no need of: "We have emptied seven sacks of flour in the last four weeks. We have had mittens, boots, etc. made that we didn't need. One little boy brought us a string of 25-30 toys made of walrus teeth. He wanted flour. We have given the children beans for dinner when they were very hungry. We have given the men and the boys flour for shoveling when we didn't need snow shoveled."

Vene lamented the practices of the white traders who came to the village, supplying the natives with alcohol and tobacco or trading unfairly. Of the effect of their visits, he said, "The natives of all ages and sexes use tobacco except some of the boys whom I have got to leave it alone. They get a bottle of whiskey from the sailors sometimes or a gallon can of alcohol from Siberia but Healy stopped the Captains trading it. Some captains give them good trade and some don't."

After nearly three years on St. Lawrence Island, Vene and Nellie Gambell welcomed their first child into the world. On April 13, 1897, little Margaret was born without the help of a physician. The birth of a ten pound baby made Nellie's recovery a difficult one.

Mrs. Gambell wrote home in early September 1897: "Mr. Gambell has had nearly all the housework to do since before Christmas. I am not sick in bed but cannot be on my feet much. Dr. Gall the doctor on 'The Bear' said I would have to have an operation performed before I would be well again. We are looking for 'The Bear' any hour now, have everything packed that can be until she is in sight. If there is any one to help me on the way down, Mr. Gambell will stay here. We are very sorry we have to leave our work now. Yahgonga, a little girl that has helped us some cried the other day when we told her 'The Bear' might come in a day or two."

Two weeks after Nellie wrote her letter, the cutter had not yet arrived at St. Lawrence Island and Vene had grown anxious: "'The Bear' is so long over-due that we are afraid something has happened to her or she has decided at St. Michaels to go south and won't come this way, so we have given up expecting to go home, but we do hope to see a steamer to send mail down on."

The Reverend Gambell proved himself a most admirable man, teaching school, taking care of his home and parishioners while Nellie could do little of that. His letter home continued with the nearest he ever made to a complaint: "I have developed into a pretty good cook. I can make good yeast bread, it is easy to make a good cake but I don't like to make pies though Mrs. Gambell says I made the best mince pies she ever ate and I don't put brandy in them either. I wouldn't mind the cooking if it wasn't for all the other work I have to do. My! But I am getting tired of canned stuff. It's 'what shall we have for dinner.' It's almost like the army song 'Beans for breakfast, etc.' to the tune the old cow died on. How I would like a rest or vacation."

Shortly after penning this letter on September 19, 1897, the cutter Bear arrived at St. Lawrence Island. With their beautiful five month-old baby Margaret, the Gambell family locked the door to their home, said goodbye to the natives whom they had come to know so intimately, and loaded their belongings onto the ship. They were ready for a welcome vacation with family in Washington and in Iowa.

Gambell family photos courtesy of the Winfield, Iowa Historical Society.

CHAPTER 4 - THE UNIVERSITY HERO

Born of two immigrants, John James "Jack" Lindsay's early life was tailored from the tough cloth of his parents. His father, Hugh, served four years in the 23rd Regiment of the Wisconsin Infantry and survived the Civil War after sustaining gunshot wounds. While Hugh was fighting in the war, Jack's mother, Kezia, taught school in Caledonia, Wisconsin. She later drove a covered wagon cross-country to Norton and Rock Branch, Kansas, where they built and operated flourmills. After Kansas, the family moved on to Rapid City, South Dakota, again building a mill. Hugh was often absent, prospecting in the Black Hills or working his claims in Montana and Idaho. While he was away, Kezia and her oldest son had to defend the family farm and property from the occasional Indian raid. By the time a fifteen year-old Jack moved to Washington State, he was a young man of tempered steel.

The Summit Hotel, 1892.

Ever the entrepreneurs, reports of John D. Rockefeller's interests in the new city of Everett brought Jack's parents west, where they invested the money from the sale of their flourmill in a tract of unimproved land. After months of clearing towering evergreens, pulling stumps, and leveling a hilltop above the waterfront, construction was completed in the spring of 1892. Guests began arriving at the Summit Hotel at Pacific and Oakes while the landscape surrounding the three and a half story structure still resembled a war zone.

While the hotel struggled through the depression of 1893, Hugh Lindsay continued working at his true passion, staking mining claims in the Cascade Mountains, on the eastern fringe of Snohomish County near Darrington. Jack's father was seldom home and often returned to other mining and property ventures in Montana and South Dakota, leaving Kezia and his oldest son to tend to their Washington business.

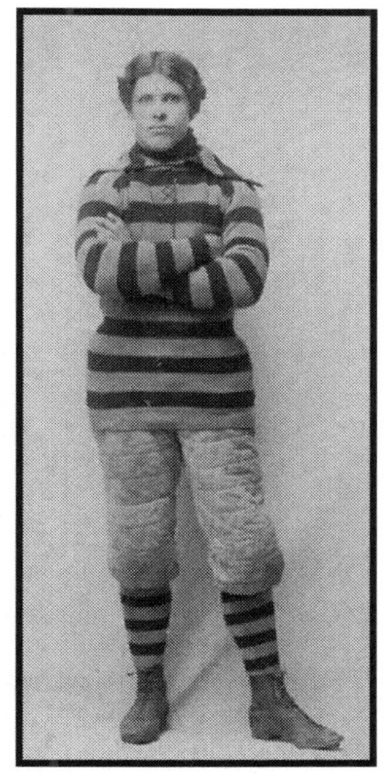

In spite of the weight of family obligations that included keeping an eye on four younger siblings, Johnnie Lindsay participated in organized and unorganized sports. During at least one rugby game between Everett and Snohomish, Everett lost 10-0 in sleet and snow. Regardless of the loss, the local paper wrote of Jack: "In the group around the ball at the time were Jack Lindsay, fresh from Wounded Knee country who had never seen either a football or baseball before." The senior Lindsay boy presented the class shoes, gave the salutatory and the oration at his Everett High School graduation, where he was one of the class of five.

Jack Lindsay roared into the University of Washington as a freshman in the fall of 1895 - the first year that classes were held at the new campus, where the board and regents had for years rallied "to remove it to a distance from the excitements and temptations incident to city life and its environments." A graduate and star athlete at Everett High School, his career at the University would surpass all prior praise.

Although the Lindsay's owned a hotel, a partner had over-expanded the property, causing financial strain on the family. In addition, the purchaser of their South Dakota lands was behind on his payments and in default on the contract. Even if that had not been the case, the Scotsman in Hugh likely would not have paid for his son's education.

Thus, college was not a free ride for Jack. And, while the University of Washington did not charge tuition to in-state residents, there were many other expenses to consider. A twenty-six mile ride (one-way) from Everett was impossible and the university did not have dorms yet. Room and board at a private Seattle home ran between $15 and $25 per month. Jack declared his major in chemistry and the lab required a $10 deposit upon enrollment. Books were an additional expense. With the time needed to maintain above-average grades, participate in athletics and school government, Jack would be fortunate if he were able to earn $40 a month. One of his first jobs was an early morning route delivering papers for the *Seattle Post-Intelligencer*. Packing bundles of print through the mud-mired, rutted hills of the city became his daily workout, an exercise that readied him for the field of sports and garnered him many valuable acquaintances.

1895 was a record year for the University of Washington football team. Ralph Nichols, a former team captain, served as coach. Martin Harrais was team captain that year, with Jack Lindsay serving as his unofficial co-captain. The season opened with a 12-0 win over the Seattle Athletic club on October 19th. A week later, the Husky boys (at the time, the team had not yet adopted that mascot and was most often referred to as the "purple and gold") tied in an ugly game against the same club. The next two wins were against Vashon College, 44-0 and 34-0. In the final season game, Clarence Larson carried a 40-yard home run and Seattle declared victory over Tacoma with an 8-4 win on Thanksgiving Day. In the slimy mud-filled fields of Pacific Northwest football, the boys of the University of Washington had finished their first undefeated season.

The years 1896 and 1897 were not as victorious in Husky football. However, Jack Lindsay had earned the confidence of his teammates and was chosen team captain both seasons. He remained a staunch character on and off the field, scoring every single touchdown during those two years. His first season as football captain also found him leading the track team, earning a state record in the fifty-yard dash. With the assistance of the history professor, Edmond Meany, he and several other students chartered the first fraternity at the University, Sigma Nu Gamma Chi, opening a house on the Old University Campus. John J. Lindsay, Arthur P. Calhoun, John B. McManus, Robert W. Abrams, George L. Andrews, and Herbert Ostrom were all founding members. Professor Meany was their brother in the faculty. Jack and many of his friends were legends in the making.

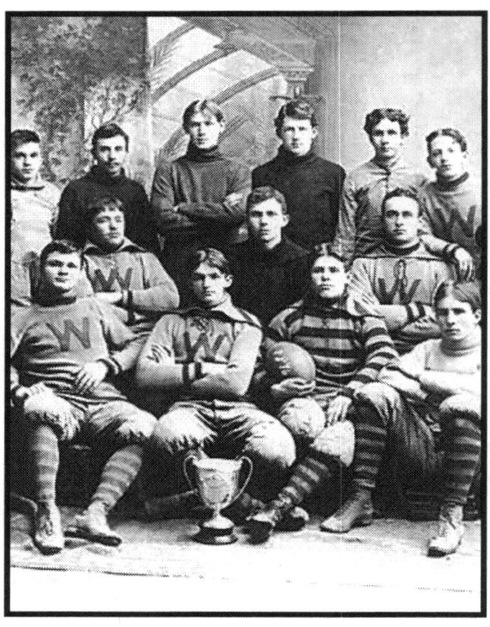

Jack Lindsay, holding the football, Victor and Conrad Schmid, center back row, 1896. Photos courtesy of the Lindsay/Diamond family collection.

Johnnie, as his buddies sometimes called him, had bigger dreams than an education at the University of Washington could fulfill. He wanted an Ivy League degree. A more prestigious college, with more prestigious connections, could pave the way for his aspirations. Perhaps, with a degree in chemistry, he could join the ranks of scientific pioneers such as Thomas Edison; or Joseph John Thomson, who had recently identified sub-atomic particles; or Marie Curie, who had made the news for her work in physics. In order to accomplish this goal, he needed more money than could possibly be earned by working at the newspaper and doing odd jobs around the city.

Ending the '97 season with a 0-16 loss at Oregon State on December 4th, Jack Lindsay finished classes at the University of Washington and readied himself for a year in the North. Ralph Nichols (who Stanford University's student manager, Herbert Hoover, had tried to poach with the offer of a free ride at the competing school), Carl Morford, and Victor and Conrad Schmid - all football players - had accompanied Major Ingraham and Prince Luigi on the ascent of Mount St. Elias.

From the reports of former classmates, gold mining was certain to provide him with the capital needed for his education. Most of the winning Husky team of 1895 was already in Alaska making their fortunes. Arthur Calhoun had gone to the Klondike before the arrival of the Portland. His brother, "Old Horse" Calhoun, the 96-97 full back, had recently joined him. Arthur Dunham, the varsity guard, had a "lay" on Bonanza Creek. Martin Harrais, the 1895 team captain who held down the position of center for four years, was working a claim at Bonanza Creek, as well as other stakes in the interior of Alaska. Norm and Bob Abrams, Clime and Arthur Hill, Arthur Crook - the list of Jack's prospecting friends was endless. Many had panned out more money in one break from studies than he had earned in an entire year of labors in the city. Some had already returned to Seattle, suddenly wealthy men, packing satchels of gold.

Two of his classmates, Victor and Conrad Schmid, were well known to Major Ingraham and had been selected for the spring expedition to Kotzebue Sound. Since all of the positions on the Major's team had been filled, Jack signed up with other expeditions. For a variety of reason, perhaps due to a lack of funds or the loss of nerve, every one of them broke up right before getting started. After the last letdown, Hugh Lindsay finally agreed to accompany his son to Alaska. But while Jack and his father were making arrangements to go north, Major Ingraham had a sudden opening. Someone had backed out at the last minute and there was now a spot for Jack. Accepting the offer, he was over the moon with excitement. Great things were about to happen.

CHAPTER 5 – CLAYTON PACKARD

Clayton Packard (holding bicycle), circa 1902. Photo courtesy of the Everett Public Library.

For Major Ingraham, having Clayton Packard on his team was a foregone conclusion. A prospector who had claims all over the country, Packard was considered the authority on gold and silver ore extraction, construction, excavation, and operation of large mines. In 1897, Packard Mining Company was developing the Nemo Mine, a 150-foot tunnel dug into the canyons above Monte Cristo in Snohomish County, Washington. At the same time, the company employed ten men at another tunnel, the O. & B. Mine, while excavating a third shaft at the Sydney Mine.

Although Clayton had other stakes in Colorado, a large number of Packard Mining Company's claims were located on the eastern edge of Snohomish County, where the Cascade Mountains soar from the forest floor to craggy vertical peaks and the steep canyon walls make glimpses of sunlight a rarity below the crests. Clayton was accustomed to packing a side arm while trekking the ridges, using the occasional mountain goat as his target. This "shooting iron" projected a foot below the tails of his coat. With his trusty firearm he could pick a gnat off a mule's ass from more than a city block away.

One of Clayton's other ventures was the *Snohomish Eye*. Originally started because of the need to publish timber and mining claim notices within the county, the newspaper did well, expanding from a four-column, four-page weekly to five columns, with additional pages, published three times a week. Packard became so well respected as a journalist that his articles were frequently reprinted in other papers around the country. It was later said of Clayton and his publication, " During all of its years in existence the Eye was a valiant advocate of clean politics, and very outspoken in its condemnation of corruption in public officials."

Packard was as fast on his feet as he was in thought. Because of his small stature, he usually appeared to be in a rush. What he lacked in height he compensated for in a myriad of other traits. Early on in his journalism career in Snohomish County, he nearly drowned attempting to save a friend and a coworker who had fallen through the ice while skating on a nearby lake. In the dim evening light, the seventeen year-old Packard slithered across the ice on his belly, extending tree branches to the outstretched arms of his buddies. A mere ten feet from reaching them, the fragile surface began to crack and he was forced to retreat. Recognizing that they would be of no assistance dead, he and another survivor ran the mile back to Snohomish for help. Although they returned to the scene of the accident too late to save the young men, Clayton's determination and reliability in a crisis were evident even then.

At the time, Clayton was working for the *Northern Star* newspaper. Eldridge Morse, the owner of the publication, was a man of unusual scientific and literary knowledge - likely even more unusual in an infantile community such as Snohomish was in 1876. Although Clayton's father, like Ingraham's, was an early abolitionist and advocate of equal rights, Mr. Morse further incubated and fostered the ideas of equality, logic, and rational thought in his reporters. In this environment, Packard's intellect grew to adulthood.

Freedom of religion in the United States of America was still a wobbling toddler in the 1800's. In some ways, it was a time of religious radicalism. Experimentation in old and new philosophies hatched scams for channeling the dead, new religions, and a whole host of other "new age" ideas. Freedom of religion had also been embraced by those of scientific mind - with the relatively new concept - freedom FROM religion. Naturalism, the predecessor to humanism and atheism, gave birth to the "free thought" movement. Following the lead of scientific minds, Clayton adopted this philosophy.

Among fellow "free thinkers," Clayton Packard counted Susan B. Anthony, Thomas A. Edison, Helen Gardener, Horace Greeley, Elizabeth Cady Stanton and a long list of others who were staunch believers before him. The essence of the "free thought" movement was to rid the human mind of beliefs instilled by some of the more absurd teachings of the Bible and other theological doctrines that there was scant evidence to support. They believed that opinions should be based on facts, scientific inquiry, and logic, instead of dogma and religion. Free thinkers were the early adopters of equality for men and women of all races and persuasions. They also believed that every man and woman should hold themselves accountable for their lot in life, provided that the rights afforded them by the Constitution of the United States of America were upheld and enforced. In the logical minds of free thinkers, "God's will" was not a legitimate explanation for good fortune or for misfortune. God didn't have anything to do with fortune.

In 1882, some time after Eldridge Morse closed down the *Northern Star*, "Clayt," as he was widely known, launched the newspaper *Snohomish Eye*. One of his partners, George E. Macdonald, would eventually write of his years at the journal with Clayton: "It was the paper the old residents took and swore by; and it deserved their confidence. No man in the county had a better reputation for honesty and squareness than Packard. His probity was unimpeachable."

Tales of Clayton Packard's exploits were legendary. "God dam it" was likely to precede the explanation of any character he thought unsavory or situation he thought lacked rationale. Some events were even absurd enough to suggest that he might have been a drunkard. However, he was not. In fact he was far from it, reportedly never smoking tobacco or drinking alcohol of any kind. Once, in a successful effort to rid Snohomish of a particularly disdained priest, whom even the local Catholic mothers were eager to be done with, Clayton organized (or at least encouraged) his removal through a tarring and feathering conducted by the priest's very own parishioners. One can only imagine what this priest's offences against the community were. Whatever the cause, women and men gathered goose down from a furniture store in Snohomish and within three days of the event, the priest had high-tailed it for California where he was retained by the

Catholic Church but never returned to the State of Washington.

From 1882 to 1897, Clayton owned and operated the *Snohomish Eye*. During those years, he married the sixteen year-old Alice Reeve, fathered three sons, established two mining companies, worked his claims in multiple states, tormented local politicians, and got divorced - all before his thirty-seventh birthday.

By late 1897, a combination of events caused Packard to make a go at the Alaska gold fields. Alice had remarried and was caring for the boys. Major Ingraham had returned from the overwhelmingly successful expedition to Mount St. Elias and Prince Luigi had already committed to funding a gold-prospecting venture to Kotzebue Sound. Then, in November of that year, a massive slide broke off rail transportation to Packard's mining operations in Monte Cristo, where profitability had always been somewhat touch and go. So, after fifteen and a half years of operating the *Snohomish Eye*, he closed down the publication. With the knowledge that Ingraham's expedition would span two or three years, and the hopes of finally striking it rich, Clayt signed on as the Major's mining expert.

CHAPTER 6 - JOHN PACEY

Initially, John Pacey may have been merely a pawn to John MacDougall and the scrooge, Henry Southwick. Perhaps he had been lured to this new company, in a new city, with promises of fantastic wages. Perhaps he found himself in a situation that once embroiled in, he could find no practical escape from - for there is certainly a fine line between those who compromise their principals under the pressure of financial obligations and those who refuse to. Eventually, John became the owner of several sailing schooners transporting prospectors to the gold rush, and a willing participant in the machinations of MacDougall and Southwick.

In January of 1886, a twenty-four year old Pacey left his job as a postal clerk in Wichita, Kansas to try his hand at homesteading in Hamilton County. The blizzards of the Kansas plains were apparently not something that he had previously considered as a regular occurrence in the life of a homesteader, for less than a year elapsed before he accepted a job as the bookkeeper at Kansas National Bank, returning to Wichita, his adopted hometown. On January 19th, 1886, the *Wichita Daily Eagle* reported:

"Mr. John O. Pacey, who left his position a couple of months since to try the blizzards of a homesteader's life in Hamilton county, returned yesterday in response to a telegram to take a position in the Kansas National bank. Mr. Pacey is a very competent accountant, probably one of the finest in the city."

By December of 1886, John was managing the bank clearinghouse. Well-known, liked and respected, he continued in that capacity until July of 1892, when he accepted a position in Seattle. The townspeople and neighbors were sad to see him leave.

Six years in the clearinghouse taught the thirty year-old Pacey much about the world of finance. He became intimately familiar with the float - the time between a check being written and the time when the funds would be deducted from the account it was written on. Bundles of checks arrived daily from each bank. There, the clearinghouse clerks sorted the checks by the names of the banks they were drawn on, tallying each stack at the end of the day. It was the most efficient way for these institutions to settle their accounts with each other. From the clearinghouses, checks went to their respective banks and funds would then be deducted for the individual accounts that the items were drawn on. All of these paper financial instruments were transported across the country by train, boat, wagon, and horseback. This meant that it could take a week or two, sometimes longer, for a check to reach the bank account that it was to be deducted from.

Check kiting, or floating, was the ponzi scheme of the pre-electronic age. It was not uncommon for a person with accounts geographically distant from each other to write progressively larger checks and deposit them into other accounts to inflate their financial position. An elaborate scheme could go on undetected for years. While illegal, many savvy business people used the float. Others just used it - regardless of the potential legal consequences. Kiting was, and still is, fraud and a felony.

Pacey was an expert at identifying banking infractions. In the retail world, he would use this expertise in other ways.

After leaving Kansas, John arrived in Seattle and went to work for the MacDougall and Southwick Company as their secretary. He soon became a board member of the corporation. On the 11th day of December 1895, one James L. Schultz, a silent partner at MacDougall and Southwick, signed Pacey's United States Naturalization papers in Seattle. At the age of thirty-four, John was no longer a Canadian citizen. And he could now legally own property, including ships sailing under the flag of the United States.

As gold rush fever blew into the Puget Sound in 1897, the company began chartering boats, eventually purchasing several with Pacey holding the title and the legal liability for these vessels. He rented his home and had no other assets on paper, making him the ideal owner in a time when ships sank, capsized, or went missing on a daily basis.

Schooners had become an economical and profitable means of transporting miners north to Alaska and the Klondike. With the only fuel costs being those needed to heat their interior, converted whalers and sealing vessels were fast, staunch and cheap. Even if they were wrecked in a storm, a schooner was often salvageable.

John Pacey acquired one of these salvaged ships, the schooner General Siglin, in the summer of 1897. Her mast had been torn off and hull filled with water in a storm near Nome. Captain Crockett, on board the schooner Willard Ainsworth, was one of the first to sight the wreck. The body of a man was visible strapped to her stern, but weather conditions were such that they could not inspect the vessel nor could they get close enough to search for survivors

When the General Siglin was later towed to Sitka and beached, the body of a little boy and $2000 were still in her hold. The corpse strapped to her stern was identified as the mate. Regardless of the fact that everyone on board died and the boat might be cursed with "sailor's superstition," John was not dissuaded from purchasing the schooner. Once a salvaged ship's repairs were complete, a reputable surveyor could certify her and render the vessel "staunch and seaworthy" - therefore insurable. The ship was a bargain, and bargains John knew in spades.

John Pacey's personal obligations may have altered the motivations of a previously honorable man. In the spring of 1897, he married Annie McGinnis, a teacher at Seattle Central School. Very soon, he would have other family members to support.

CHAPTER 7 - THE PRINCE WIRES $10,000

While rumors of Major Ingraham's next venture had been circulating since before Christmas of 1897, the details of his agreement with Prince Luigi were as yet undisclosed. That changed in the early spring of 1898 when the clerks at a Seattle bank started the local tongues wagging.

Pacey's relationships within the financial world likely set fire to the rumors - since the MacDougall and Southwick Company had dealings at the Dexter Horton and Company Bank, a block away from their store at the southwest corner of First and Columbia. Being a close friend of Dexter Horton, Major Ingraham banked there as well. Ingraham, publisher of the *Seattle Guide* and owner of the Calvert Company, held an office at First and Marion – just another block from MacDougall and Southwick. John Pacey knew exactly how much money Prince Luigi had wired and set about making plans to ensure that a large portion of the funds ended up in the outfitting firm's coffers. On by March 26, 1898 the headline was splashed across the *New York Times*:

"ITALIAN EXPEDITION TO ALASKA

Major Ingraham to Lead Gold Hunters Backed by Prince Luigi.

SEATTLE, Washington, March 25. – Prince Luigi of Italy is to be the backer of an expedition to Alaska which is to leave here in May under the leadership of Major E. S. Ingram, who accompanied Prince Luigi on his ascent of Mount St. Elias last summer.

The party will consist of fifteen persons, and will include a number of Italians. With Kotzebue Sound as a base, an exhaustive prospecting for gold will be made. It is stated that Prince Luigi would accompany the party were it not for the desire of King Humbert that he lead an expedition to the north pole."

On March 30th, five days after the story broke, John G. Pacey, secretary of the MacDougall and Southwick outfitting firm, made an offer on the schooner Jane Gray for $6,000. Built in Bath, Maine as a whaler in 1887, she was relatively young and had already had a successful career sailing the Pacific for ten years, hunting seals and selling their hides in Japan. She was just shy of eight-three feet in length and twenty-two feet in breadth, with a net capacity of 107 tons. Pacey spelled out the conditions of the purchase:

"Capt. F. H. Kandy,

City.

Dear Sir:

I will give you for the schooner Jane Gray $6000 cash on her arrival in Seattle provided on inspection on arrival she is satisfactory to me and as represented. Built in Bath, Maine 1887 – 107 net tonnage 82.7 keel, 22 feet breadth, 9.2 hold, spars and hull in first class condition, copper painted on bottom and hull painted within ten days past, new running gear, 2 suits of sails, one suit having made but one trip; usual supply of anchors and chains, sheathed with iron wood for ice; as a whole the vessel being in good condition and ready for sea; all spare gear of all sort and description to go with vessel, spare boat, etc. except chronometer, which if I retain I will pay owner $5.00 per month for use of.

I will further agree to pay you any legitimate bills you have been put to from Feb. 23d, viz.,-groceries, provisions, dockage, etc. on your presenting the bills to us. In other words take all expense of the vessel off your hands from the date of your charter except the charter money of $250 you have paid. It is understood however, that all groceries and supplies whatsoever that may remain shall be mine; also the freight money shall belong to me, you to give us an order on the Captain of the Jane Grey so we will have full and complete charge of vessel the minute she arrives.

Respectfully,

J. G. Pacey"

And on April 3rd, another newspaper article, this time in the *Kansas City Journal,* the publication of Pacey's former residence, read:

"LUIGI PAYS THE BILLS

ITALIAN PRINCE RESPONSIBLE FOR AN ALASKAN EXPEDITION.

WILL GO TO KOTZEBUE SOUND.

WILL TAKE WITH THEM EXPENSIVE AND COMPLETE OUTFIT.

Major Ingraham, the Mountain Climber, Solicits With Success the Nobleman's Financial Assistance in a Gigantic Undertaking.

Prince Luigi of Savoy, who last summer expended $26,000 in a pleasure expedition to Mount St. Elias, the summit of which he attained, is the backer of another expedition, which is to leave Seattle in May for Alaska. The object of this expedition, however, will not be for pleasure, but for the acquirement of gold.

The leader of the new expedition will be Major E. S. Ingraham, says the Post-Intelligencer, who has a wide reputation as one of the most experienced mountain climbers in the United States and who accompanied Prince Luigi on the Mount St. Elias expedition. The prince has untold wealth, and when he learned by letter that the Seattle mountain climber was desirous of leading an expedition to Alaska and would not object to being backed for the undertaking, he at once forwarded to Seattle at a cost of $64 a cablegram, which instructed Major Ingraham to immediately make all necessary preparations for the trip. Major Ingraham has since called at one of the banking institutions of Seattle at the request of the cashier and was informed that an amount of money had been forwarded from Italy by Prince Luigi and awaited his pleasure.

The expedition would have been accompanied by Prince Luigi himself had he not been commanded by King Humboldt to lead an exploration party which is to start soon for the North pole. It is the intention of Major Ingraham and his companions, however, to make an exhaustive exploration of the Arctic region in their search for gold. Under the plans which have been formulated, and which at present they intend to follow, they will first land at Kotzebue sound, and from there commence their explorations.

Major Ingraham said that he would prefer that the amount furnished by Prince Luigi remain unknown to the public, but said it was sufficient for him to accomplish the tremendous undertaking, and that, if necessary, he could secure still more funds from the same source simply by asking.

Under the Arctic Circle.

'Our party to Alaska will number about fifteen.' Major Ingraham said. 'We shall leave Seattle in May, our destination being Kotzebue sound, which is under the Arctic circle, at a point 200 miles north of St. Michael on a direct line. To reach Kotzebue sound it will be necessary to pass through the Bering strait. Our method of travel will be on a schooner, which we shall either charter or purchase. I shall know definitely in a few days which proposition will be adopted. The party will probably be composed of four Italians from Biella, Italy, relatives of Senor Sella, who was the photographer of the Mount St. Elias expedition, and most of the others will likely be from Seattle, although there is a party coming to Seattle from Turin, Italy, who are anxious to join us.'

An Extensive Outfit.

'I am going on a line of information which gives me every reason to believe that our party will be successful in striking rich diggings. We will leave Seattle with an outfit just as complete as the most extensive and thorough experience can suggest, and we will be prepared to remain away from the United States for a period of at least two years, and possibly longer. We will have a ton and a half of provisions to each man, and the other portions of our outfit will be complete in every detail.'

'We will be provided with the required number of boats and also with a steam or vapor launch of the very best manufacture, as I have been instructed by Prince Luigi not to proceed to the Arctic regions equipped with an outfit which would not bear the closest inspection. It is very evident that the prince has implicit faith in Alaska, and I have not much doubt that he would have joined the expedition and made the trip more for pleasure and curiosity than a desire to acquire additional wealth, had he not recently received a commission from King Humbert, of Italy, to lead an expedition to the North pole.'"

Major Ingraham's reliable source was the missionary at St. Lawrence Island. Vene Gambell reported that the natives in the Kotzebue Sound region had confirmed that gold was found on beaches in the area. He shared this information with the crew on the revenue cutter Bear. And while the word of natives was not always reliable, for they would often tell white people whatever they thought they wanted to hear, this rumor found wide open ears in the gold-frenzied streets of Seattle.

Miners were dying of scurvy and starvation in the Klondike. In an effort to slow this greed-induced death march, the Canadian government passed a law requiring all miners coming north be equipped with a years worth of provisions - amounting to approximately one ton per person. In order to encourage miners to spend their money at businesses in the Klondike, the Canadians had also enacted a hefty import tariff on merchandise brought in by the prospectors. The same outfit tonnage became the benchmark for those heading to the Alaska Territory. In combination, these facts provided a new sales advantage for outfitters in San Francisco and Seattle: by promoting the rumors of gold in the Kotzebue Sound region, they could advertise the savings to be had in bypassing Canada. Merchandisers all along the West Coast rubbed their hands together, feeling the cold hard cash that would pass through their fingers with the sale of every one-ton "outfit."

While neither newspaper article revealed the amount of money that the Prince had wired to Major Ingraham, John Pacey was fully aware of the sum. And if $10,000 was the figure that Ingraham intended to spend for fifteen men on an expedition to Alaska, the MacDougall and Southwick Company stood poised to make a handsome profit. Perhaps Ingraham would even become a silent partner in ownership of the boat.

As secretary and bookkeeper, Pacey had done the math prior to making the offer on the Jane Gray. This wasn't his first rodeo and he was bucking for a promotion. He could charge fare for passage as well as make money from sales at the store. Fifty passengers at $100 a head would bring in $5000, in addition to profits from their purchases. If each man spent $200 at MacDougall and Southwick, the company would likely net at least another $5000 - conservatively estimating a 100% markup from wholesale to retail - and conservatively estimating the amount each passenger would part with in amassing their respective "outfits." Later evidence indicates that many prospectors spent no less than $1000 each on their way to Alaska. Even if some prospecting agents were given discounts, after expenses for the vessel were deducted, one trip to Alaska with fifty prospectors could bring MacDougall and Southwick something in excess of $10,000. At a time when an average man in Seattle might earn $1,000 a year, this was a king's ransom.

On April 7th, John Pacey's offer on the Jane Gray was accepted. The $6000.00 check, drawn on the schooner General Siglin's account at the Bank of California, took a full week to clear the Dexter Horton and Company Bank in Seattle, allowing more time for financial maneuvering.

Prior to the check clearing and Pacey receiving title to the schooner, MacDougall and Southwick signed an order for a $100 full-page advertisement in the *North American Transportation & Trading Company*'s book, All About the GOLD FIELDS OF ALASKA, with Prince Luigi and Major

Ingraham headlining this latest production. The ad also touted their store as the one-stop shop for all of your outfitting needs: "Tickets can be purchased for $100 at the MacDougall & Southwick Company, 717, 719, 721, 723 First Avenue in Seattle." MacDougall and Southwick's advertisement continued, stating, "We have for years and are now conducting stores in the Alaska mining regions. We own and operate a fleet of vessels between Seattle and Alaska ports. The experience we have gained in our extensive operations is at your disposal for the asking. We will readily answer any inquiries, either in person or through the mails, and will not expect you to trade with us in return."

The day after writing a check for the Jane Gray, Pacey paid off the crew of the schooner at Port Townsend and penned a contract with Major Ingraham. In the memorandum, John agreed to transport a party of no more than sixteen men, at a fee of $50 per person, from Seattle to the mouth of the Kowak River in the Kotzebue Sound region. Knowing full well that the vessel had a net capacity of one hundred and seven tons, he further agreed to transport, free of charge, about a hundred thousand pounds of provisions and outfits - and this was solely for the Ingraham group.

$800 hardly seems adequate fare for fifty tons of goods and sixteen passengers, so who really owned the boat?

CHAPTER 8 - LAST PREPARATIONS

By the end of April 1898, newspaper and magazine articles across the country were herding droves of prospectors to Seattle. Surrounding MacDougall and Southwick's ad in "All About the Gold Fields of Alaska," one prospector is quoted as saying that the "Kotzebue is richer than Klondike," and it is the "richest spot on earth." Within ten days, the miner had reportedly taken out $50,000 in gold nuggets from the banks of the Kowak River. This same man went on to say that starvation was nearly impossible and that "there need never be any fear of famine there, as deer are plentiful and fish can be caught in abundance all year round. In the winter you can break a hole in the ice and catch enough salmon and trout for a meal in ten minutes." Absurd publicity such as this intensified the rush for riches in the Kotzebue Sound region.

At about the same time as the advertisement went to print, John Pacey hired Ezekiel Crockett as master of the Jane Gray. Although only thirty years old, he owned the Yukon Rapid Transit Company and his career had already included the command of sealing schooners and steam ships all over the North Pacific. As the captain, he was given full charge of hiring and management of the crew. In search of qualified seamen, Crockett headed to Ballard, the little Scandinavian community just north of Queen Anne Hill where Swedish and Norwegian were spoken as often as English, and sailors were as thick as fish in a barrel. His first hire was the mate, John Hanson. The rest of the crew would arrive as soon as word spread through town.

Image courtesy of the Sella Foundation, Biella, Italy.

One block down the hill from the MacDougall and Southwick Company store, the two-masted schooner lay tied up to the dock at Railroad Avenue and Columbia. The surveyors, declaring the vessel "staunch and seaworthy," had come and gone. Post-inspection modifications to the ship were in progress. Under the supervision of Pacey and Crockett, the mainmast boom was being raised to allow room for the seven-foot overheads of a new forward cabin. Within the eighteen by twenty-two foot structure, three tiers of eight beds lined each outboard wall. If passengers slept with their feet toward the keel and others with their heads against the bulkheads, the cabin, although cramped, could accommodate forty-eight to fifty men, double-berthed.

Other crewmembers arrived as the sailing date neared. Andrew Carlson and his brother, Charles, took two of the three remaining positions as seamen. Andrew had just completed a stint as a deckhand on the City of Champaign. Charles Carlson had been working as a longshoreman on the docks, loading and unloading ships. Captain Crockett hired Charles Oleson from the steamer Greyhound as cook, and Albert Johnson from the steamer Fairhaven as assistant cook. The only positions that remained unfilled were that of the waiter and an additional deckhand - jobs that could be done by almost any able-bodied person wandering the docks in search of employment.

In an attempt to get ahead of the tidal wave of miners heading for Kotzebue Sound, The Jane Gray was thought to be one of the first vessels leaving Puget Sound that spring. The advertised date of departure was May 15, 1898 and her passengers had already assembled in the city.

~~~

Charlie Aiken arrived from Sacramento early, negotiating his passage on the schooner before anyone else. Buying up shovels, an unassembled boat kit, cold weather gear, and all of the other things that would make up his outfit, he became a regular at the dock, dropping off his purchases at the Jane Gray and watching preparations as repairs were being made to the ship. He visited the dock every day, meeting Mate Hanson and Captain Crockett's father-in-law, Claude Brown. After some discussion, Charlie and Claude decided to finish purchasing their outfits together and became partners in their prospecting operation.

~~~

After the journey from Iowa, the Gambells took a break with relatives in Tacoma. Nellie enjoyed the extended convalescence with her family and had completely recovered from her surgery. After her comfortable vacation, she likely did not look forward to returning to their home and the difficult life on desolate St. Lawrence Island, however, as a devoted Christian wife, she needed to obey her husband's wishes. And Vene wanted to get back. He hoped to book passage home on the Bear or one of the other revenue cutters. The venerable Reverend Sheldon Jackson was relying on them to continue their work with the natives. On Sunday, May 15th, they attended services at the Presbyterian Church in Tacoma, where Vene's brother, Herbert, was a devout parishioner. While everyone was admiring baby Margaret, Vene learned that many of the revenue cutters had been enlisted for service in the Spanish-American War, causing a shortage of government vessels making the run north. Now, he needed to hurry to find tickets on another ship.

~~~

For six months, Edwin Taylor had been negotiating wholesale contracts in Seattle on behalf of the family business. (The S. P. Taylor Company produced a novel product of the times, the first square-bottomed paper bag.) Bombarded with talk of wealth in Alaska, Edwin also caught the gold virus. In addition to selling their paper products in the booming mining towns, perhaps they too could stake mining claims. He returned to San Francisco just long enough to convince his younger brother, Fred, to come north with him.

After a successful sales pitch, Ed once again said goodbye to his wife, Nellie, on Thursday, May 4th. With his brother Frederick, he hoped to make enough money in gold rush
~~~

country to save their paper manufacturing company. Fred's wife, Kate, and their two young daughters, Edna and Frances, as well as another Taylor brother, James, were there to see them off at San Francisco. Along with Burrey Spencer of the Union Paper Company, and Charles Wilkinson, foreman at Valeau and Peterson's Pressrooms, the party of four arrived in Seattle a week before the Jane Gray was scheduled to depart for Alaska.

~~~

James Blackwell assembled his prospecting party by the second Monday in May. The forty-three year-old Blackwell was a master at organization, both by birth and by education. His father, Moore Carter Blackwell, was a captain in the Confederate Army. James' first wife, Lucretia Virginia McLean, was the daughter of Major McLean, the very same man who owned the house at Appomattox in which General Lee surrendered to General Grant. Blackwell graduated as a first lieutenant at Bethel Military Academy in Warrenton, Virginia, with a degree in civil engineering. He soon became the federal supervising architect in Washington, D. C. After Lucretia died, he left his two children in the care of his parents in Virginia and moved to Washington State, where he worked on the first dry dock at the Bremerton Naval Shipyard. With the support of his second wife, Eleanor, he became active in the community, serving on the town council and later serving a term as mayor. By 1898, his other projects included the Louderback Building and the Vorhee's grain elevator in Tacoma and the Puyallup Opera House. For the mining expedition, Blackwell chose eleven men to accompany him. Seven decided to buy their outfits together, while the others purchased theirs individually.
~~~

From his Seattle home at Twelfth and Marion, Blackwell assigned responsibilities to each member of the party.

James Livengood came in from Nebraska to join his older brother, Silas, on the Blackwell expedition. William Weaver arrived from Muncy, Pennsylvania, accompanied by William Deterling and William Otten of Arlington, Minnesota. Although traveling separately, George Boak also arrived from Pennsylvania. All were part of the Blackwell group.

After inspecting ships along the waterfront, William Weaver and James Livengood made their way through the Seattle circus. Harnessed dogs pulling sleds advertised lessons for the novice "musher." Children chased the sleds down Railroad Avenue. Men on the corners pitched the advantages to their respective models of "gold rockers." Every manner of mining frivolity lined the streets. Dodging horses, trolleys, and potholes filled with water deep enough to drown an entire mule team, they negotiated a course through stacks of bagged coal to the MacDougall and Southwick Company store on First and Columbia. After a predictable good-cop, bad-cop conversation with Pacey and MacDougall, they successfully haggled the fare for twelve on the Jane Gray. The price for passage and the amount of freight allowed agreed upon, the two men headed to Seattle Grocery, a block over on Second and Marion, where they purchased three thousand pounds of dry goods, cases of canned goods, and miscellaneous other supplies. George Boak, following their lead, bought over a thousand pounds of goods for himself at the same store.

Photo courtesy of the Tacoma Public Library.

Meeting up with the Blackwell party, Charles Chard had already resigned from his post as a clerk in Seattle and commenced purchasing items needed for the trip north. His first stop was at Louch, Augustine, & Co. Grocers between Marion and Columbia on First Avenue. There, he stocked up on tobacco and smoking supplies, not only for personal enjoyment, but also for trading with the Alaskan natives.

Chard and Blackwell spent most of the week visiting every outfitting store in Seattle, buying up coats, boots, rubber blankets, guns, ammunition, tents and any other conceivable item that might be needed for two years in the Arctic.

In addition to mining gear and supplies, James Blackwell picked up merchandise and trinkets that could be used for trade with the Alaskan natives: 500 yards of calico fabric, one lot of assorted fancy beads, 150 pounds of "battle axe" chewing tobacco, and 13 Indian robes and shawls, spending $95.10 in all. George Boak bought a batch of combs and mirrors for the same purpose.

~~~

Percy Davenport and Frank Ginther took leave from their jobs as railway postal clerks in early April. Departing Harrisburg, Pennsylvania, accompanied by George Hiller, with more than $3,000 between them, they had already invested an entire year planning their expedition to the gold fields. Once in Seattle, they also met up with the Blackwell party.

~~~

Erminio Sella and his group arrived from Biella, Italy in the first week of May. After the trip across the Atlantic, they retraced the route across the United States that the prince's 1897 expedition team had taken, traveling from New York City to San Francisco and on to Seattle by train.

In Northern Italy, the history of the Sella family is as legendary as the Alpine mountain range north of their home. Erminio's uncle, Quintino Sella was a mathematician who taught geometry in Torino before becoming the Italian minister of finance. Erminio's father, Giuseppe Venanzio Sella, was a scientist and pioneer of Italian photography, founded the Italian Alpine Club (CAI, or Club Alpino Italiani), and owned a textile mill. Quintino and Giuseppe also founded the financial institution "Gruppo Banca Sella." Erminio's brother, Vittorio, who was the expedition photographer for Prince Luigi on the ascent of Mount St. Elias, continued their father's work - documenting mountain ascents around the globe through his exquisite vision and masterful use of the latest photographic equipment. Thus far, although he had graduated from the University in Torino with a degree in mechanical engineering, success had been elusive to Erminio. The youngest child of Giuseppe Sella and Clementina Mosca Riatel, he planned to step out of the family shadows and return to Italy a wealthy, successful man.

Erminio was accompanied by his sister's husband, Edoardo Gaia, and three other men, employees and family friends who were to help pack their camera equipment and mining gear. Abele Ceria, a farmer in charge of lands near the Sella family home in San Gerolamo; Secondo Bissetta, an employee at the woolen mills operated by Maurizio Sella; and Bissetta's cousin, Secondo Bianchetto, were all members of their team. Rounding out the party of six was Hans Wachter, an alpinist and mountain climber from the Austrian-Italian border.

~~~

With the backing of his father, a wealthy cattle baron, banker, and Seattle real-estate tycoon, Ben Snipes (Junior) resigned from his job as a bookkeeper at Oceanic Packaging Company. Ben lived at the Rainier Hotel, where Manuel Roberts was the janitor and night watchman. Nellie Sawyer, the sister-in-law of the hotel manager, paid $100 for Manuel's ticket and allowed him to charge his gear to her account at the MacDougall and Southwick outfitting store. Ben and his friend Mannie booked passage on the Jane Gray three days before she sailed.

~~~

Lured by the advertisement displayed by MacDougall and Southwick, more passengers made their way down for a tour of the ship, where a large white banner blaring "Kotzebue Sound" hung suspended high in the rigging.

C. J. Reilly and J. H. Conture, from Hartford, Connecticut, bought over two tons of supplies after negotiating the price to their tickets with John Pacey.

John Stutzman left his job as a florist and his wife and children in Westfield, New Jersey. After the long trip west, he also bought a ticket for Kotzebue Sound on the Jane Gray.

~~~

The following day, May 17th, John G. Pacey took out a Fireman's Fund insurance policy from MacDougall and Southwick, who were also insurance brokers. The vessel and all of its gear were valued at $7,000 and the premium of $500 bought him $5,000 worth of coverage. The following terms and conditions were of particular note:

"RULE X.

All losses shall be payable sixty days after proof and adjustment of loss of interest, and if payment be anticipated, interest shall always be discounted for the time so anticipated, at the current rate of interest at the time of payment. Provided however, that General Average claims, and losses of other descriptions, amounting to less than (500) five hundred dollars, may be paid without discount, so soon as ascertained; and nothing herein contained shall apply to sums paid in compromise.

RULE XI.

Wages and provisions in general average.

The schedule of allowance for wages and provisions in General Average shall be fixed as follows:
~~~

Wages: The actual wages paid, at the prices specified upon article.

For Masters $1.50 per day

For Mates $.75 per day

For Seamen and others $.40 per day

And the period for which wages and provisions shall be allowed, shall be from the day or bearing away for a port of distress, until the vessel is ready for sea."

Pacey put the policy on a time-payment plan. With $125 down, he signed three promissory notes, equaling the balance, payable on the 17th of the month, every three months until the policy would be paid in full on February 17, 1899.

This very same day, Pacey advanced some of the crew wages for the voyage. Captain Crockett received $147.50, Mate Hanson $104.15, Charles Oleson $77.25, Andrew Carlson $52.50, Andrew Johnson $29.00, and Charles Carlson $39.90.

On Wednesday, May 18, 1898, already three days past the Jane Gray's scheduled departure date, The *Seattle Post-Intelligencer* published another article about the impending expedition:

"PRINCE LUIGI'S BIG PARTY

Leaves This Afternoon for Kotzebue Sound in Search of Gold

MAJOR E. S. INGRAHAM LEADER

It cost the Italian Nobleman $10,000 to Outfit the Party, Which Will Remain in the Far Northern Country Two Years—Schooner Jane Gray Will Convey Them to Destination—Mr. Ingraham Talks.

Maj. E. S. Ingraham's party of gold-seekers that is headed for Kotzebue sound in the interests of Prince Luigi, of the Italian royal family, will leave for the north this afternoon on the fast schooner Jane Gray.

Fifteen strong men, some of the most experienced miners and prospectors, make up the party that will for two years put forth their best efforts to enrich themselves and to pour a stream of Arctic gold from their Kotzebue sluice-boxes into Prince Luigi's coffers. They are as well outfitted as any party of the size that has left for the north this year. It cost the prince and other backers of the expedition some $10,000 for the two years outfit, but there is every prospect of a royal return.

Maj. Ingraham, who is in complete charge of the men of the expedition, is one of the best known mountain climbers on the Coast. Time and again he has ascended the higher peaks of the Cascades, and last year came into even greater fame by piloting Prince Luigi and a party of Italians of royal blood to the top of Mount St. Elias. It was through that trip that Maj. Ingraham was able to interest Prince Luigi and his money in the gold hunting trip. The prince first heard of the wonderful gold resources of the interior of Alaska while north on the schooner Aggie on his mountain climbing trip. When Maj. Ingraham decided to head a party, Luigi was quite ready to go in.

Maj. Ingraham was seen yesterday by a Post-Intelligencer reporter and said:

'After many weeks of preparation and expenditure of some $10,000, our two years' outfit is now on board the schooner Jane Gray and we will sail tomorrow afternoon. The Jane Gray will be at the entrance of Bering straits when the ice goes out. We will go into the interior at once and establish a base of supplies by building a large cabin and storehouse. The building will be frame and of sufficient size to accommodate the men, as well as store seventy-five tons of supplies.'

'Prospecting will be done under my direction on all of the rivers flowing into the sound. We will have four separate prospecting parties, working in different directions from the base of supplies. These parties will be headed by C. H. Packard, W. H. Gleason, S. W. Young and G. H. Pennington. One party will work with the launch which I have had built especially for the trip. She is thirty feet in length. We will be gone at least two years, and will do our best to get gold out of the Kotzebue country, if there is any there.'

Two members of Maj. Ingraham's party are well known to Seattle. C. H. Packard has for years been a prominent mining man in Snohomish county, and was one of the first men to locate in the Cascades. At one time he owned more claims than any other man in the country. He formerly published the Weekly Eye at Snohomish. Jack Lindsay, captain of the University of Washington football team for the last two years, is also a member of the party. The others are W. H. Gleason, W. A. Johnson, V. J. Smith, L. M. Lessey, C. G. Smith, P. C. Little, S. W. Young and W. D. Millan, of Seattle; C. H. Packard and G. H. Pennington, of Snohomish; J. J. Lindsay, of Everett; Horace Palmer, of Lebanon, O.; F. G. Saulsberry, of Minnesota; A. B. Dunlap, of Dwight, Ill.

The Jane Gray is in command of Capt. Crockett, formerly of the steamer Townsend. She has forty-one passengers outside of the Ingraham party. Among them is a party of four from California, which has just purchased a big outfit here. The men are C. W. Wilkinson, E. M. Taylor, B. S. Spencer and F. S. Taylor."

CHAPTER 9 - DEPARTURE DAY

THURSDAY, MAY 19, 1898

As the black of night gave way to a gray dawn, horse-drawn carts, heavily laden with prospecting supplies, clattered across the tracks on Railroad Avenue. All along the waterfront, steamer ships awaited an influx of passengers, their stacks billowing black smoke from the coal-fired boilers. From the muddy slurry of Denny Hill, where the steep slopes were being re-graded by wooden culverts blasting water, south beyond Main Street, the masts of sailing vessels formed a nautical forest lining the piers and wharves of Seattle.

Last minute provisions began arriving on the dock at the foot of Columbia Street. Sacks of turnips, rice, oats, and flour were dropped off and loaded into the holds of the Jane Gray. Gulls spread their wings above the Sound, unleashing a cacophony of noise as they search for any stray morsel or kernel of dropped grain.

As more gear was unloaded, Erminio Sella's team went to work inventorying their delivery from Vulcan Ironworks. Consisting of blades, pulleys and fittings for a portable sawmill, the equipment would be used to construct a large dormitory and storehouse once the group reached Alaska.

The sun had not yet risen above the Cascade Mountains when Major Ingraham's group assembled, cobbling together a conversation with the Italians. Victor and Conrad Schmid were well acquainted with Erminio's brother, Vittorio, from the prior year's expedition to Mount

St. Elias. Although none of the men in the Sella party spoke English fluently, they were all at least somewhat conversant in German and the Schmid boys spoke that language well. Their father, Vitus Schmid, emigrated from Germany as a teenager and at his urging the brothers had taken two years of the language at the University. Jack Lindsay had been a their classmate in the same studies. With the help of Hans Wachter, the Austrian mountaineer who spoke German and Italian, the group discussed details of the trip while Erminio set up his camera and photographed the momentous day.

Ingraham's party was the largest group making passage on the Jane Gray. By noon, the sun had burned off the morning haze, and the rest of the team had arrived. William Gleason, the Seattle contractor who would be in charge of one of the sub-teams, was accompanied by his wife and eleven year-old daughter, who were there to see him off. Another prominent member of the team was the sixty-two year-old Spencer Young, a veteran miner and log dealer. George Pennington, a familiar face in the Snohomish County mining brotherhood, arrived with Clayton Packard. Bard Dunlap, the twenty-eight year old son of Major Ingraham's cousin, Eliza, made the trip out from Dwight, Illinois for the opportunity of a lifetime. By the time everyone showed up, twenty-two prospectors, including the Sella party, and the large crowd of family and friends gathering on the dock lent to a festive mood.

Jack Lindsay could barely contain his excitement. For two years he played football and attended classes with the Schmid boys. This was a new game, on a new playing field, and their enthusiasm could be heard above the din of activity on the waterfront. Clayton Packard, whose father served in the Wisconsin Infantry with Jack's father, was the leader of their prospecting team. In him, the boys of the University could not have asked for a fiercer, more reliable fellow to guide them on this adventure to the gold fields.

As more travelers arrived, fifty-six stowed their gear. Forty-three were housed in the new forward cabin, the rest in the aft quarters. With Victor and Conrad Schmid, Jack Lindsay and all of the members of the Ingraham team claimed bunks in the new deckhouse. Luther Lessey, the Seattle dentist who scaled Mount Rainier with the Major on numerous occasions, shared a berth with Horace Palmer, who arrived from Lebanon, Ohio to be the engineer in charge of the steam engines and other mechanical equipment. Will Millay, who studied under the Major when he was the young principal in South Thomaston, Maine, grabbed a middle bunk, while Packard claimed the one below him.

The Gambell family, unable to secure passage on one of the revenue cutters, purchased accommodations in an aft stateroom on the Jane Gray. Compared to the hoard of prospectors, they were traveling light, stowing a mere 250 pounds of sundries in the hold.

Over at the Hotel Seattle on First Avenue and James, Ed and Fred Taylor finished up last minute business. They traveled from San Francisco, arriving early the prior week with two other paper industry men, Burrey Spencer and Charles Wilkinson. During the week preceding departure, they purchased most of their outfit in Seattle. The brothers were hopeful that this venture would bring much needed revenue to the family business, the S. P. Taylor Company. Their father's death and the subsequent financial crisis of 1893 had left their mother and siblings over-mortgaged and mired in debt. After checking out of the hotel, Ed paid one cent for postage to drop a letter to his wife, Nellie, in San Francisco.

The Hotel Seattle, circa 1898. Photo courtesy of the Seattle Public Library.

Captain Crockett and Mate Hanson, aided by John Pacey, made a detailed accounting of the weight of passenger's provisions. The ships stores weighed in at 120,843 pounds, not including the 64 people and their luggage. Below deck, the hold was packed to the rafters with dry goods and provisions: 34,500 pounds of flour; over 17,000 pounds of corn meal, rolled oats, rice and beans; 11,000 pounds of bacon; 1,500 pounds of candles; 18,500 pounds of sugar, baking powder, salt, dried fruit, coffee and tea; 5,720 pounds of dried potatoes, barley, peas and pilot bread; and 32,500 pounds of canned goods, butter and miscellaneous other sundries.

Patrick McKelvey was the last person to buy a ticket from John Pacey. His purchase was so tardy that a record of his freight was never entered into the MacDougall and Southwick ledger.

Arriving after the rest of the crew received an advance on their wages, the final hired hands were Leon Ausprung, seaman, and John Hawco, waiter.

By five o'clock that evening, the dock at the foot of Columbia Street was crowded with family and friends bidding farewell to a schooner packed with local and international celebrities. Victor and Conrad's parents, Mr. and Mrs. Vitus Schmid, as well as their sister Theresa, who was also a university student, embraced the young men. Phil Little's father, Frank, wished his son well, as did Arnot Johnston's mother. University men and women yelled football cheers to their hero, Jack Lindsay.

On deck, the passengers and crew posed for a photographer from the *Seattle Post-Intelligencer.*

The Ingraham Party of sixteen: Major Edward S. Ingraham, officer in the Washington State Militia, former school superintendent, educator, mountaineer, and publisher from Seattle; Dr. Luther M. Lessey, dentist and mountaineer from Seattle; Victor J. Schmid, University of Washington student and football player from Mercer Island; Conrad G. Schmid, University of Washington student and football player from Mercer Island; John J. Lindsay, University of Washington student, team captain and football player from Everett; William D. Millay, from South Thomaston, Maine; Clayton H. Packard, former owner of the *Snohomish Eye,* mining expert, and journalist from Snohomish, Washington; George H. Pennington, from Snohomish County, Washington; William H. Gleason, contractor, from Seattle; Philip C. Little, from Seattle; Spencer W. Young, veteran miner from Snohomish

County and Seattle; Horace Palmer, engineer, of Lebanon, Ohio; A. Bard Dunlap, from Dwight, Illinois; Frank G. Saulsbury, of Minnesota; V. S. Hamilton, from Illinois; and W. Arnot Johnston, from Seattle.

The Sella and Gaia Party of six: Erminio Sella, Edoardo Gaia, Abele Ceria, Hans Wachter, Secondo Bianchetto, and Secondo Bissetta, all from the region surrounding Biella, Italy.

Charles Williams, from Olympia, Washington, traveling solo.

B. S. Frost, of San Francisco, traveling solo.

Conture and Reilly, party of two: J. H. Conture and C. J. Reilly, from Hartford, Connecticut.

Johnson and Doxsey, party of two: Job Johnson, of Long Island, New York, and Wilbur P. Doxsey, from Lynbrook, Long Island, New York.

Weston and Ritter, party of two: Coney Weston, of Skowhegan, Maine and Edward F. Ritter, from Poughkeepsie, New York.

John M. Stutzman, of Westfield, New Jersey, traveling solo.

F. W. Ginther, party of three, traveling with the Blackwell group: Frank W. Ginther, Percy J. Davenport, and George Hiller, all from Harrisburg, Pennsylvania.

Kingsbury and Ranney, party of two: A. G. Kingsbury, of Boston, Massachusetts, and Bernard D. Ranney, of Mexico City and Kalamazoo, Michigan.

Aiken and Brown, party of two: Charles C. Aiken, from Sacramento, California, and Claudius Brown, from Seattle.

Nick Hederlund, traveling solo.

Charles E. Chard, of Seattle and part of the Blackwell party, but listed as traveling solo.

The J. E. Blackwell Party of five: James E. Blackwell, from Seattle; William S. Weaver, of Muncy, Pennsylvania; Silas Livengood, of Seattle; William F. Deterling, from Minnesota; and William Otten, of Minnesota.

George Rupley Boak, of Hughesville, Pennsylvania, part of the Blackwell party but listed as traveling solo.

The Taylor Brothers, party of four: Edwin M. Taylor, Fredrick S. Taylor, Burrey S. Spencer, and Charles W. Wilkinson, all from San Francisco.

Ben E. Snipes, Jr. and Manuel F. Roberts, of Seattle.

Patrick McKelvey, from Eau Claire, Wisconsin, traveling solo.

The Gambell Family, party of three: Sylvenes Gambell, from Ohio and St. Lawrence Island, Nellie and Margaret Gambell

The crew of eight: Captain Ezekial E. Crockett; Mate John Hanson; Charles Carlson, Andrew Carlson, and Leon Ausprung, all seamen; John Hawco, waiter; Charles Oleson, cook; and Albert Johnson, assistant cook.

Waiving to the throng of well-wishers, Charlie Aiken was the last to cross the gangway before the mooring lines were cast off.

The Jane Gray and the Moonlight were two of the first ships to leave Seattle for Kotzebue Sound that spring. Since it was widely believed that the Jane Gray was the faster vessel, her crew expected to beat the Moonlight to Unalaska in less than three weeks. Charles Thornton, who had been a porter on the Mount St. Elias expedition with

Ingraham and the Schmid brothers, and wrote for *Overland Monthly* and *Out West Magazine,* was on board the Moonlight. He engaged his friends in a wager as to who would be the first to arrive at their destination. Tied against the hull of the same steam tugboat, the celebration and playful joking continued well into the night.

CHAPTER 10 - INTO THE STRAITS

FRIDAY, MAY 20, 1898

Without even "the shadow of a wind," the tug pulled the two sailing vessels north under the black sky of a new moon, passing between the heavily timbered banks of Bainbridge and Whidbey Islands before heading west toward the Pacific. Approximately eight hours later, the tug Queen cast her lines off of the Jane Gray and the Moonlight in the Straits of Juan de Fuca near Port Townsend, Washington, before sunrise.

Although both vessels raised all of their sails, they were caught in the slack of flat calm between incoming and outgoing tides around 4:00 a.m. Winds were elusive and the passage to the Pacific remained a millpond during the morning hours.

Climbing over passengers and freight at first light, the two Carlson seamen, Charles and Andrew, along with Leon Ausprung, worked to secure gear and supplies that would not fit in the hold. A dory, sides of beef, unassembled boat kits, sleds, and lumber covered the forward cabin. Forty sacks of coal, stacked four high; barrels of water, beef and pork; and bags of vegetables stacked between the two cabins made moving about topside nearly impossible. The poop deck carried two large steam launches overhanging the forward roof of the aft cabin. Both of these launches were packed with provisions and prospecting gear. The only place where a foot could touch the deck was in front of an improvised toilet room outside the door to the forward cabin.

The cook, Charles Olson, and his assistant, Albert Johnson, prepared a morning meal for the passengers. Some of the men found seats on sacks of coal. Others wedged themselves between lumber and gear on the deckhouses. The waiter, John Hawco, passed breakfast to anyone who made it out onto the deck.

From most accounts, it seems that the passengers enjoyed this peaceful opportunity to get to know each other.

Vene and Nellie Gambell brought baby Margaret up on deck. Most of the men were fathers, some even grandfathers, and they doted on the little girl, quickly naming the happy toddler the ship's mascot. The Gambells told stories of the natives on St. Lawrence Island who had stared through the windows of their cabin for the slightest glimpse of the baby, often commenting on the length of her hair and her beautiful disposition. The Inuits would soon be shocked to see how much Margaret had grown while the family was stateside. Talk veered to the problems of alcohol consumption among the native population - and how they would trade themselves into starvation for even a taste of it. In spite of their differing opinions on the value of converting the population to Christianity, both Ingraham and Packard agreed with Vene's viewpoint on banning alcohol - they too had seen the horrific effects that it had on people who lacked the ancestral European genes that would have provided them greater tolerance.

Victor and Conrad Schmid, with the help of Hans Wachter, spoke with Erminio Sella about his photographic techniques. The young men were familiar with the work of his brother, Vittorio. They had packed his equipment up

Mount St. Elias, erected his black photograph development tent, and seen the results of his labors. Once they learned that Erminio had accompanied his brother on many of his other mountain ascents, they were anxious to learn more about the Italians and their treks over the Alps.

Al Kingsbury spent the morning hours on deck with the other engineers. A man of diverse talents and interests, he had acquired a franchise for the distribution of electricity in 1887 and founded a company in DeLand, Florida. There, he built an ice-making plant with two-foot thick walls and operated an ice delivery service. Kingsbury constructed a generator to power the lighting. This was at a time when the long-range distribution of electricity had not yet been perfected and the incandescent bulb was still in its infancy. By 1893, he operated a telegraph service, was the editor and publisher of the monthly commercial publication *Irrigator*, and had traveled extensively throughout the United States and Mexico, setting up irrigation and electrical projects. Kingsbury was also a noted author who wrote articles for *National Magazine*. Another engineer, Horace Palmer, had worked at a flourmill in Lebanon, Ohio, before joining the Ingraham party. James Blackwell, who had worked on the James River and Kanawha Canal in Virginia before joining the offices of the federal supervising architect in Washington, D. C., also found the conversation enlightening, and talked of the obstacles that he had encountered while constructing the Bremerton dry dock and his other projects in Portland, Tacoma, and Seattle.

Between conversations, the men worked at securing their belongings for the long voyage across the North Pacific. Some tied down gear on deck while others carefully packed precious medical supplies and anything that might sustain damage from exposure to salt water away in their cramped cabins.

The Straits remained glassy most of the day, and once they felt confident that their gear was secure, the Sella party sat down for a game of cards. Secondo Bissetta taught Erminio "tressette," which literally means "three sevens," and is a trick-taking game played with a forty-card Italian deck. Bissetta dealt ten cards to each player, explaining that the object was to gain twenty-one points.

For the American's watching, the value and order of the cards was likely as baffling as Bissetta's instructions. And to the Italians, American English was as equally disorienting, making "Port Townsend" sound like "Porthansen" to them.

After the game, Secondino Bianchetto regaled everyone with the tale of "Palo di Ferro." In the late 1400's, Leonardo da Vinci had designed a giant crossbow, the "Pole of Iron," while working as the military engineer for the notorious Cesare Borgia. To engineer a weapon twenty times larger than those carried by men on horseback, Leonardo had applied "geometrical mathematics of the laws of motion" to the design. Secondino's grasp of Leonardo's concepts caught everyone by surprise.

The story had not yet reached its conclusion when a southbound schooner passed near the Jane Gray. Returning from the Copper River, the crew of the other vessel told of good weather to the north while Captain Crockett shared news of the latest American victory against the Spaniards. As dusk settled in, a breeze began to blow out of the southeast. The vessels parted ways and continued on their respective courses.

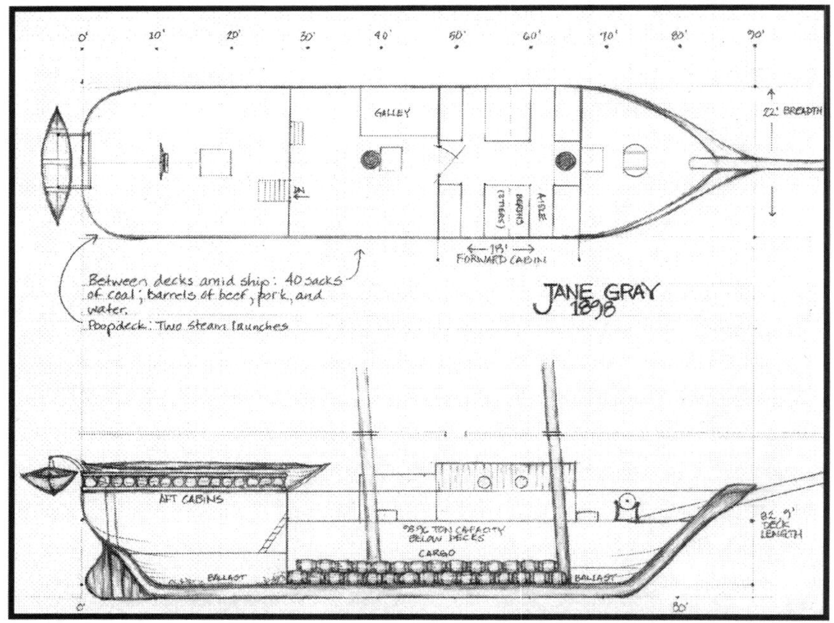

Illustration based on vessel description and evidence file, by Michelle Merritt.

The wind gained speed and strong incoming ocean swells began to batter the little ship. Under other circumstances, burdened with her usual cargo, she would have slipped through the waves like a hot knife through butter. That was not the case on this day. Every time the Jane Gray's bow went under a wave, gallons of water swept over the forward cabin, onto the deck amid ship, and a great deal of it washed through the doorway of the new house, where there were no drains or outlets.

The ship pitched and rolled all evening, water sweeping across the floor inside of the forward cabin. The sacks of coal and other supplies on deck became sponges, restricting the water from escaping through the scuppers that were not blocked by the new deckhouse.

As the seas grew rougher, water washed into the port side galley. The cook and his assistant were wet to the knees. Grumbling to the passengers that the ship should be put back to Neah Bay or the nearest port, they refused to prepare an evening meal.

The boys in the forward deckhouse of the Jane Gray were experiencing what would soon become a hell of a ride. Those in the outboard upper bunks began to feel the full effects of the cross-swells from the Pacific as the ship rocked from side to side. With no moonlight and very few portholes to view the horizon, their equilibriums were tossed into chaos. Soon most of them were leaning over the bulwarks "feeding the fish." And nausea bred nausea. Those who were unable to make it on deck remained miserable in their bunks, fighting a hopeless battle against the devilish curse of seasickness. Even the experienced mariners on board had difficulty with the rolling motion of the ship.

During the night, the water forward got so deep that Clayton Packard got drenched in his lower bunk. The situation was bad enough that in order to have any dry clothing by morning, he had to move everything out of his berth and up off the floor. After stacking his belongings on a table, Packard crawled into the middle berth where he slept with another member of the Ingraham team, Will Millay. Before long, even some of the middle berths were drenched. Moving their gear as high above the deck as possible, the rest of the men abandoned the lower berths. Those who were unable to find a spot in the forward cabin moved aft, where they doubled and tripled up in the driest place on the ship.

William Gleason, Spencer Young, Jack Lindsay, the Schmid brothers, Millay, Packard and the rest of the Ingraham and Sella party tried to sleep in the forward cabin as the Jane Gray plowed through the surging seas.

The schooner held her westward course all night, and with every swell she encountered, water continued to flood the forward cabin.

CHAPTER 11 - THE STRAITS BECOME DIRE

SATURDAY, MAY 21, 1898

Around midnight, the Jane Gray had made approximately one hundred miles, running into the Pacific Ocean, midway between the Olympic Peninsula and Vancouver Island off Cape Flattery. They had lost sight of the Moonlight the prior evening and the race was on. The wind continued to blow out of the southeast, the waves gaining height as the vessel headed out to the open sea.

Three members of the Blackwell party; Charles Chard, William Weaver and George Boak, shared one of the aft staterooms with C. J. Reilly and J. Conture. George Hiller and Frank Ginther shared an adjoining cabin, while Reverend Gambell and his wife and daughter occupied another aft stateroom next to theirs.

At five in the morning, Weaver was feeling extremely sick and climbed the aft companionway onto the deck. Blackwell, bailing water from the forward cabin and fighting his own case of seasickness, told Weaver that he was uneasy. Water had been pouring through the anchor chain holes and was already so deep that everyone forward had to abandon the lower bunks during the night. Tables and gear from the starboard cabins had been disrupted and were floating around in a foot of water.

Sitting near the pump amid ship, Weaver watched the water washing between the two cabins faster than it could escape from the scuttle holes, which there were very few of. Blackwell and some of the men in the forward cabin attempted to stop the flow by placing a board at the bottom of the door. It proved to be a fruitless endeavor.

Weaver did not stay on deck long. Nausea sent him back to the aft cabin where he crawled into the upper berth he shared with George Boak, who was also sick. Charles Chard came aft and propped the door to their cabin open with a bag of salt, affording the miserable members of his party some fresh air and a view of the deck. With the exception of a few trips to the top of the steps, Weaver and Boak stayed in their bunks all day Saturday. Their berth put them at eye level with the outside deck and they could hear everyone complaining about the water in the forward cabin as well as see the happenings outside.

The ship was in turmoil with gear all over the deck and most of the passengers sick in their cabins. Of the Sella party, Edoardo Gaia and Secondo Bissetta lay prostrate, unable to move, while Erminio attempted to save the photographic equipment that they had packed with such care.

George Pennington, the forty-eight year old lumberman from Ingraham's team, spent the day helping the crew as they continued to stow and secure the gear on deck. All of the men had donned rubber-coated canvas slickers and knee high boots to keep from getting completely soaked by the oncoming waves.

While supervising the placement of cargo and periodically ordering men into the rigging, Captain Crockett and Mate Hanson managed navigation of the vessel from the aft helm.

Vene Gambell brought his baby topside several times during the day. Nellie wasn't feeling well, so she stayed below. Captain Crockett had a five month-old baby boy and couldn't resist the happy one year-old little girl with big brown eyes and wavy auburn hair. Neither could James Blackwell, Coney Weston, nor William Gleason - all of whom had little girls at home. The Taylor brothers crawled out of their bunks for a short time, but not even the little mascot could distract them from their incessant nausea. They were as sick as Boak and Weaver and quickly returned to their stateroom. Vene followed them down the aft companionway to check on Nellie. Soon, he too was overcome by seasickness.

Major Ingraham stayed at the helm with Crockett and the mate, discussing what should be done about the flooded forward cabin. Around noon, the decision was made to bring the ship around and head back to Neah Bay. Unhappy with the vessel's behavior and the complaints of the passengers in the forward cabin, the captain turned the schooner on a southeast heading. With the wind then blowing against her starboard side, he hoped the ship would straighten up long enough to bail water from the forward cabin and better evaluate the situation. Even with the sails close-hauled, the Jane Gray would not sail windward. The crew continued to fight the wind and the seas for several hours. After improvising stoppers for the hawser holes from bags of coal and vegetables, the ship was returned to her west-southwest course. Running under a moderate gale, winds gusting up to forty miles per hour, the waves sometimes reached twelve feet in height throughout the day.

James Blackwell's apprehension grew as water continued to slop over the sides amid ship for the entire afternoon. Wilbur Doxsey, an eighteen year-old boy from Long Island, New York, and George Pennington had the same concerns and also remained on deck. The three of them were determined to remain vigilant and in spite of their own nausea.

With the majority of passengers sick in their cabins, the galley didn't bother putting out any meals and the cook continued to complain to anyone who would listen that the ship should be put back to the nearest port.

Almost everyone in the Sella party remained in their bunks. In a desperate attempt to save his cameras, Erminio had disassembled and strewn the equipment all over one of the upper berths. After that was done, he made a bed for himself inside of their steam launch on the aft deck.

Mate Hanson, who had been at the helm and managing the crew all day, pumped the holds every hour. Even though the forward cabin was still swamped, the water didn't appear to have entered the lower cargo area. Each time he pumped, little more than a bucket or two of water was found. Near the end of the captain's watch, Hanson pumped out the hold again with the same results. By the time the remaining passengers had gone to bed, he felt confident enough in the ship's behavior to encourage the captain to get some rest.

Around nine o'clock that night, Captain Crockett ordered the crew to lower all of the sails except the foresail and the staysail. Hove to, with the ship as stable as she could be when at sea, he hoped to afford everyone some reprieve from the pitching and rolling. After this was done, the captain retired to his cabin, leaving the mate in charge.

Johnnie Lindsay and his companions never left their bunks in the forward cabin. Weakened from two days of seasickness, none of them had the energy to stand or walk about the deck, let alone eat.

James Blackwell returned to his bunk in the leaky deckhouse and laid half-awake listening to the creaking ship and snapping sails as they were battered by the wind and roughening seas.

At ten o'clock, a horribly ill William Weaver found a seat in a chair in the aft cabin, attempting to quell his nausea. While unable to find the strength to climb back into his bed, a violent lurching of the vessel threw him out of the chair and across the room. Charles Chard, who was less prone to seasickness, heard Weaver's cries and helped him into the upper berth, then propped the door open again with the bag of salt. Weaver and Boak lay awake watching the deck.

Mate Hanson pumped out the bilge at the end of his watch. Blackwell heard him call, "Eight bells and all's well!" and remained half-awake in the forward cabin. Packard, who had recovered from a slight case of seasickness, couldn't sleep either and listened from his berth in the forward cabin.

Charles Carlson and Leon Ausprung took over the night watch when the mate went below deck at midnight.

Major Ingraham remained dry under a rubber tarp, resting peacefully in his sleeping bag between the two launches on the roof of the after cabin. He woke occasionally under a star-filled blanket of ebony sky. His father and uncles were mariners. And every mariner knows that some of the most effective antidotes for seasickness are watching the horizon or staring at a fixed point - on a dark night - the stars. And they also know to find a center point on the ship, low to the deck, to minimize the confusing effects that a rolling sea can have on the equilibrium. For an hour and a half after the mate's cry of "eight bells and all's well," not a single sound disturbed his slumber.

CHAPTER 12 - ON HER BEAM ENDS

SUNDAY, MAY 22, 1898

The sea continued to roll under a moderate gale, waves crashing over the decks of the schooner, but everything seemed much as it has been for the past twenty-four hours.

Around one-thirty in the morning, the Jane Gray was heading south-southwest when a minor squall came on her from the southeast. The wind and waves crashed against the port beam, causing her to list on her starboard side. Charles Carlson, the third mate, strapped the wheel to keep her steady, climbed between the two launches, over Ingraham, and went forward to lower the peak of the foresail. Major Ingraham was awakened from his peaceful sleep by the sudden activity on deck. Men were working with the sails as the ship heeled over on her starboard side.

While the crew was trying to right the ship, William Weaver had been unable to sleep. From his aft bunk, he watched the deck through the open cabin door and noticed water coming down the steps into the companionway. Thinking that something must be wrong, William elbowed his bunkmate, George Boak, and asked if they should alert a crewmember. George had been severely weakened from a relentless case of seasickness, but rallied and got the attention of the cook, Charles Oleson, who then woke Mate Hanson. The mate got up, climbed the steps and closed the door to the aft cabin, at the same time placing a board at the bottom to block water from coming in the companionway.

Hanson realized something was seriously amiss. Within seconds of closing the door, he returned to the companionway, leaping onto the darkened deck. "Hard up the helm!" he barked to the seaman at the wheel, ordering Carlson to force the tiller as far windward as possible.

The starboard rail was hugging the crests of the waves, water threatening to flood both cabins as it pushed through the hawser holes and surged over the top of the bulwarks. Waves pounded the port quarter. Heavy winds blew hard against the foresail, pinning the schooner over on her starboard rail.

Mate Hanson knew that all hands were needed to correct the vessel's position and sent Charles Carlson, who was on watch and acting as mate, down the aft companionway. Pounding on the captain's door, Carlson yelled that something was wrong with the ship and that the master was needed on deck at once.

Seaman Leon Ausprung, the least experienced hand, was on watch with Charles Carlson. Andrew Carlson, the second mate, heard the call from his fellow crewmembers, ran to the deck and began working in the rigging.

In the forward cabin, Blackwell had been lying half-awake for most of the night and heard the mate and the seamen calling to the captain that something was wrong with the ship.

Shortly before two o'clock Clayton Packard was alerted by the call, "All hands on deck." The other men who were awake in the forward cabin thought that the mate was only calling for the crew to come on deck. The Schmid boys, Jack Lindsay, and Phil Little had all been seasick and eaten nothing for several days. They were completely unaware as to what was happening outside.

Captain Crockett quickly pulled on his trousers, jacket, and boots while pushing his way through the stream of water rushing down the stairs into the aft companionway. The assistant cook, Albert Johnson, and the waiter, John Hawco, heard the call and followed him on deck. Cook Oleson rushed out ahead of them. Charles Chard helped William Weaver out of the aft cabin and up the stairs where Weaver clung to the side of the Italian launch that was secured to the roof of their quarters.

Just as the captain got on deck, Blackwell hurried out of the forward cabin, pulling on his rubber boots and slipping a wool sweater over his head. Horace Palmer, J. H. Conture, Manuel Roberts, Ben Snipes, and Luther Lessey followed him.

Clayton Packard heard the ruckus and woke Millay, telling him that he was going out to see what was happening. With no light to find his own gear, Clayt pulled on Will's boots and went out on deck. His bunkmate rolled over and went back to sleep, oblivious to what was about to transpire.

Shit was happening so fast that nobody could be certain of the outcome. The night was dark. While the stars twinkled in the sky, there was no moon. Wind howled through the spars and lines. Waves beat against the hull. On deck, the scene was organized chaos.

Erminio Sella, asleep under the cover of the launch, was suddenly awakened by excited voices. Although he couldn't understand much, he was able to comprehend the phrase "all sails down" and jumped up to see what was happening.

The Jane Gray was lying over, forty-five degrees to starboard, her lee rail under water. With every wave and gust of wind, the schooner listed further starboard. Captain Crockett once again called, "All hands on deck." This time adding the order, "Get on the weather rail," sending every man available into the rigging and onto the port rail in an attempt to right her.

Reaching the deck, Packard noticed a dozen men up in the rigging. The Captain and crew were attempting to get enough weight on the port side to offset her starboard list. One of them yelled to him to get up with them and try to right the vessel. Packard knew that his slight frame would be of little help, but climbed into the rigging anyway.

Recognizing that the ship was not responding, Captain Crockett bellowed, "Lower the foresail!" in the hope that he could bring the Gray into the wind and that she would right herself.

"Set the forestaysail!" The Captain's next order roared over the water-swept deck.

Loud and long, Captain Crockett barked more orders, "Everybody on deck! Everybody on deck!" Followed by, "Cut away the launches."

Packard had come down from the rigging and gone forward to launch the dory that lay on the top of the forward deckhouse. He almost had it loose from the lashings when Captain Crockett issued the order, "Set the jib!" As Carlson and Hanson were obeying the captain's orders, the halyard parted and the jib boom came down with a bang, covering the dory. This was a last ditch effort to get the vessel back up. The Jane Gray had failed to respond to all attempts to right her.

Reverend Gambell, who had been watching the efforts of his fellow passengers and the crew, came on deck carrying his daughter and immediately returned to the cabin. A distraught Mrs. Gambell, with the skirts of her nightgown whipping around her legs, followed him back down the stairs.

At this point, the vessel listed even further starboard, her rail barely above the waves. She was sinking rapidly, everything on deck and under the deck quickly being soaked by incoming water.

While working to cut away one of the other boats on the forward cabin, Horace Palmer talked with Dr. Lessey and Clayton Packard for a moment on deck. Perhaps seeing no possibility of survival, he told them, "This is a hard way to die, isn't it. The only thing I mind is leaving my wife and children."

Major Ingraham and others were working with the fastenings of the steam launch Kennorma while Sella's team of Italians tried to get their boat loose from the port quarter, which was now well above the waves on the windward side. Pulling out the only six life jackets onboard, Erminio called to his men. One by one, he adjusted the straps of the canvas and cork devices as the members of his party found their way to him through the darkness.

Fighting the heavy seas made handling the smaller ship's boats difficult and when one of them was being lowered from the davits, a rope parted. The boat filled with water once the other line was let loose. The crew released it, focusing on the boats that were more likely to save them.

The Kennorma was the first launch to float off the quarterdeck. Mate Hanson and George Pennington sprang into the boat and pushed her away from the side of the schooner, preventing her from being smashed against the hull.

Supposing that the launches were being cut loose in order to lessen the weight on deck and right the ship, Major Ingraham held to the fore rigging. Others thought the same and did not jump into the boats.

Leaving Nellie and Margaret in their aft stateroom, Missionary Gambell returned topside and mutely watched the operations of the men organizing their escape from the Jane Gray. Every few minutes someone remembered his wife and child and asked if they have been brought out of the cabin. Caught up in his own thoughts, he gave them no answer.

While Mr. Gambell stood on deck, his wife called to him from the aft companionway, "Father, what shall we do? What shall we do!" Standing in water that was soaking the heavy folds of her skirt, she repeated her plea, "What shall we do?" The Reverend returned to the cabin and told his wife, "The boat is doomed; we might as well all die together."

The men on deck thought that Gambell had gone below to get his wife and baby and would soon bring them on deck.

Suddenly realizing the gravity of the situation, Wilbur Doxsey hurried down to the aft cabins where he told his bunkmate that the boat was taking on water and that the captain had ordered everyone on deck. Launches were being cut loose. Job Johnson immediately leapt out of bed, telling Doxsey to get in the first boat. Grabbing some clothes and a hat, Job made it topside as men were beginning to fill the Kennorma. He rushed toward the launch, but stopped when he heard one of the men call out, "Let the woman and child have the first chance."

George Boak grabbed some clothes, passing Ginther while rushing from the aft cabin. Without shoes or a hat, he made his way to the port side while putting on what belongings he had time to retrieve – a gauze undershirt, lightweight corduroy trousers, and a coat. Frank Ginther followed him out. Many of the other men scrambling on deck barely had time to put on clothing. Some were barefoot and wearing little more than their nightshirts. The ship was listing so hard to starboard that water five or six inches deep was now running into the aft companionway.

Gripped by disbelief that the schooner was sinking, many failed to understand the need to abandon ship. Others thought that they must wait for Mrs. Gambell and the baby. When Captain Crockett realized this, he jumped into the Kennorma and issued the order, "All hands get into the launches." Three or four men leapt into Ingraham's boat with the captain while others followed by stepping off the rail into the launch. Still others slid into the water and swam for it. The captain and the mate threw the boiler and excess gear out of the Kennorma to make room for more passengers. Fearing that the little boat would be smashed against the hull of the Jane Gray, the men struggled to keep her close enough to the ship for others to gain their escape without drowning.

Weaver was still on deck, hanging onto the Italian launch, when he decided to make a go for Ingraham's boat and got washed overboard. In the churning sea, wreckage hit him in the chin and right shoulder. He pushed it away and grabbed the bow of the launch, where several men were holding the little vessel to the end of the ship's mast with a boat hook.

Erminio Sella and some of his men stepped into the waves. After making it to the launch, they found it nearly impossible to climb into the boat. The bulky life jackets kept them afloat, but because they were unable to get over the side, other men scrambled on top of them, using the bodies of the Italians as a rope ladder.

Finally, someone pulled Erminio in. After laying in the bottom long enough to catch his breath, he realized that two of his men were still clinging to the side, just as he had been, restricted by their lifejackets, getting pummeled by waves and other passengers frantically trying to get into the launch.

A man in the bow of the Kennorma yelled to Weaver, who thought that they were having a quarrel until an outstretched arm pulled him onboard. It was then that he realized that the man was an Italian who was only trying to help save him and the other men; all desperately fighting for their own lives.

The Italian launch was now in the water, floating over the stern of the schooner, but had apparently been smashed by the rigging while skidding off of the poop deck.

Kingsbury, below deck in the aft cabin, was awakened from a sound sleep by the voices from outside calling all hands to get out. Scrambling from his berth while trying to locate his trousers and jacket, he stepped into water well above his knees. The dining table was turned up on end near his cabin door from the ship careening to the starboard. He looked around and saw no one else in the cabin except Mr. Gambell and his wife in their stateroom. Their cabin door was open. As he dressed, Kingsbury overheard Mr. Gambell telling his wife, "We are all lost; there is no chance for us."

Making his way back on deck, Charles Chard passed Kingsbury's door, met the Reverend in the aft companionway and heard him saying to Nellie that there was no hope for them.

With barely enough time to put on a jacket and pants, Kingsbury turned to go up the companionway and onto the deck, passing Mr. Gambell on the way. The Reverend was leaning over with his back turned, quietly speaking to his wife. Kingsbury, in an urgent tone, told the family, "Come, let's get out of this quick!"

Reverend Gambell remained with his back turned and did not acknowledge the plea of his fellow passenger.

A frustrated Kingsbury grabbed the Reverend by the shirt and turned him around. Gambell refused to leave the cabin and repeated, "There's no chance for us. We are lost."

Growing desperate, Kingsbury issued a forceful plea, "Give me the baby and get your wife. We can take the boats."

Gambell replied again that it was no use. Nellie Gambell looked up as Kingsbury spoke the last time. The look in her eyes said that she would do anything to save her daughter. She was ready to try for the launch. Kingsbury repeated the rational argument that there were boats on the ship, and that they could at least make an attempt to save their own lives. Then he told them that he would go up the stairway and reach down for the baby, and for them to hand her up. Kingsbury felt certain that if he could get baby Margaret, the mother's instinct would lead Mrs. Gambell to follow him and perhaps then the family would try to save themselves.

Kingsbury mounted the companionway, thinking that the Gambells were going to hand him the baby and follow. He called twice to them to give him the baby, but they did not answer

At this point it was every man for himself. No one has had time to drag the men from the forward cabin. Some of the men remained on deck, uncertain of what action to take, apparently waiting for someone to help them. Many were unable to swim while others were simply resigned to take their medicine and go down with the ship.

But their little girl, their "mascot," they could not forget. From the launch, a voice carried loudly across the black sea, "Save the child!"

The other men in the boat raised their voices in chorus, "Yes. Save the babe. We can't lose our mascot!"

From the aft companionway, Kingsbury heard the captain call everyone into the boats and abandoned his valiant attempt to save the Gambell family. Just then he heard the scrape of another mans boots against the metal of the unlit companionway. Water was pouring down the stairs, filling the cabins below.

As Kingsbury made the deck, Claudius Brown, Captain Crockett's father-in-law, himself a father of five and a grandfather, hurried below in a final effort to persuade the Reverend Gambell and his wife to bring their daughter and get into the launch. Within seconds of Kingsbury's escape, the after cabin filled with water. No one else emerged.

The waves were rolling high, the wind whipping the sea into a frenzy. With only the dim starlight illuminating the night, it was difficult to distinguish anything or anybody.

Packard hesitated about getting into the first launch, thinking she already had too many men in her, and did not do so until Captain Crockett yelled, "Hurry up and fill this boat." At this point the launch was alongside, near the stern of the Jane Gray. As he jumped for a chance at safety, Packard caught a glimpse of two other members of the

Ingraham party, Bard Dunlap and Horace Palmer, who were both helping with the other boats.

Barely ten minutes had passed since the crisis began. Men were now rushing the Kennorma, realizing the necessity of leaving the schooner.

Major Ingraham held to the fore rigging until the last moment then leapt for the twenty-seven foot Kennorma. Landing in the water, he grabbed the side of the launch and became a human fender as the two vessels collided, the force of the waves against the boat slamming his body into the hull of the Jane Gray. Clayton Packard pulled him over the bulwarks and into the rapidly filling lifeboat.

Identifying items that might be necessary for their survival, Mate John Hanson managed to get back onto the Jane Gray. The schooner's main boom was sweeping over the passengers in the Kennorma with every rock of the ship. As Hanson threw boxes of provisions into the launch, the boom hit him in the head, nearly knocking him overboard. The ship was rapidly settling under the weight of water filling her holds. Those in the launch pulled the men in as fast as they came to the rail. Mate Hanson was one of the last to leave the ship.

The Jane Gray was now completely over on her starboard side, the spars kissing the peaks of the waves.

After letting go of the port rail, George Boak crawled out the mast and onto the aft boom, which was lashed in place. The Kennorma was directly below him - the deck of the Jane Gray nearly perpendicular to the ocean swells. Falling from the rigging, he dropped onto the bodies of the men already piled in the craft.

From the starboard rail, Kingsbury, one of the last men to escape the aft cabin, slipped in to the sea and made for the launch, diving under the wreckage several times. As he swam, he noticed the other launch with four men in her. He thought that he could make out Ranney and Ginther in the boat, but couldn't identify the others. The Italian launch sat low in the water as if it was half sunk. When he reached the side of the Kennorma, the hands of fellow survivors pulled him into the crowded boat.

Conture, Ben Snipes, and Mannie Roberts stood at the rail, waiting for a chance for one of the boats. Mannie saw a launch off the stern of the Jane Gray and said to his partner, "Ben, I guess it's off with us. I guess it's in the water." Following Conture's lead, Mannie and Ben jumped in, pulling long strokes to reach their only hope for survival.

Weak from seasickness and wearing a heavy sweater and long rubber boots, James Blackwell stepped into the water and frantically swam for the launch, now some sixty feet from the sinking schooner. Thoughts of his wife and children pushed him to his very limit. Limp and exhausted from extreme exertion, he reached a line trailing behind the little craft and was pulled on board by one of the passengers.

Although they could not see anyone, the men in the Kennorma heard the cries of those who were still clinging to the Jane Gray. Without oars, it was impossible to return to the ship. Each wave and wind gust pushed them further away from the sinking schooner. Captain Crockett and the men in the launch continued to call out over the roaring sea, pulling in every man who had been able to swim within reach of the little boat.

Job Johnson, waited too long for the Gambell family and missed his chance for the Kennorma while she remained near the sinking ship. Hanging on to the schooner's port rail as she went down, he too could see the Italian launch with four men in her. A sudden lurch of the vessel threw him through the rigging. Falling and striking a boom, the impact bruised him severely and tore his clothing. Fearing that he would be entangled in the rigging, Johnson swam deep under water before emerging in the midst of the wreckage. Unable to see either of the launches or anyone else above the crests of the waves, he swam to an overturned boat, found a grip on the side and floated in the sea.

Reilly and Gleason also held to the railing of the Jane Gray until the last possible moment. Reilly dove in first, swimming through the frigid water to a pile of boards. Gleason followed and got a hold of the other end of the same boards. Out of breath, cold and tired when he finally reached the lumber, William Gleason gasped to Reilly that he did not think he could hold on very long. The much younger Reilly tried to cheer him up, optimistically saying that they would soon be picked up. He had seen both of the launches get away from the ship with men in them.

Before dawn broke the darkness, Gleason spoke his last words to Reilly, "I'll have to give up. Goodbye." Letting go of the lumber, he sank beneath the waves.

All alone in the moonless night, clinging to a pile of boards in the dark, icy sea, somewhere between Vancouver Island and Cape Flattery, a horrified C. J. Reilly watched Gleason's body disappear from sight.

In the launch Kennorma, Kingsbury looked for his partner in the darkness. He called out for Ranney, but received no response. Others called the names of their partners while the captain began a head count of the survivors. Conture called out for Reilly. Again, there was no reply.

As they drifted away from the wreck, no more voices could be heard. Soon, the noise of wind and waves were the only sounds that broke the silence of the night. The men huddled in the launch, stunned speechless by the events of the last hour.

The sea was running high with ten to fifteen foot swells threatening to swamp the overcrowded vessel, but the Kennorma steadily rode the waves. As their sight gradually adapted to the blackness of the night, the passengers scavenged anything floating by that might later prove useful in saving their lives.

About an hour and a half after abandoning the Jane Gray, at the first glimmer of sunrise, the survivors heard a voice echoing over the waves. It was Job Johnson, clinging to an overturned boat. He had been drifting in the wreckage for several hours, the seas carrying him and scattered pieced of debris in the same direction as the launch. An experienced mariner from the northeast, he was more accustomed to the frigid waters and had been able to hang on longer than most could have.

Within fifteen minutes of pulling Johnson into the boat, the deep bass voice of C. J. Reilly rang over the sea. The men in the Kennorma, using improvised oars, poled the launch through the dim light in the direction of his voice. They found him locked in a death grip with the bundle of lumber, exhausted to the point of delirium - so much so that two men had difficulty prying his hands free from the makeshift life raft. After being dragged into the crowded launch, an overcome Reilly told how Gleason let go of the lumber and died before his eyes.

Under the dim pre-dawn light, the men in the launch could see the Jane Gray. Her hull now full of water, she had righted and the topmasts were vertical above the waves. Soon, these too disappeared.

At about ten o'clock in the morning, the group of survivors fashioned a sail from a tarp and ran north before the wind. From his last reckoning, Captain Crockett estimated that they were about ninety miles northwest of Cape Flattery and forty miles west of Vancouver Island. The launch did not head toward the coast, but parallel with it.

Major Ingraham and Captain Crockett covered the boat with a tarp to prevent the water from splashing in as the waves broke over the bow. The clear morning sky was soon obscured by heavy gray clouds and the canvas folds of the roof became a catch for rainwater.

Water pooled on the floorboards. The captain feared that the boat may have been damaged, but was uncertain and assigned one man to constantly bail. The men alternated this duty, tired, but warmed a bit by the exhausting exercise. Some of the passengers refused to help with the bailing. Others were downright disagreeable and did everything that they were asked not to do. Packed one on top of the other, soaking wet, the men tried to shift their weight in an attempt to regain circulation in their limbs. As the Kennorma was less than twenty-eight feet long by seven feet four inches beam, the close quarters meant that the twenty-seven men could neither lie nor sit. Any sudden movement threatened to swamp the little boat.

The men in the launch sailed until five o'clock Sunday afternoon. Both Captain Crockett and Major Ingraham had an idea of their position. Fearing that they would blow north into the wide-open Pacific and miss the opportunity to make land, the engineering minds on board constructed a drag using a propeller, the tarp, and pieces of rope and canvas. Throwing it over the stern to steady the boat, the drag was also hoped to slow their course. They rode the sea until four o'clock Monday morning when a slight change in the wind made it possible for the vessel to head directly west, where it was believed that they should run into the coast Vancouver Island.

CHAPTER 13 - SURVIVORS

After riding the ocean all night in virtual silence, the half-clothed, freezing survivors replayed the horror of the night in their minds. Although they didn't realize it yet, only ten of the forty-three men in the forward cabin made it into the Kennorma. And nothing had been seen of the Italian launch since drifting away from the Jane Gray. The missing faces among the group haunted them, as did the loss of their little mascot, Margaret. Stiff, exhausted and overwhelmed with grief, some of the passengers grew cross and uncooperative. Few could muster the desire to eat any of the turnips or prunes that were saved by Mate Hanson.

Dawn cast its early rays across the wave tops as the wind caught their makeshift sail, pushing the little vessel toward shore. At eleven o'clock on the morning of Monday, May 23rd, the passengers finally made out the rocky northwest headlands of Vancouver Island.

Three hours later, thirty-six hours after abandoning the Jane Gray, the twenty-seven survivors poled the launch through an opening in the jagged rocks to a calm cove on the southern banks of Kyuoquot Sound. After pulling the boat up onto the shores of Union Island, everyone unfolded their rigid limbs, stretching their legs on the beach while gathering mussels and wood. The group built a fire, making a meal of roasted mussels. For most of them, it was the first food they had tasted since entering the Straits of Juan de Fuca on Friday morning.

The men who had been able to make it on deck fully clothed shared what little they had with their fellow shipmates. While scavenging lumber from the wreck, a sack of garments had been found floating in the water. This was now divided among those most in need. Until this very moment, the full realization of their losses had been unrecognized. Passing out clothing, it was no longer possible to ignore.

Of Major Ingraham's team, only four of the sixteen remained. Erminio Sella's party was short two men. Blackwell had also lost two. Kingsbury's partner did not make it. Charles Wilkinson was the lone survivor of all of the San Francisco men.

The loss of the Gambell family was a bitter pill that was particularly difficult for Packard and Ingraham to swallow, senseless in so many ways. How many men had sacrificed their own lives in the attempt to save them?

Even after the last thirty-six hours crowded in the launch, it seemed inconceivable that they had lost so many.

As evening approached, the sun hovered low over the waves of the Pacific and a native hunting deer from his canoe passed their camp. He told them that his village was not far away. Promising to lead them to his home when he returned in the morning, the native continued on his hunt.

Making camp on the rocky beach, the survivors huddled around the fire, attempting to dry out and thaw their bones while awaiting the Indian who would lead them to the nearest settlement.

Dawn broke again and, at five o'clock in the morning, the damp, frozen survivors returned to the Kennorma. With the same makeshift oars that had brought them across ninety mile of rough seas, the men paddled six miles to the north, following the native in his canoe to the village of Kyoquot. The trip took them another four hours.

Upon their arrival at the Indian settlement, the men from the Jane Gray found the schooner Favorite at anchor in the flat waters of the harbor, where the vessel was wind bound on its return from the northern sealing grounds. Captain McLellan, master and owner of the Favorite, agreed to transport the survivors to Victoria once favorable winds arose.

For two days, the survivors of the wreck, wearing what clothing they had been able to salvage, scavenge, or borrow, remained on the decks of the Favorite, awaiting winds that would allow them to make the passage south. The few who had cash in their pockets were able to purchase goods in the village. With nothing but time on their hands, they discussed the possible causes of the disaster. Rumors circulated. Was she cursed?

Captain McLellan was aware of an incident involving the Jane Gray and recounted the story. When she was only a year old, the schooner was caught in a gale off Point Barrow. It was August of 1888. The sailing barks Fleetwing, Young Phoenix, and the Mary and Susan were wrecked in the ice during the storm. All were abandoned. The Jane Gray lost her anchors, drifted about sixty miles northeast of the point in the same gale. Instead of risking starvation waiting for help, the crew of the schooner made their way overland. Captain Healy, on the Bear, rescued some of them, while the rest found their way to the nearest port. Another revenue cutter, the Thetis, found the Gray capsized in the ice, determined that she was salvageable, and towed the ship to Sitka. There, her hull was repaired and a contingent from the cutter's crew sailed the schooner back to San Francisco. After that, the same ship had a fairly successful career sailing the Pacific while engaged in the sealing trade. She had once been impounded by the government for illegal sealing and remained in government possession until the owners paid the fine, got her back, and sold her in San Francisco.

The survivors of this sinking talked of compensation. The MacDougall and Southwick Company was a large, powerful operation. Had they any knowledge of the Jane Gray's past? Perhaps the group would have better odds of recouping some of their money if they presented a united front. James Blackwell still had his water stained ticket in the pocket of his trousers. The stub clearly stated that the very least they were entitled to was $100 each for lost baggage. It was decided that Blackwell, Reilly, and Kingsbury would speak for those who had been left most destitute by the tragedy.

Memorial Day, Monday, May 30, 1898, was surely a solemn day for the survivors on board the schooner Favorite as she sailed south for Victoria. Captain Crockett pondered the wreck of the Jane Gray, telling James Blackwell, "there was no sea to cause the loss" of the ship and that "he hated to lose his vessel in a hatful of wind." For five full days the ship battled headwinds, often drifting with no wind on the return to the southern tip of Vancouver Island.

Upon their arrival at Victoria Harbor, early on the morning of June 1st, Captain Crockett immediately sent a telegram to John Pacey at the MacDougall and Southwick Company in Seattle:

"J. G. Pacey, Seattle: The Jane Gray foundered ninety miles west of Cape Flattery. Twenty-seven saved, brought here by schooner Favorite. Authorize me to draw on you for $270 to pay passage on schooner. CROCKETT."

George Hiller sent a message to his mother in Harrisburg, Pennsylvania: "I am safe. Vessel foundered. Ginther lost." James Blackwell also got a telegram off. Since cables to transmit telegrams had not yet been laid across the floor of Puget Sound, the messages were hand carried to the first steamer leaving for Seattle. Traveling at about fifteen knots per hour, the seventy-four mile trip brought the messages to Western Union by 10:00 a.m. on the morning of June 1st.

At the office of the American Consul in Victoria, arrangements were made for travel to Seattle within a few hours. The crew of the Jane Gray was allowed free passage, while the survivors were given half-priced fare on the City of Kingston. George Pennington, Seaman Carlson, and the cooks, Johnson and Oleson, caught an evening trip on the North Pacific. All four were interviewed while waiting at the consulate. Crewmembers Charles Oleson and Albert Johnson recounted their feelings about the behavior of the ship on the Saturday before she went down. Both stated that the day water was first found in the forward cabin, they had told the passengers that the ship should be taken back to Neah Bay or the nearest harbor. When asked if either of them told the captain of their concerns, they replied that the captain no doubt "knew his business better than they did." Pennington refused to express an opinion on any possible causes for the wreck, telling the reporter that he was not a seaman and therefore not qualified to do so.

CHAPTER 14 – FIRST NEWS

The messages arrived at the telegraph company as soon as an errand boy could run them up from the steamer. However, before the kid made the two blocks from the waterfront, reporters from the *Seattle Daily Times* and *Post-Intelligencer* intercepted the telegrams and word of the disaster began to spread throughout the city.

When the eleven o'clock edition of the *Seattle Post-Intelligencer* reached print on June 1st, newspaper peddlers cried out from the street corners, "The Jane Gray Goes Down off Cape Flattery! Thirty-Four Lost!"

N. WEDNESDAY, JUNE 1, 1898.—TWELVE PAGES.

THIRD EDITION

—11 A. M.—

SCHOONER JANE GRAY LOST AT SEA.

THIRTY-FOUR LIVES LOST OFF CAPE FLATTERY, MAY 22.

MAJOR E. S. INGRAHAM'S PARTY OF FIFTEEN ABOARD.

FULL PASSENGER LIST AND THE SURVIVORS.

Image courtesy of the Seattle Public Library.

Every resident of Seattle stopped dead in their tracks, aghast as they viewed the headlines.

Effie Young, the seventeen year-old daughter of Spencer Young and an employee at Western Union Telegraph Company, was one of the first to hear the news. Her father was one of the missing. From the offices at 113 Cherry Street, Effie held her skirts and nearly ran the fourteen blocks to their home at 811 Pike. Making the trip in less than fifteen minutes, the teenager broke the horrible news to her mother, Cordelia.

Many local seafaring men were indignant at the implication in Crockett's telegram that the shipwrecked passengers were charged fare to return to the nearest port. Down on the docks, rumors flew. The Jane Gray had been wrecked before. She was overloaded. They never should have built that forward cabin on a vessel designed as a whaler.

A great many held their breath, hoping that there had been a mistake, that perhaps the *Seattle Daily Times* had the names wrong when publishing the list of the lost and survivors:

LOST—34: Signor Gaia, Italy; Signor Secondo, Italy; Jack Lindsay, Everett; W. H. Gleason, Seattle; W. A. Johnson, Seattle; V. J. Smith, Seattle; C. G. Smith, Seattle; P. C. Little, Seattle; S. W. Young, Seattle; W. D. Millan, Seattle; Horace Palmer, Lebanon, O.; F. G. Saulsberry, Minnesota; A. B. Dunlap, Dwight, Ill.; B. D. Ranney, Mexico City; B. E. Snipe, Jr., Seattle; John M. Stutzman, Westfield, N. J.; E. M. Taylor, California; F. S. Taylor, California; B. S. Spencer, California;W. P. Doxey; Edw. F. Ritter; F. W. Ginther; B. S. Frost; W. F. Levering; William Otter; O. F. McKelvey; C. Brown; C. C. Aikins; N. Hederlund; Charles Williams; V. C. Gambell, wife and child, missionary on St. Lawrence Island in the Bering Sea. And one other (subject to correction).

SAVED—27: Capt. Crockett, Seaman Hanson, Seaman Carlson, Seaman Oleson, Seaman Johnson, Major Ingraham, L. M. Lessey, C. H. Packard, G. H. Pennington, J. E. Blackwell, S. Livingood, C. E. Chard, George R. Boak, Wm. W. Weaver, C. J. Reilly, J. H. Conture, Job Johnson, George Hiller, P. J. Davenport, Signor Sella, Signor Bianchitts, Signor Ceria, H. Waechter, A. G. Kingsbury, M. F. Roberts, Coney Weston, C. W. Wilkinson.

News of the disaster caused a large crowd to gather at the dock awaiting the arrival of the City of Kingston. Carriages filled with family and friends anxiously watched as the steamer tied up to the pier. All eyes were strained, desperately scanning the figures on deck for a glimpse of their loved ones. The bedraggled, weary survivors were surrounded as soon as they set foot on the planks of the wharf. Mothers and wives, in search of their sons and husbands, rushed from man to man, pleading for news. Many collapsed, sobbing at the realization that theirs were not among those on board the steamer.

Erminio Sella was overwhelmed by the reception and, through his own tears, told one of his fellow survivors, (translated) "The welcome I received today somewhat alleviates the immense pain I feel; it is one of those spontaneous demonstrations that is very good and that I will never forget."

Those who were able to locate friends and relatives loaded them into waiting carriages and whisked them to their homes. The captain, James Blackwell, and several others immediately headed for the MacDougall and Southwick store.

Besieged by the anxious relatives of the members of his party, Major Ingraham's, charged with the safety of so many young men, struggled to maintain his composure while repeating the tale again and again. Before he was able to go home and change out of the clothing that he'd been wearing for a full week, a reporter from the *Post-Intelligencer* drew him out of the crowd to a waiting carriage and whisked him away to the private offices of the newspaper. The man who had scaled mountain peaks, commanded militia, and supervised thousands of students wept as he told the story that would go to print the following morning.

Speculation about the cause of the disaster began within minutes of the arrival of Crockett's telegram from Victoria. Immediately following the headlines announcing the list of passengers, gossip from the docks in regards to the history of the Jane Gray earned its own block of print in the same newspaper:

"SAILOR'S SUPERSTITION.

The schooner Jane Gray was built in 1887 at Bath, Me., and has had an adventurous career. Her length was 82.7 feet; breadth, 23 feet; depth, 9.2 feet. Her gross registered tonnage was 112.70 and her net 107.07. She was owned by Mr. J. G. Pacey of the MacDougall-Southwick Company, and was thoroughly inspected before leaving this port. Capt. Burns of the Board of Underwriters and Capt. Milnor, The Times' inspector, both pronounced her staunch, safe and seaworthy, and as being in much better condition than many of the sailing vessels that have left this port for Alaska this season. Before the vessel left port there was much talk along the water front about her being unfortunate in the past and being afflicted with a sailor's "hoo-doo," but such talk came only from the superstitious, who wagged their heads the more because she left here on a Friday.

These, however, were taken as merely the effervescence of idle talk and such they really were, for the gentlemen who said she was seaworthy before she sailed insist upon it now and claim that only some extraordinary weather or unusual mishap could have befallen her."

CHAPTER 15 - HEADLINES

By June 2, 1898, the sinking of the schooner Jane Gray headlined every major newspaper across the country, from New York to Kansas City to San Francisco.

Some publications even noted Prince Luigi's fortunate escape. Remembering that the Duke of Aosta would have been a member of the prospecting party, had it not been for the fact that his uncle, King Umberto, had directed him to conduct an expedition to the North Pole, the *Boston Herald* commented: "Prince Luigi will regret the tragic fate of the Alaska expedition, but he is scarcely human if he does not go into the nearest church and leave a thank offering because he was not aboard the ship that foundered on the Vancouver coast. He might have been."

And while Monday's column in the *Seattle Daily Times* declared that thirty-four were lost, the *Seattle Post-Intelligencer* provided the most comprehensive coverage of the tragedy, adding the names of U. S. Hamilton, Andrew Carlson, and John Hawco while omitting C. C. Aikins and Nick Hederlund from the list of missing men. Charles E. Chard and George R. Boak did not appear on the list of survivors. Even more confusing, the head count didn't add up. Were sixty-three on board, sixty-four or sixty-one?

"DRAWN TO DEATH BENEATH THE WAVES OF THE PACIFIC.

Thirty-Six Lives Lost in the Foundering of the Schooner Jane Gray.

TWENTY-SEVEN SURVIVORS ARRIVE IN THIS CITY.

Most of the Victims Are From Seattle—Of Major Ingraham's Expedition of Fourteen But Four Survive—Complete List of Victims—Disaster Happened Sunday Morning, May 22, at 2 O'Clock, While the Vessel Was Hove-to Ninety Miles Off Cape Flattery—No Storm at the Time—Occurs So Suddenly That Many Had Not Even Time to Leave Their Bunks—Refuge Taken in a Launch, in Which Vancouver Island Was Reached—From There to Victoria by Schooner—Heartrending Scene on the City of Kingston's Arrival With the Survivors of the Wreck.

The schooner Jane Gray, freighted with lives precious to this city, foundered ninety miles off Cape Flattery Sunday morning, May 22. The ship and thirty-six people were lost. Twenty-seven, including a number of Seattle men, were saved. Following is a complete list of the lost and the survivors:"

THE LOST—36

William H. Gleason, of Seattle; W. Arnot Johnston, of Seattle; Philip C. Little, of Seattle; Spencer W. Young, of Seattle; Ben E. Snipes, Jr., of Seattle; Claudius Brown, of Seattle; S. Gaia, of Biella, Italy; Secundo Bissetta, of Biella; V. J. Schmid, of Mercer Island, Wash.; C. G. Schmid, of Mercer Island; W. D. Maloy, of La Conner, Wash.; John J. Lindsay, of Everett, Wash.; Horace Palmer, of Lebanon, O.; U. S. Hamilton, of Illinois; A. B. Dunlap, of Dwight, Ill.; F. G. Saulsbury, of Minnesota; John M. Stutzman, of Plainfield, N. J.; B. D. Ranney, of Kalamazoo, Mich.; E. M. Taylor, of San Francisco; F. S. Taylor, of San Francisco; B. S. Spencer of San Francisco; W. P. Doxey, of New York; Edw. F. Ritter, of Poughkeepsie, N. Y.; F. W. Ginther, of Harrisburg, Pa.; B. S. Frost, of San Francisco; W. F. Deterling, of Pennsylvania; William Otter, of Pennsylvania; O. F. McKelvey, residence unknown; Charles Williams, residence unknown; Wm. C. Gambel, St. Lawrence Island, Bering Sea; Mrs. Wm. C. Gambel and child; Andrew Carlson, seaman, of Seattle; John Hawco, waiter, of Seattle.

THE SAVED—27

Major E. S. Ingraham, of Seattle; J. E. Blackwell, of Seattle; Capt. Ezekial Crockett, of Seattle; Silas Livengood, of Seattle; M. F. Roberts, of Seattle; Dr. L. M. Lessey, of Seattle; C. H. Packard, of Snohomish, Washington; George Pennington, of Snohomish, Washington; W. S. Weaver, of Muncy, Pennsylvania; C. J. Reilly, of Hartford, Conn.; J. H. Conture, of Hartford, Conn.; George Hiller, of Harrisburg, Pennsylvania; P. J. Davenport, of Harrisburg, Pennsylvania; A. G. Kingsbury, of Boston; Coney Weston, of Skowhegan, Me.; C. W. Wilkinson, of San Francisco, California; Erminio Sella, of Biella, Italy; Secondo Biancaetto, of Biella; A. Ceria, of Biella; Hans Wachter, of Tyrol; John Hanson, mate, of Ballard; Charles Olson, cook, of Seattle; Albert Johnson, waiter, of Seattle; Charles Carlson, seaman, of Seattle; Job Johnson, seaman, of Long Island, New York.

"The Refuge of Startled Men.

The Jane Gray opened her seams and began to sink at 2 o'clock in the morning. Ten minutes after the first alarm only her topmasts were visible above water and a few feet from where she had ridden the waves a tiny launch was bobbing up and down in the starlight, the refuge of twenty-seven startled men. In that brief ten minutes thirty-six souls had passed out of this life, and one of the most horrifying disasters of the North Pacific ocean had occurred. The stars blinked down compassionately on those twenty-seven, who strained their eyes in the darkness toward the wreckage and wondered what had happened. It was as though a mighty hand had reached up from the ocean's depths and pinched the laboring schooner until her ribs cracked and the urgent water had rushed through the crevices and filled the hold; had stolen into the state rooms and coldly lapped the feet of the sleepers, rousing them to horrors indescribable; and the hand had drawn down and the waters had risen until the vessel was engulfed. No great outcry came from the lips soon to be stilled forever. The utmost bravery and unselfishness was displayed by the suddenly awakened passengers. Some did not even leave their bunks. Others refused at the last moment to abandon the vessel for fear of swamping the steam launch, which offered the only means of escape from the wreck. 'If we must die,' they said, 'let it be like men.'

The ill fated schooner sailed from Seattle for Kotzebue sound Thursday, May 19, with sixty-three people aboard, including Capt. Crockett and eight men. Maj. E. S. Ingraham, with the party of fourteen men equipped for Prince Luigi, at an expense of $10,000 was on board, and another expedition of Italians under Erminio Sella. The schooner carried no cargo save the outfits of the passengers. On the deck were two steam launches. In one of these all who escaped the wreck found refuge. Had it not been for the launch not a life would have been saved.

On Saturday night, May 21, the Jane Gray hove-to ninety miles off Cape Flattery in latitude 48:40, longitude 126:55. Nothing disturbed the peace of the night until 2 o'clock in the morning, when the startling order came, "Everybody on deck." This was repeated again and again, and was heard by everyone on the ship. The vessel was sinking rapidly, and the two steam launches, loaded on the deck, were soon afloat. In one, the Kennorma, belonging to Ingraham's party, were crowded twenty-seven people.

When last seen the other launch held four men, whose identity could not be distinguished because of the darkness. The launch seemed to be half full of water and was somewhat damaged. No hope in entertained that it stayed above water. In the Kennorma room was left for three of four more survivors.

The only woman aboard perished with her husband and child under romantic circumstances. Rev. V. C. Gambel, missionary at St. Lawrence Island, in the Bering Sea, was returning to his station, accompanied by his wife and baby daughter. They were in the lower cabin when the alarm was sounded. The missionary came on deck long enough to see what was happening. "We are doomed," he exclaimed. "There is nothing left but to die." He then went below and locked himself in the cabin with his wife and child. Efforts to get him on deck once more were fruitless; neither would he consent to the rescue of his wife. "We shall die together," was all he said in answer to entreaties.

On being freed from the wreckage the launch Kennorma, with the survivors aboard, was propelled to Vancouver Island and there a schooner was found which brought the weary victims to Victoria. The first news of the disaster cabled from Victoria reached here early yesterday morning and created the utmost excitement in the city. The Jane Gray had so many well-known Seattle people aboard that the news carried poignant sorrow everywhere.

The announcement that the survivors were coming to Seattle on the steamer City of Kingston attracted a great crowd to Yesler dock. As the steamer drew in from Victoria a forlorn party was seen standing by the forward rail. The men were roughly dressed and their features were pinched and drawn from suffering and exposure. As they came silently down the gangplank they were seized by waiting men and women, who clasped their hands and gave fervent thanks for their safety. Women with tears in their eyes pleaded for news of those whose faces they did not see among the saved. At the words, "All lost," they turned away in an agony that brought sympathetic sobs from the breasts of strong men."

Major Ingraham's interview from the prior evening followed: "The Jane Gray foundered Sunday morning, May 22, at 2 o'clock, ninety miles off Cape Flattery, in latitude 48:40, longitude 126:55. I am accurate as to the hour, since my watch stopped as I sprang into the water. We left here Thursday, May 19, and got outside the Straits Saturday morning. A strong southeast wind was kicking up a heavy sea, and a majority of the passengers were very seasick. We carried all sail that day and made ninety miles. No attempt was made to get meals, and the food passed around was partaken of very lightly. A number of the passengers were so sick they had taken to their bunks.

At 9 o'clock Saturday night we were hove-to under a foresail and staysail. The captain said he did this for the sake of the sick passengers and not because he feared danger. I slept on top of the cabin in my sleeping bag. Several times I awoke. The stars were shining and all seemed well, and I dropped back to slumber with a feeling of the greatest security. Just before 2 o'clock I heard Capt. Crockett say:

'Lower the foresail.'

"The schooner seemed to be listing to starboard and he evidently hoped to right her. The Gray failed to respond. She was plainly waterlogged and even then was sinking rapidly. The captain now called out in a voice heard all over the ship:

'Everybody on deck. Get on the weather rail.'

"The next order was 'cut away the launches.'

"At that time I was clinging to the fore rigging. I supposed the launches were to be cut away in order to right the ship. Others thought as I did. As soon as a launch was cut loose she floated off the quarter deck of the schooner. No one jumped into the Kennorma, which was first to float off, and Capt. Crockett sprang to her and ordered:

"'All hands get into the launches.'

"The other launch had also been cut loose in the meantime and floated over the stern of the schooner. There were four men in it. The necessity of leaving the ship was now causing a rush for the Kennorma. The launch lay alongside, now washed near by rising on a wave and again falling away with the sweep of the sea. I clung in the fore rigging of the Jane Gray until the last moment, and then sprang into the water, making a lucky grab for the launch's rail as I did so. As I clung to the rail the launch was dashed violently against the schooner, my body acting as fender. The blow caused me to cry out, and I was drawn into the launch in the nick of time.

"We were without oars, and had great difficulty in warding off floating wreckage. It was quite dark, for, though the sky was clear and the stars shone bright, there was no moon. After getting away from the schooner we heard cries, and could dimly make out a man on a pile of wreckage. We pulled him out and found it was Job Johnson, of Long Island. Fifteen minutes later another shout was heard. It was C. J. Riley, of Hartford, Conn. We turned our attention to him and he was soon aboard. Riley said he had left the Gray when her rail was only eight or ten inches from the water. For a time he had as a companion on the wreckage W. H. Gleason, of Seattle. The latter had been unable to hang on, and had sunk beneath the waves without a moan.

"It was now growing light and we could just see the topmasts of the schooner sticking above the water. These, too, disappeared. The vessel had first careened over on her starboard side until her topmasts lay in the water. She had then sunk to her port rail and had straightened once more, sinking at last in an upright position.

"We improvised a tarpaulin sail and ran before the wind. We did not head toward the coast, but parallel with it. We sailed until 5 o'clock Sunday afternoon, then made a drag, using a propeller, the tarpaulin, pieces of rope and canvas, and threw it over the stern. We rode there until 4 o'clock Monday morning. At that time a slight change in the wind made it possible for us to head direct for the land. At 11 o'clock we caught sight of the highlands of Vancouver Island.

"As we approached the shore we saw rocks and reefs, with hardly a visible channel. At last an opening, a few cable lengths wide, was made out and we succeeded in passing through and rounded what afterwards proved to be Rugged point. We found ourselves in a quiet cove in Kyuquoit sound, about sixty miles from the north end of Vancouver island.

"We landed at 2 o'clock Monday afternoon, just thirty-six hours after we had left the wreck. There had been no suffering from hunger or thirst on the launch. A bag of prunes and some turnips were almost untouched. It rained part of the time and we caught plenty of fresh water. The terrible scene through which we had passed deprived all of appetite. The boat had been covered with an awning to prevent the water splashing in, as the waves broke. One man was kept constantly bailing and we discovered after we had landed that two planks had been smashed near the water line. As the boat was only twenty-eight feet long by 7 feet 4 inches beam, you can understand what close quarters it was for twenty-seven men. We could neither lie nor sit.

"After landing we took an hour to limber up, and then built a fire. Some mussels were gathered and these we baked for the evening meal. About 5 o'clock on Monday afternoon we saw an Indian in a canoe and learned of a settlement about seven miles from our camp, where stores could be obtained. The Indian had been hunting deer and promised to come back Tuesday morning and show us the way to the village.

"At 5 o'clock the next morning we boarded the launch once more and, following the native's pilotage, reached Kyoquot four hours later. There we found the schooner Favorite, of Victoria, owned and commanded by Capt. McLellan. She was wind bound on her way home from sealing grounds. Capt. McLellan received us with great hospitality and readily agreed to take us to Victoria as soon as the wind would permit us to sail.

"We succeeded in getting out of the harbor at noon on Thursday, May 26, and after battling with head winds and drifting with no winds, reached Victoria harbor this morning at 4 o'clock.

"Capt. Crockett reported our loss to the American consul and he gave transportation to the crew to Seattle. The rest of us were given a half rate on the Kingston. Several of the survivors are practically destitute, since neither money nor clothing could be saved in the confusion of the moment. A few of the outfits were insured."

The twenty-seven survivors of the Jane Gray almost to a man secured new clothing as soon as they arrived here. Many were borrowed garments and others were clad in the rough clothes they wore on board the ship. A committee appointed by the passengers on the Favorite visited the MacDougall & Southwick Company yesterday and presented what they said was a fair demand upon the company, which they considered as operating the Gray. This committee consisted of Mr. Blackwell, Mr. Reilly and Mr. Kingsbury. It is understood that the men claim $100 each in money and a new outfit of wearing apparel.

Mr. Blackwell stated that the committee had not completed its adjustment with the MacDougall & Southwick Company. The great majority of the survivors were, however supplied with new clothes at the company's store on First avenue.

Mr. MacDougall said last night that the company had nothing to do with the Gray any more than that she was advertised by them. He said: "The schooner was owned by J. G. Pacey and others. Our arrangement as to the new supplies for the survivors will be made with him and his associates. All we want is to do the right thing by the men."

"Packard Tells of Some Horrors.

Clayton H. Packard, one of the best-known mining men in Snohomish county, and formerly publisher of the Tri-Weekly Eye, at Snohomish, was one of the men who survived the foundering of the Jane Gray. He joined Maj. Ingraham's expedition as a mining expert. To a Post-

Intelligencer reporter yesterday Mr. Packard gave the following story of his experience:

'Trouble began for the sixty-three persons on the old whaler Jane Gray on Friday morning. Even before we got out of the Straits the forward cabin was awash. Every time her bow went into the swells gallons of water swept over the deck, and a great deal of it found its way into the forward cabin through the hawse holes. I had a lower berth and woke up Friday morning to find a half-foot of water sweeping around the cabin. With every wash of the vessel I was flooded. I got my personal outfit on the table and after that bunked with W. D. Maloy, of Skagit county, who had the middle berth.

'Although the water was pouring into the galley, we managed to get breakfast Friday morning. Many of the boys were seasick, and did not care to leave their bunks. The schooner was kept on her course Friday and Saturday, for the storm was not a heavy one. The water, however, continued to come aboard with every swell. We did not have another meal after getting out of the Straits. When we went to bed, on Saturday night, the schooner's hold had just been pumped out, and very little water found.

'I could not sleep after midnight (Sunday), although I had recovered from a slight spell of seasickness. Shortly before 2 o'clock Sunday morning I heard the mate, who was standing watch, call out: 'All hands on deck.' He had noticed that the vessel was keeling over more than she should when lying to. The men in the forward cabin who were awake thought the mate was calling for the crew. As I could not sleep, I said to Maloy that I would go and see what was going on. I pulled on his boots and left the cabin. Maloy turned over in his bunk, and in less than ten minutes had gone down to his death.

'On reaching the deck I noticed a dozen men in the rigging. One of them yelled to me to get up with them and try and right the vessel. I saw that this was useless, with tons of water holding down the other side, which was all awash. Water was rushing into the after cabin through a companion way in a perfect stream. Capt. Crockett, who had been asleep in his bunk, after spending hours on deck, was awakened by the mate's cry and pushed his way on deck through the stream of water. Several of the passengers followed him.

'I got down out of the rigging and went forward to see if I could not launch a dory that was lying on top of the deckhouse. I almost had the boat loose when they lowered the foresail with a bang. It covered up the dory, and I could not get at it. Maj. Ingraham and others were working with the fastenings of the steam launch Kennorma. Several of the Italians were trying to get their boat loose. Our boat finally floated off with several men in it. When it came back to the schooner we caught hold of it, and the men who where saved began to pile in.

'The missionary, V. C. Gambel, was on deck, watching these operations. Every few minutes some one would remember his wife and child and ask if they had been brought out of the cabin. He gave them no answer. Finally he went back into the cabin, we thought after the woman and baby. He met one C. E. Chard, of Seattle, coming out. Gambel said: 'The boat is doomed; we might as well die all together.' With that he went into the stateroom and locked the door.

'I hesitated about getting into the first launch, as I thought it would be too full, and did not do so until Capt. Crockett said: 'Hurry up and fill this boat.' The launch was alongside near the stern of the vessel when I got in. As it floated away from the vessel on a wave Maj. Ingraham fell into the sea. He swam back to the schooner and was hanging on to the side when the launch came back. It caught the major and crushed him quite badly. I grabbed him and got him into the boat. At first we thought his injury was serious, but he came around all right.

'Mate John Hanson behaved with great bravery. He threw a number of boxes of provisions into the launch from the deck of the schooner. With every rock of the boat the main boom would sweep over us. Once it caught Hanson in the head and nearly knocked him overboard. The schooner was settling fast and we pulled the men into the boat as fast as they came to the rail. Finally we broke away from the schooner and drifted out of sight in the darkness. We had nothing but two poles to work with and could not go back for any more men. There were twenty-five in the boat at that time.

'The sea was running high, but the Kennorma rode the waves like a duck. An hour and a half after the schooner sank we picked up Job Johnson, of Long Island, N. Y., who had managed to keep afloat, by clinging to one of the overturned boats. He was hanging to the schooner's rail when she went down. A sudden lurch of the vessel threw him through the rigging. In falling he struck a boom which tore a big hole in his gray flannel shirt and bruised him severely. He went down into the water a considerable distance and while under the water started to swim for fear that he would become entangled in the rigging. The last he saw of the Italian launch was a minute before the schooner went down. It had been knocked against the main mast and its side partially crushed in. There were four men in the boat. When he came up he could see nothing of it. He got to the overturned boat and floated with it until we picked him up. He was not exhausted in the least although he had been in the water a long time.

'C. J. Riley, of Hartford, Conn., had the narrowest escape of any of the survivors. About 4:30 o'clock Sunday morning, we heard some one calling lustily about 200 yards away from the launch. We managed to pole in the direction of the cries, and soon came upon Riley hanging to a bundle of lumber. He was almost exhausted, and did not know whether he was above or below the water. He had a grip on the lumber that two men could hardly break. In spite of this he was yelling in a deep bass voice. He had jumped from the schooner just as she went down, and had seen nothing of the Italian launch afterward.

"Riley saw W. H. Gleason, the Seattle contractor, die. Gleason got hold of one end of the pile of boards that Riley managed to reach. He was tired out when he got to the lumber, and told Riley that he could not hold on very long. Riley tried to cheer him up, and told him they would soon be picked up. According to Riley, his last words were: 'I'll have to give up. Good-by.' With that he let go his hold and went down.

'It was not the most pleasant thing in the world to drift around in that little launch. Some of the passengers made things very disagreeable by refusing to help, and by doing everything they were told not to do. There were some of the ship's stores in the boat, so we did not suffer for want of food. Strange to say, that although I had not eaten a meal since Friday morning I was not hungry. From the time we left the schooner till we landed on Vancouver island Monday evening I ate nothing but a dozen prunes. We caught rain water in the folds of the canvas cover of the launch. There was about two inches of fresh water in the launch's tank, but none of the men on the boat knew it save Maj. Ingraham and myself. We were saving it for an emergency, but fortunately did not need it.

'I can give absolutely no hope that any one else was saved from the wreck. The Italian launch undoubtedly went down. If it did not, the men in it were without water and provisions and would have little chance. I believe that the Schmid boys, Jack Lindsay, Ben E. Snipes, jr.; P. C. Little and several others in the forward cabin, knew nothing at all of the foundering. They went into eternity without a thought. All had been very seasick for several days and had reached a stage where they did not care whether the ship went down or not. There was no time to go back into the cabin and pull them on deck. It was every man for himself, and many of those who perished were too sick to think of getting out. I saw A. B. Dunlap on the deck of the schooner, but did not see him when the launch drifted away. I talked with Horace Palmer, of Lebanon, O., for a moment on the deck of the schooner. He said:

'This is a hard way to die, isn't it. The only thing I mind is leaving my wife and children.' I think he was working with the other boat, but I did not see him again.

'Too much cannot be said about the bravery displayed by Capt. Crockett, Mate Hanson and the other members of the crew. They were up night and day from the time we got into the straits and displayed great coolness at the time of the wreck. The survivors passed resolutions thanking them. I do not attempt to explain the cause of the Jane Gray foundering. We were given to understand that she was a very staunch clipper whaler, yet, after passing through no storm at all, her seams opened up and she sank almost without warning. There was not a life preserver or life raft aboard. I have nothing more to say about this until some matters have been adjusted.'

"Capt. Crockett's Statement.

This is the account of the disaster given by Capt. Crockett to a Post-Intelligencer reporter yesterday afternoon in the private office of the MacDougall & Southwick Company:

'My opinion is that a butt in the Gray sprung open during Saturday night and let in enough water to sink her. There is nothing in the theory that her load of freight shifted and caused her to list to starboard. There was no very heavy storm; that is, sufficient to wreck such a staunch vessel as the Gray. We were carrying practically no sail and were hove-to when I was called on deck at 2 o'clock on Sunday morning. It was my watch, but the mate and one seaman were on the deck at the time, while I was down below.

'We sailed from Seattle May 19, being towed as far as Port Townsend. There we set sail early on the morning of May 20. The wind was light and we made slow progress to the straits. We passed by Cape Flattery Saturday morning, May 21, at 4 o'clock. The wind was from the southeast. Saturday evening at 8 o'clock, we reduced sail and hove-to. The foresail alone was up. The wind was stiff and blew harder in the night. It was what I would call a moderate gale. There was a heavy sea running, but not heavy enough to swamp any seaworthy ship.

'The water was pumped out of the hold Saturday night at midnight. The vessel had been making some water, but not enough to cause apprehension. I went to bed believing that everything was all right and with as much confidence in my safety as if I had been on shore.

'I was called, as near as I can judge, at 2 o'clock on Sunday morning, May 22. I can only tell the time by the fact that the watches of the men who were in the water all stopped at 2 o'clock. The mate called to me that something was the matter with the ship. I hurried on what clothing I could and jumped on deck. I immediately saw that there was something serious the trouble with the schooner. She had a heavy list to starboard and with every sea the list grew worse. I ordered the foresail lowered, hoping that she would right, but there was no change. Then I called for all hands to come on deck and told the men to clear away the boats.

'I gave particular directions for the men to get the woman, Mrs. Gambel, and her child, from the cabin. Then I turned my attention to getting the boats launched and to seeing that all of the passengers were placed aboard them safely.

'The plight of the ship grew quickly worse. Indeed there was no time for anything. At the same time there was no excitement. We lowered the big launch first and before we could get the other boats in readiness for the passengers, the water carried them off the davits. Two of the smaller boats were lowered all right. The heavy sea made it difficult to handle them, however.

'Before we had time to place provisions or oars on the launch we were compelled to get on board. Three of four of us jumped into the launch and others followed by stepping off the starboard rail into the water and swimming to the launch. Those who came alongside were helped in. We drifted rapidly away from the schooner, which was slowly sinking. It was pitch dark and difficult to distinguish anything or anybody.

"Ten Minutes and All Was Over.

'There was not over ten minutes of time from the moment I stepped foot on the deck until we were compelled to jump into the launch for our lives. The spars of the ship were already under water and she slowly settled on her beam ends. There were two launches, two seal boats and a dory. The other launch was smashed in the rigging, but I saw four men in it. It was half full of water, however, and I have very little hope for the poor fellows that got in it. None of the smaller boats was manned.

'I took charge of the launch and cleared her away from the wreck, calling to all within reach to join us. We drifted around for perhaps two hours and then day broke. An hour after dawn Reilly and Johnson, who were floating on wreckage, drifted to us and were saved. The schooner was nowhere in sight. At about 10 o'clock we rigged a sail of a piece of canvas in the bottom of the launch and headed north, driven before the wind.

'Sunday evening at dark we rigged a drag so as to steady the boat. The next morning, not long before noon, we sighted land, which proved to be the coast of Vancouver Island. We made shore late that afternoon in Kyuquot sound. We landed without difficulty and immediately set about building fires and making ready to camp. We dug some mussels and ate them and obtained the first fresh water we had had for over thirty hours from a spring hard by. The following day we were piloted to the Indian village of Kyuquot, where the British sealer Favorite lay at anchor. I arranged with Capt. McLellan to take us to Victoria. We were wind bound until Thursday, but after that made good time until we reached Victoria at 4 o'clock this morning.'

"What was the cause of the sinking of the Gray?

'She must have sprung a butt,' said Capt. Crockett. 'The ship's cargo was well trimmed and she appeared to be in every respect sound and seaworthy. Had she not I would not have gone on her as master. The accident was in many respects one of the most remarkable occurrences I have ever heard of. The break must have come very quickly. There was no premonition or warning of danger when I turned in near midnight on Saturday night. All I can say is this: the ship was all right as far as any one could see until shortly before I was called at 2 o'clock. We had shipped some water forward through the hawser holes, but this did not cause any alarm. Whether the disaster was due to a structural weakness or not I am not prepared to say. There was no time to make an investigation. The water got into her hold some way through her side and then she filled and sank. That is all there is in the story.'

"Capt. Crockett emphasized the fact that there was no excitement. He said that after the launch was floated he and the others waited for the passengers to bring Mrs. Gambel to the deck and go aboard of the launch with her child. Not until they had to jump for their lives did the men on the boat, he said, desert the ship.

'I sent Claudius Brown, my father-in-law, down below after Mrs. Gambel,' he said, 'but her husband would not let her come. In this manner Brown lost his life.'

"I WILL NEVER FORGET THAT SCENE.

"James Blackwell Tells a Story of His Experience in the Disaster.

"James E. Blackwell, the well-know civil engineer, who was in charge of the construction of the Port Orchard dry dock, was a passenger on the Gray. Mr. Blackwell lives on Marion street near Twelfth avenue with his wife and family. The first intimation that Mrs. Blackwell received that her husband had encountered bad luck was contained in a telegram from him dated at Victoria yesterday morning, and informing her of his safety. Mrs. Blackwell was at the wharf when the Kingston arrived, and her delight at the safe return of her husband may be better imagined than described.

'I have no opinion to express concerning the cause of the loss of the Jane Gray,' said Mr. Blackwell yesterday. 'I am not a seafaring man, and therefore am not qualified to give testimony concerning the reason for the disaster. I was up nearly all night on Saturday night. Why? Because the ship had shipped water Saturday morning and I felt that there was some danger. More than that, I had been terribly seasick and had not tasted food for two days.

'I first became uneasy when water poured into the forward cabin early Saturday morning. It reached almost to the second berths and it grew steadily deeper. I learned that it came through the hawser holes. The captain ordered the ship put about and headed toward Cape Flattery, but the holes were stopped up and then we turned again and headed for the north.

'During the afternoon and evening the ship made water more or less, all the time. I mean that she shipped seas over her sides about midships. Some of it slopped into the cabin of the deckhouse forward. I made up my mind to stay awake, so that if anything happened I could be ready for whatever fate had in store.

'At midnight, the sea was rough. I heard the watch sing out 'Eight bells, and all's well!' Still I remained half awake. Two hours later, I heard the watch call to the captain that something was wrong with the ship. I hurried on deck and saw that we were in a bad fix. The ship careened badly to starboard and was unmanageable. Capt. Crockett came on deck about the time that I did. He ordered the foresail lowered, in the hope that he could bring her into the wind and that she would right herself. Then he sang out, 'All hands on deck!' and I knew that we were in for it. The men on the ship bundled out quickly, some without hats and others without shoes and socks. Many did not have more than enough clothes to cover their bodies. The captain told us to get on the port rail, thinking perhaps that our weight would right the now sinking schooner. This, too, was in vain. Then the captain ordered the boats cut away. This was the last resort.

'If I should live to be a thousand years old, I will never forget that scene. The night was pitch dark. The ship lay rolling under us, sinking lower and lower into the waves. Many of us were too terrified to speak. There was no great outcry and no excitement. It was too tragic for that. Many of the passengers seemed at a loss to comprehend the true situation, or at least were unable to do anything towards saving their lives. They seemed to be waiting for some one. It was all done so quickly that even now it seems hard to tell all that did happen in those few awful minutes from the time we were aroused till the darkness and the waves hid the Jane Gray from sight.

'Some of the poor fellows on the ship saw that they were lost and resolved to take their medicine. Others jumped into the water and swam for the launch after it started to drift from the ship. Others again tried to clear the other launch and boats from the rigging, and others still waited for some one to make provisions for their safety. We all waited for Mrs. Gambel to come from her cabin until we had to jump into the sea to keep from being drawn down into Davy Jones' locker with the wreck. And amid all the terrible confusion the wind blew almost a gale and the waves rolled high around us.

'Finally, the launch was cleared away and I saw the men climbing into her. Some of them stepped from the ship to the launch, but many more swam through the waves. I had on a heavy sweater and a pair of long rubber boots. I was weak from seasickness and want of nourishment. Thinking of my wife and family, I summoned all the will power I possessed and stepped off into the waves. I called on every muscle in my body for the life and death task before me. The launch was sixty feet or more from the ship, but I reached it and laid hold of a line that floated out behind. Some one helped me aboard. I was limp and exhausted and could not even move for hours.

'The last I saw of the Gray there were three or four hapless fellows on her deck waiting to go down to their destruction. In a few minutes we were out of sight of the schooner and then we waited through the long night for dawn. The rest you already know.'"

"WELL-KNOWN VICTIMS.

Something of the Lives of the Local Men Who Perished.

Probably no other victim is better known in the city than Ben E. Snipes, jr., one of the youngest men to meet death in the disaster. Snipes was the son of Ben. E. Snipes, who in his time figured very prominently in the history of Seattle. Young Snipes made his home here for years and was a member of the Agayne Club, a local society organization. He was about 22 years of age and well and favorably known in Seattle. He had contemplated going to Alaska for a long time. When the Portland returned to this city with her famous gold treasure he made arrangements to go north, but about this time a position was given him in the city which caused him to abandon the Alaska journey. The gold craze, however, lived with him and when, a few weeks ago, the opportunity to go north again presented itself, he took advantage of it.

The accompanying cut of the Jane Gray and some of the unfortunate passengers who were aboard her is drawn from a photograph taken the day before she sailed. The men stood while being photographed on top of the forward house, in which so many of the Seattle boys met their death.

The point where the Jane Gray foundered is indicated on the map by cross and the course of the rescuing launch, north to Rugged Point, is shown by the dotted line."

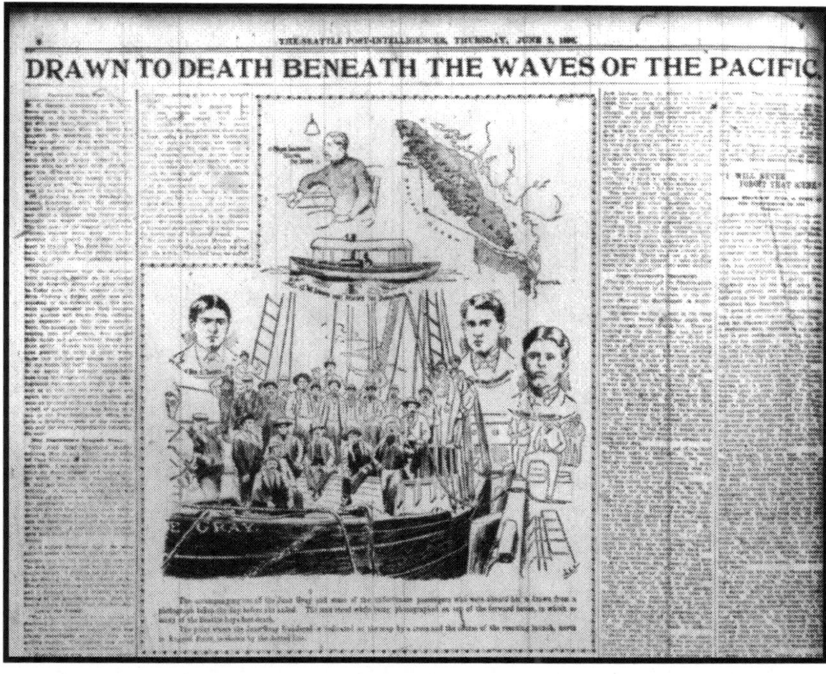

DRAWN TO DEATH BENEATH THE WAVES OF THE PACIFIC

Image from the Seattle Post-Intelligencer, courtesy of the Seattle Public Library.

CHAPTER 16 - THE WRECKAGE

In the aftermath of the wreck, nobody seemed to know exactly how many lives were lost. Names were misspelled or misreported and the hometowns of many of the victims were unknown. Even John Pacey couldn't say with absolute certainty who all was on the ship and the *Seattle Post Intelligencer* asked the question:

"Were These Men Lost?

The names of N. Hedelund and O. C. McKelvey appear on the list of the Gray's passengers who were lost. A dispute has arisen concerning these men. One authority has it that they were not on board the boat, but the passenger list furnished the Post-Intelligencer by Mr. J. G. Pacey gives their names as among those who embarked. Mr. Pacey believes that both were on the ship. McKelvey bought a ticket just before the Gray sailed. He was alone, and there was no record as to where he came from. It may not be definitely known for some time whether Hedelund boarded the Gray or not."

The only thing that was certain was the number of men who survived - twenty-seven.

Each day, more information about the missing passengers and crew was published in newspapers across the country, some of it contradicting other reports. In a *New York Times* interview with Captain Crockett, his story changed slightly when he was quoted as stating, "We were lying to, to mend our foresail." He continued, "A moderate gale was blowing and the seas were running high. I had gone to bed and was sound asleep when the watchman awakened me with the announcement that something was wrong. I arose at once and found the vessel leaking. A hurried investigation showed that she would soon sink, and I at once notified the passengers of the situation. Most of them were asleep underneath the deck. A scene of confusion took place and it is impossible to give any detailed account of the events that followed."

This was the first time that mending the foresail had been mentioned. Most other accounts stated that everyone remained calm and that there "was no excitement," while abandoning ship.

On June 2nd, under the headline, "Penned Up Like Sheep Many Persons Drown," the *Tacoma Daily Ledger* printed another version of the sinking, repeating the opinion of many others that the Jane Gray "was not fit for passenger service." She was built for whaling, which she did well. But that forward house and all of those passengers. The modifications and overloading were again cited as the "fatal mistake."

The last two paragraphs of the article in the *Tacoma Daily Ledger* detailed Vene Gambell's connection to Tacoma:

"Rev. V. Gambell, who with his wife and baby went down with the Jane Gray, is the brother of H. F. Gambell, for eight years and still a clerk in the Tacoma post office. He also has a brother, Dr. H. F. Gambell, now in Tacoma on his way to Unalaskilk, Alaska, seventy-five miles beyond St. Michael, where he is to be a physician in connection with the government reindeer station in the vicinity.

V. C. Gambell, the lost, was enroute to St. Lawrence, in the Bering Sea, as a missionary. He had been on the island in the same work three years and was returning after a vacation to the states. Last fall he came south, and went to Iowa to visit his old home in Winfield, that state. Mr. Gambell was thirty-five years old. He and Mrs. Gambell were in Tacoma with their child between May 7 and 14, and during the time became acquainted with quite a number of the members of the First Presbyterian Church. Mr. Gambell's parents live in Winfield. The father is J. C. Gambell, a man of sixty years old".

While some thought the death of the Gambell family romantic, perhaps kneeling in prayer, that they would go down together, many thought it was downright idiotic and that the Reverend had surely lost all of his senses. The latter sentiment became the prevailing opinion once George Pennington was reported to have said "Mrs. Gambell could have been placed in the launch without wetting her feet."

Major Ingraham, a husband and father who lost most of his expedition team, and along with them, his cousin's son and two Italian friends, remained tormented by the events surrounding the sinking. The reverend's actions that night, which very likely caused many others to sacrifice their own lives, were particularly galling. He confirmed Pennington's account of the Gambell tragedy in his interview with the *San Francisco Call*:

"I don't know when I will finish telling the many incidents of that awful trip or of those which occurred just before the Jane Gray disappeared. W. C. Gambel, a missionary bound for St. Lawrence Island, in the Bering Sea, was aboard with his wife and little babe. In the midst of it all maniacal ideas took possession of him, and as a result his wife, his babe and himself had their lives snuffed out. When the water started to rush over the deck he was with us. His wife and babe were below. We had been referring to the latter as our mascot and as a big wave swept over the deck and we saw that if we were to escape at all it must be at once, one of the boys cried:

'Save the child.'

"For a minute we forgot all else and from a dozen—yes, two dozen—throats came cries of 'Yes, save the babe; we can't lose the mascot.' The missionary made a wild dash into the cabin. On the way he met one of the boys and cried out: 'The ship is doomed. We will all die together!' With that, this man, changed in a second from a human being of good mental faculties to a maniac, rushed into his stateroom, shut the door, locked it, refused even upon pleading to open it, and when the Jane Gray went down to her doom the Alaska missionary, his wife and his child—'our mascot'- breathed their last."

While Ingraham and the well-known Seattle men were subjected to seemingly endless interviews, the survivors who had nowhere to go were put up at the Hotel Brunswick. With an "elevator, steam heat, and modern improvements," a block from the waterfront, some of the weary men were finally able to let loose and have a little fun. Suddenly celebrities, they rarely escaped the eyes of reporters and were caught horsing around in front of the hotel. The *Post-Intelligencer* reported on their antics: "There was some merriment among them, showing the disposition of men safely out of impending trouble to jest at their misfortunes. 'Job Johnson and C. J. Reilly are going to immortalize themselves in a play,' said one of the survivors yesterday. 'They floated around for nearly two hours on wreckage after the ship sank, and now it is proposed that they go on stage and do a 'tank' act. It would be great.' Point is given to the jest when it is remembered that Mr. Reilly was formerly engaged in the theatrical business."

Manuel Roberts, the night watchman at the Rainier Hotel who had been accompanied by his now missing friend, Ben Snipes, needed to clear up a few things. First, that there might still be hope for the men who made it into the second launch. He told a correspondent from the *Seattle Post-Intelligencer*, "I don't know who they were...but there is in my opinion a possible chance for them." Mannie agreed that the other vessel sat low in the water, perhaps partially sunk, however, he continued, "I do not want to quell any faint hopes in the belief of any who had friends or relatives on the Gray, but my opinion is that there is just a possibility that the Italian launch might have lived."

The second thing he needed to clarify was the fate of others in the forward cabin: "I want to correct the statement that Snipes and others lay in their bunks in the cabin without making any effort to get out. I was Snipes' partner and we stood together on the ship's side as she lay in the final struggle in the trough of the sea. Conture was the first to leave the ship. I followed him and then came Snipes. We stood together on the deck of the Gray waiting for a chance to get into one of the boats. The ship was healing over more and more with every wave. I stood at the rail and said to Snipes: 'Ben, I guess it's off with us.' Just then I saw the launch drifting astern and plunged into the water. I did not stop to look as to whether Snipes followed me." Once Mannie was pulled into the Ingraham launch, he saw men in the other boat and assumed that Ben had made it to the other vessel. The darkness made certainty impossible, but he remained hopeful.

The Tacoma postal clerk, Herbert Gambell, had difficulty accepting the reports of his brother's behavior on the night of the disaster. While he and his father were in Seattle investigating the tragedy, they had an opportunity to speak with Silas Livengood, one of the survivors who gave them a more appealing account of Vene's actions that fateful night. A. G. Kingsbury, who waited at the top of the aft steps for the Gambells, corroborated the possibility that Vene and Nellie intended to escape, but were overcome by water when they hesitated too long. Although the story was at odds with that of most of the other survivors, it offered some solace to the grieving Gambell family. On June 9, 1898, no longer able to tolerate the negative stories that seemed unjustly perpetuated by every member of the press, Vene's brother submitted a letter to the editor of the Christian publication, the *Home Mission Monthly*:

"LOST AT SEA.

The reports concerning the disaster which overtook our missionaries, Mr. and Mrs. Gambell and their little child, while on their return to St. Lawrence Island, Alaska, as published in the daily press, were so erroneous that our readers will appreciate the following communication from a brother of Mr. Gambell:

Tacoma, Washington, June 9, 1898.

"To the Editor of the Home Mission Monthly:

You perhaps have heard of the awful catastrophe that overtook my brother, his wife and child, a few weeks ago on the Pacific Ocean; but thinking you might wish to know the full particulars and to have a correct report to give your readers, I have decided to give you what I know to be the facts.

Vene C. Gambell was born at Winfield, Iowa, March 8, 1863, and was thirty-five years of age at the time of his death. At the age of eighteen years he began teaching school, and after a few years he entered the Ames Agricultural College at Ames, Iowa, from which he graduated. After leaving college, he was principal of schools at Rhodes, Iowa, and also, later, at Wapello, Iowa. While at Rhodes, Iowa, he became acquainted with Miss Nellie F. Webster, who afterward became his wife. She was born April 12, 1874. Resigning his position as principal of the Wapello, Iowa, schools, he left at once, with his wife, for the mission field on St. Lawrence Island. They reached San Francisco in the latter part of June, where they remained for two weeks, when they went aboard a sailing vessel, in July, 1894, and began their long journey to the far off island, which for years was to be their home. After sailing for five weeks, they at last reached St. Lawrence Island to find about 375 natives waiting for them, but their island was bleak and barren—no trees or shrubs of any kind—covered only by grass and lava rock. They took with them provisions and coal for one year, and lived almost entirely on canned goods. Many were the hardships endured. However, they could catch plenty of codfish and shoot ducks and other wild fowl, making a variation from the canned goods that became so tiresome.

In April, 1897, Margaret Gambell was born, and such a wonderful baby the natives thought that they had never beheld; they wanted to see her constantly, and stood looking into the windows, to catch even the least glimpse of her, and as she grew older were curious to know why she did not have the hair shaved from the back of her head, as did their children.

Mrs. Gambell's health made it necessary to come home for treatment, which they did, reaching Tacoma in November last. After remaining here for one week, to rest before leaving for their long overland journey, they went to Iowa, visiting Mrs. Gambell's home and later the home of Mr. Gambell, where they spent Thanksgiving. Mrs. Gambell was then taken to the Presbyterian Hospital at Chicago, where she remained about two months, and later to the hospital at Keokuk, Iowa, where she remained two weeks.

In January Mr. Gambell was sent to Juneau, Alaska, to take charge of the Government school for white children; he remained there for two months, when he returned to his home at Winfield, Iowa, to find his wife so much improved in health that they at once decided to return to their home and shepherdless flock on St. Lawrence Island. They reached Tacoma May 14, and remained over Sunday, attending services at the First Presbyterian Church, where they knew many of the members, and where they felt they had a church home. On Thursday evening, May 19, they went aboard the sailing vessel "Jane Gray" at Seattle, and were towed out to sea. The first night out they were happy, and little Margaret was bright and in a playful mood, and at once made many of the passengers her warmest friends. Friday, Mrs. Gambell became sea sick, and Friday night and all day Saturday she and her husband were very sick. At two o'clock in the morning the alarm was given for everyone to get on deck, and my brother hurried above, without hat or coat, to find the vessel careening badly and the waves breaking over the ship. He soon realized—even though the night was dark—that the vessel was doomed, and was then sinking rapidly. His wife was calling from below, asking if she should come up—and knowing how sick and weak she was--he answered, 'No, dear, I will come down.' As he descended the steps the water was pouring in from all sides, and reaching the cabin the water was almost to their knees. Mr. S. Livingood, a Christian gentleman, whose home is in Seattle, Washington, and who was rescued, was with Mrs. Gambell when my brother returned. He stated positively that neither the captain nor any members of the crew, nor any of the passengers came below to help them. Mr. Livingood saw my brother step into the stateroom, pick up their baby girl, and come out as if to go above, and thinking they were following, he started forward; as he gained the step the water reached to his waist, and glancing back he saw my brother, with his baby in his arms, and his wife, clinging to him, step back into the stateroom as if to get something they wished to take; he never saw them again, for they sank to the bottom of the deep with the vessel. Realizing his own life in danger, and that if he would save his own life he must act at once, he fell forward sick and weak and threw up his hands to grasp something, when some one above grasped his arm and drew him out almost exhausted; he could not stand, but slipped to the side of the ship, where he reached the launch, and was one of the twenty-six persons that were saved. Terribly cramped and piled one upon and across the other, for thirty-six hours they were tossed about and finally reached the shore of Vancouver Island, too weak and exhausted to stand; here they were taken care of by some Indians, and were later picked up by a passing ship. In addition to my brother, his wife and baby girl, about thirty-four others were drowned—many of them never leaving their berths. In ten minutes after the alarm was given, the vessel had sunk—almost one hundred miles from land!

In great sorrow, but with a firm trust in God.

Yours very sincerely,

Herbert F. Gambell"

The sense of grief reached across the entire country and when George Hiller's telegram to his mother, "I am safe.

Vessel foundered. Ginther lost," made the rounds in Pennsylvania, where Frank Ginther and Percy Davenport were popular railway postal clerks, the *Scranton Tribune* reported on the loss of one of their own, complete with inaccurate details:

"HARRISBURG PROSPECTORS

Three of the Lady Jane Gray Passengers Were from Pennsylvania.

A telegram which reached Harrisburg tonight told briefly of the death of Frank W. Ginther, a former postal clerk, in the foundering of the steamer Lady Jane Grey on the way to the Klondike on Sunday, May 22.

The telegram came from George Hiller, jr., of this city, and informed his mother that he was safe, but that Ginther, his traveling mate, had gone down to death in the wreck. In the early part of April, Ginther and Percy Davenport, a fellow postal clerk, with young Hiller, left Harrisburg for the Klondike going to Seattle whence they took passage for Alaska. Ginther was one of the Klondike prospecting company organized in the city last fall with $3,300 capital. He was one of the largest stockholders and a director. Ginther went out as the agent of the company and intended to do the prospecting and to take a hand in the work, Davenport and Hiller going with him. They sailed for the Alaska territory about the middle of May and on Sunday, May 22, the vessel foundered and all but 27 of the sixty-one souls on board were lost near Cape Flattery.

It was said among postal clerks tonight that the last word from the party was that Davenport was going by another way and there are possibilities that he is safe. Hiller is at Vancouver. It is not known if he saved any of his own or Ginther's property.

Ginther had over $3000 with him when he left. This represented the stock of the company and his own cash."

The wreck consumed conversations at every table and street corner. Residents of Seattle discussed what should be done about the others who were still missing. Perhaps there was a slim possibility that some of these hearty men also made the shore at Vancouver Island. After all, the survivors had seen at least four people in the Italian launch and all of the other ship's boats had reportedly floated free of the wreckage. George Pennington had seen the launch and felt that there was a chance. Manuel Roberts agreed with that opinion. Maybe there were more survivors in one of the coastal villages with no means of communication. Perhaps they were hiking overland to Victoria. Every possible scenario was played out. On Friday, June 3rd, The *Tacoma Daily Ledger* printed the latest proposal:

"SUGGEST A SEARCH FOR THE MISSING

Government Vessels Proposed to Look for Possible Other Survivors of the Jane Gray.

In consideration of the view taken by some that a boat from the foundered Jane Gray may yet be afloat with several persons from the vessel, it was suggested by a shipping man yesterday that the government gunboat Wheeling and the revenue cutter Perry, both on the lower Sound, be dispatched to search off Cape Flattery for such a boat.

Some severe criticism was also heard as to the overloading of sailing vessels bound for the North and of the piling of mining apparatus and other freight around the upper works of craft to make the long journey to the Yukon until they looked like a glimpse of the streets of Cairo, and of the permission of superannuated hulks to essay the long voyage."

The Canadians joined in the chorus of condemnation, blaming United States shipping laws "which do not provide for the inspection of sailing vessels" and the owners for modifying a ship that was built as a whaler. The *Victoria Colonist* said that the "fatal mistake" was the construction of a house on the foredeck and the stopping of the scuppers.

Speculation as to the cause of the sinking ran rampant in Seattle, with a number of men saying they "knew she would sink" and "said so when she left port." Of course, all of these men had failed to mention their fears to anyone aboard the Jane Gray prior to her departure. Theories of a hidden defect were floated about. The surveyors who inspected the vessel before she left port were sure that anything above the water line would have come to their attention. The *Seattle Daily Times*, after consulting all of the experts, including their own surveyor, concluded that the vessel was severely overloaded:

"The theory now generally accepted is that she was overloaded and that too much of that load was on her deck. From her forecastle to nearly amidships there was a house in which forty-three people were berthed. On the port side of the roof of this house was a skiff intended to be used as a lifeboat. On the starboard side of this roof was a dory belonging to the Italians, and between these two boats were piled: Two knocked-down boats belonging to the Blackwell party, two knocked-down boats and two sleds packed with hardware and tools belonging to the Taylor party, two canvas boats belonging to Snipes; and about three tons of iron rods, pipes and machinery for a sawmill, pumps and forges, belonging to the Italian party.

All this stuff was on the roof of the house on the forward deck and the boom of the foresail had to be elevated very high to clear this mass of freight." Detailing the rest of the cargo that covered nearly every inch of the Jane Gray's decks, The *Times* concluded that this water logged load made the vessel top-heavy.

Around Seattle, talk had begun to focus on the MacDougall and Southwick Company and their response to the accident. It was not flattering. The *Times* reported:

"Although J. G. Pacey is the reputed owner of the vessel, yet for reasons not known the actual owners are alleged to have been MacDougall-Southwick Co., and much criticism is now being passed upon this method of doing business, it being alleged that Mr. Pacey is merely a clerk in the company's employ and that his financial responsibility is a question not fully settled in the minds of those most deeply interested. And it is further alleged that the company simply used him in the matter in anticipation of just such a contingency as has now arisen."

Suspicions of dirty dealings were not unwarranted. After the 1889 Seattle fire consumed the inventory of the Singerman department store, an employee by the name of John B. MacDougall found the cash to buy out the business. One of his partners in the purchase was Henry C. Southwick. As often happens in business take-overs, not all of the obligations of the previous owner were paid by the new MacDougall & Southwick Company, a corporation. Singerman subsequently opened another store - either in competition or to redeem himself in the eyes of the community at large.

The relationship between John B. MacDougall and Henry Clay Southwick likely began in New York City, when a young MacDougall was fresh off of the boat from Scotland and an employee at one of the retail outlets where the Southwick family dealt in all manner of merchandise. Grooming secretaries was a long-held practice for them. A job well done often led to financial backing in another venture, with the secretary becoming president and a Southwick assuming a lesser role in the corporate structure of the new company.

Henry Southwick was born a ninth-generation American. His grandfather, Royal Southwick, was a Quaker of the Whig party. Royal earnestly opposed slavery and believed that black men should be bestowed the same respect as white men. His conviction in this belief was so firmly held that he took Frederick Douglass and Charles Lennox Remond into his home when they were mobbed at an anti-slavery rally in Lowell, Massachusetts. However, Royal was not just any man on the streets crying "equality." His convictions were well financed by family funds and those of his own labor. Royal's son - Henry's uncle, John Claflin Southwick, became partners with Jackson S. Shultz, Esquire, a genius at business and a purported pioneer in medical products of the time. When Shultz died in 1878, he left an estate in excess of $3,000,000.00 (three million dollars, in 1878!) - and the Southwicks were partners in many of his retail operations.

When John MacDougall bought out Singerman in 1891, the Southwick department store chain boasted forty-two stores in the United States and Canada. Seattle became their flagship operation.

The *Seattle Daily Times* continued its commentary on the outfitting firm's treatment of the survivors:

"The survivors in most instances are without a dollar; they are absolutely penniless, in fact, and it is not believed that the people of this city will tolerate any efforts on the part of the real owners to avoid the just responsibilities devolving upon them under the circumstances, even if they should be disposed to dodge that responsibility behind a stool-pigeon or through other means."

Beyond the boundaries of Seattle and the State of Washington, news of the identities of the missing continued to trickle in as family members from around the country learned of the loss of their loved ones. On June 4th, the *Sacramento Daily Record-Union* printed a condemning story:

"IT WAS WHOLESALE MURDER

HOW THE JANE GRAY WAS SENT OUT TO SEA.

The Trip That Cost Charles C. Aiken of Sacramento His Life.

David Falconer of this city, who is now in San Francisco on his return from Dyea and Seattle, writes to the "Record-Union" the following account of the condition in which the ill-fated schooner Jane Gray was sent to sea. One of her passengers was Charles C. Aiken of Sacramento. Mr. Falconer says:

'By the recent wreck of the whaling schooner Jane Gray Sacramento has lost one of her best-known and popular going men, Charlie Aiken. He was for years foreman under Victor Lemay in the repair department of the Southern Pacific Company. He left the shops about two months ago, and went north to Seattle to get ready for a trip up the Yukon.'

'Mr. Aiken was one of the very first to engage passage on the unfortunate ship for Kotzebue Sound; and took great interest in everything that was done on board up to the time the lines were cast off, and was the last man to cross the gang-plank before she sailed.'

'He had made every preparation for a protracted stay, taking two years' provisions, picks, shovels, tents, knock-down boats and all manner of clothing to withstand the cold climate. His many friends in Sacramento will be pained to hear of his sad death. Mr. Senitz, in charge of the construction department of the railroad company, visited him at the schooner when in Seattle on his vacation.'

'The last thing Charlie did was to exchange watch-chains with me, and ask me to write to his sister, Mrs. Dundes of Sacramento, in case I learned of any thing about the schooner on her way up, and I would I had a more pleasant task to perform than the one now before me.'

The Jane Gray was loaded to within two feet of the main deck. Her forward part was built on with staterooms for the sixty-five passengers, so that there was no possible chance to work the ship to advantage in severe weather. With the deckload of water casks, lumber, machinery, boats and staterooms, and the forward hatches open, there was no possible way for the waves that struck her to escape. Why vessels are allowed to leave port in such condition, jeopardizing the lives of the passengers, seems beyond all comprehension.

The Jane Gray was sold a short time ago for $5,000. Her sixty-five passengers paid on an average $150 passage. She carried nearly 100 tons of freight at $25 a ton, making the total receipts $12,250, or over $7,000 above the original cost, for a sixty days return trip, with a crew of eight men only. A rotten place was found in her mast, which was cut out and patched up the day before she sailed."

On June 6th, the *New York Times* reported on a victim from Plainfield, New Jersey:

"Mrs. John M. Stutzman of Westfield yesterday received news confirming the report that her husband, who started for the Klondike gold fields five weeks ago, was one of the passengers in the wreck of the Jane Grey in the Pacific who lost his life. One of Stutzman's objects in going on the trip was the hope that it would benefit his health, though he was in hopes too, of finding wealth. He had lived in Westfield for many years and was a florist, being considered an authority on the growth of violets. Besides his wife he leaves three children."

By June 7th, six days after the weary survivors disembarked the City of Kingston in Seattle, news from Vancouver arrived that seven bodies, presumably from the Jane Gray, had washed ashore near the Kuyoquot Indian Reservation. The report was reprinted in the *Boston Evening Transcript*:

"A special from Alberni says that the bodies of seven white men, supposed to have been victims of the Jane Gray disaster, have been picked up on the beach near Kuyuquot reservation by Indians, while a sack of clothing with an Italian name on it was washed ashore not far from Clayoquot.

Coupled with this information comes the news by the return of the steamer Willapa that considerable wreckage from the lost schooner, including four of the boats, has been discovered at different points along the coast. The launch belonging to Major Ingraham's mountain climbing party has also been found by Indians. It floated upright, although the sea had flooded it. There were a number of books and papers in the boat but no bodies, and the natural supposition is that the six men who were seen in the boat when it left the schooner have all been washed overboard.

The Nootka sound Indians picked up another boat, the dory belonging to the Jane Gray and which was referred to by several of the survivors in their stories of the wreck."

While some still believed that there was a slim chance that more men could have survived, others could not. In Everett, Washington, Hugh and Kezia Lindsay met with their friend, Clayton Packard, and heard his account first hand. Holding out no hope that Jack survived the awful night, they grieved the loss of their oldest son. On June 7th, the *Everett News* printed a memorial to the football hero. The *Seattle Daily Times* added to the tribute:

"JOHN LINDSAY

A Tribute to His Memory by the Everett News.

Among those who were lost on the Jane Grey none were better known in Seattle than Jack Lindsay. Being captain of the University football team and a nice fellow generally, he became a favorite. His home was in Everett, and the Everett News pays this tribute to his memory:

'Clate Packard thinks that Johnnie Lindsay went down while still asleep in his bunk, and this is probably true; for had he been awake he would surely have taken care of himself—or others, for he was made of that kind of stuff that would have developed the hero in an emergency like this. No boy ever grew up in Everett who was so universally respected and highly esteemed. He was a young man of splendid character, and was destined to become a useful and honored citizen. His sudden taking away is one of fate's cruelest pranks, which has lodged poignant grief, not only in the hearts of his family, but of a wide circle of sincere friends. As captain of the University football team for two years, he was known all through the Northwest in athletic circles, and he has never received a word of condemnation—for he was an honest, manly young fellow who commanded admiration.'"

The morning after Jack Lindsay's memorial made the paper, survivors and family members of the other lost men gathered at the Seattle City Council Chambers in City Hall. Initially the meeting was planned to explore the possibility of sending a steamer to the West Coast of Vancouver Island in search of survivors, however, that plan changed with the news of bodies being found. All that they could hope for now was that they might be able to identify their loved ones and bring them home for a proper burial.

Those in attendance included: "Manuel Roberts, Clayton Packard; Vitus Schmid, the father of Victor and Conrad Schmid, lost; P. J. Draper, Charles Chard, George Hiller, William Weaver, Percy Davenport; M. H. Salisbury, brother of F. G. Salisbury, lost; Erminio Sella representing Edoardo Gaia and Secondo Bissetta, lost; Frank Little, the father of Philip Little, lost; Major Ingraham; Frank Olsen and H. W. Carroll representing Edwin and Fredrick Taylor, lost; Ben E. Snipes representing his son Ben, Jr., lost; Dr. Luther Lessey; and Mr. Gleason, whose brother was lost."

Major Ingraham, Frank Little, and Ben Snipes had previously volunteered to take the steamer City of Kingston to Victoria that very evening, meet the southbound steamer coming in from the west side of the island, and make arrangements for any bodies that may have been found. Frank Olsen, secretary of the board of public works and a representative for the Taylor family, knew many of the residents on the West Coast and had volunteered to go along and question the natives in the coastal villages. By the end of the meeting, hoping that other news may arrive, all in attendance decided to await the return of the Kingston before taking any further action.

The following day, June 9th, brought word to Seattle that the report of finding bodies was false. The story had apparently originated from the meandering comments of a drunken passenger on board the Willapa. However, it was still thought there was a very slim chance that some of the survivors may have caught the southbound steamer. The *Seattle Daily Times* printed an exclusive:

"JANE GREY

The Report of Finding Bodies False.

A FAINT HOPE.

A faint hope is entertained that some of the survivors have been picked up by the steamer Athenian, which passed Wilapa about the time the launch of the Italians was found by the Indians. The launch was waterlogged but upright.

The Mischief, with correspondents aboard, it is thought, will be back tonight. The Seattle delegation is here awaiting her return."

Before this story hit the newsstands, the group, a committee charged with exhausting every possibility of finding those lost, dead or alive, boarded the steamer, City of Kingston, and was already heading for Victoria.

From Canada, The *British Colonist* reported their arrival on June 10th:

"A HOPEFUL PARTY

Relatives of Those Missing on the Jane Grey Disaster Arrive in Town.

On the City of Kingston from the Sound yesterday morning there arrived a party of seven friends and relatives of those supposed to have been lost at sea in the Jane Grey disaster of a week ago. They had heard of the searching expedition now being made by the Journal-Examiner representatives, which left here on the steam schooner Mischief at the beginning of the week and came over prepared to follow in its wake. They brought along a dozen homing birds, and as they obtained news they intended allowing anxious friends at home know the latest news by dispatching one of the birds. On arriving here, however, their hopes were somewhat lessened, those who arrived by the Willapa advising them that it was useless to make the trip down the coast. They therefore liberated the birds here and some of the party returned to the Sound on the North Pacific last evening. The personnel of the party is as follows: Dr. Lessey and Signor E. Sella, two of the Italian party which left on the Jane Grey; T. N. Little, superintendent of streets in Seattle, whose son, Phil C. Little, is among the missing; Professor and Mrs. August Melhorn, representing the Smith brothers; M. N. Salesbury, whose brother is among the missing, and Ben E. Snipes, father of Ben E. Snipes, another of the missing."

At every turn, a city learned that one of their residents was somehow involved in the disaster or had disappeared beneath the waves on the dark night when the Jane Gray went down. Monday, June 13th found another article, this one opening with A. G. Kingsbury, the well-known East Coast miner, engineer, and author, recounting how the Reverend Gambell and his family drowned, published in the *New York Times*:

""A.G. Kingsbury of Boston gives perhaps the clearest account of the last moments of Mr. Gambell and his wife and child. Mr. Kingsbury made this statement: "I was awakened from a sound sleep by the voices from the deck calling all hands to get out. It must have been after the majority of those in the cabin had emerged because I looked around me and saw no one in the cabin except Mr. Gambell and his wife in their stateroom, the door of which was open. I heard him say just as I was dressing: 'We are all lost; there is no chance for us.' Gambell had gone on deck, as I subsequently learned, and after taking a survey of the surroundings, had returned to his wife and child in the cabin. As I stepped from my berth I got into water perhaps two feet deep. The dining table had been turned up on end when the ship careened to starboard, and stood not far from my door. I was next to the companionway. I stepped out of the way of the table and reached for my shirt and cap. Then I saw that we were in great danger. As I turned to go up the companionway on to the deck, I passed Mr. Gambell. His back was to me and he was leaning over talking in low tones to his wife. I said: 'Come, let's get out of this quick!' or something to that effect. He did not appear to hear me. I again spoke to him, turning him around and grabbing him by the shirt. He said: 'There's no chance for us. We're lost.' I said, 'Give me the baby and get your wife. We can take the boats.' He replied again that it was no use. Mrs. Gambell had looked up as I spoke the last time, as if she was interested. I told them that there were boats on the ship, and that we could at least make an attempt to save our lives. Then I told them that I would go up the stairway and reach down for the baby, and for them to hand it to me. I knew that if I got that baby the mother's instinct would lead her to follow it wherever it went and that perhaps they would come out of the cabin and try to save themselves."

"All this passed through my mind much quicker than I can tell it. Every wave washed into the companionway and down into the cabin, each freshet being larger than the rest. As I turned to go, I thought I saw in their faces a look as if they understood me and would comply. As I mounted the companionway and reached the deck, I turned and looked down, expecting Gambell would hand me the child. I called twice for him to come and give the baby to me, but he did not reply again. Then I heard the Captain tell every one to get into the boats. I turned and saw that the ship was already sinking; that the starboard rail was under water, and the schooner was on her beam ends. Just then I heard some man going down the companionway, heard his boots scrape against the metal covering of the steps. This must have been Brown, whom the Captain sent down after the woman and child. In another minute I had slipped off the boat and into the sea. Then I made for the launch, diving under the wreckage several times, until I reached its side. I was helped into her, and looked around to see the Gray disappear in the waves and the darkness of the night."

"I believe that Mr. Gambell and his wife meant to come out on deck and try to get into the boat, but that before they could make a move, the water rushed into the cabin with such force and in such quantity as to make their escape impossible. It was all over in a minute. Within two minutes at the most after I got on deck. I slipped into the water from the starboard rail and swam to the launch."

"For a time there was nothing said on the launch. The men appeared to be too horrified at what they had passed through to speak. There was no room for thought and none for words; for nothing but horror at the awful fate of the good men who were still on the Gray sinking to the depths below and from which we had escaped. After a while I called out for Ranney, who was my partner. There was no response, and I knew that Ranney was lost. Some one called for Reilly, and there was no reply. Then I believed that he, too, was gone. And so it was for an hour or more, as the dark night gave way slowly to the broadening beams of the sun."

"At dawn we heard a voice come over the waters. It was a loud, heavy voice, and we knew it was Reilly. He was on a piece of wreckage, and was very nearly gone, but had strength enough left to sing out good and strong. Then Job Johnson floated along, and he, too, was helped into the launch."

"As I swam out to the launch I noticed the other launch with four men in her. I thought I recognized the forms of Ranney, who was my partner, and of Ginther. The other two I did not recognize. The launch sat low in the water, and appeared to have considerable water in her. I do not know whether she lived long after the wreck or not. The darkness settled down like a pall between us and the sinking ship, and when day broke we could see nothing but rolling waves and bits of wreckage strewed here and there."

CHAPTER 17 - MORE OF THE MISSING

At a time when overloaded ships often sailed with hoards of undocumented passengers, the all-star cast of prospectors on board the Jane Gray expedited identification of many of the missing.

The name of William D. Millay, whose identity had been erroneously reported as W. D. Maloy, Malloy, Millan, and Miller, of Snohomish, Washington, was clarified by Major Ingraham and reported in the *Seattle Post-Intelligencer*:

"Mr. Millay was 30 years of age and was well acquainted with Maj. Ingraham, having been a scholar in the South Thomaston schools when the major, as a young man, and before coming to Washington, was the principal of the graded schools of that town. When Maj. Ingraham began to organize his party, Mr. Millay was one of the first whom he invited to join him, knowing his physical and mental worth to an expedition of this nature. Beside his father, Mr. Millay leaves to mourn his tragic death his mother and one sister, Mrs. John C. Newburg of Mattapan, Mass."

The name "Levering" was also corrected when it finally came to light that he was William F. Deterling, who came to Seattle from Arlington, Minnesota, instead of Pennsylvania. And his traveling partner was William Otten, not William Otter as had been previously stated.

The parents of U. S. Hamilton learned of his demise days after the sinking. The *Daily Illinois State Journal* of Springfield reported on June 3rd:

"Ashland Boy Drowned.

Was a Prospector on boar the Schooner Jane Grey.

Ashland, June 3.-(Special)-Mr. and Mrs. Samuel Hamilton of this city today received the sad intelligence of the death by drowning of their son, Uehl Hamilton, on the schooner Jane Grey, which foundered Sunday, ninety miles west of Cape Flattery. The schooner was baound for Kotzbue, in the Klondike country and young Hamilton was a prospector.

The details of the foundering of the Jane Grey were told in The Journal Thursday morning but the dispatch did not contain the name of young Hamilton. Today the sad news reached the parents who are heart broken.

When the ship went down sixty-one passengers were on board and thirty-four were drowned. The remainder escaped by embarking in a launch. It is probable that the body will never be recovered as the ship went down many miles from shore.

Hamilton left home several weeks ago to seek his fortune in the Klondike country and he was well equipped for the journey. He was a young man, not quite 25 years old, of excellent moral character and popular among his associates. He worked for his father in the grain business for a number of years, but when the stories of Klondike riches ran high, he began to make preparations for the journey. For a number of hears he was a leader of the Ashland band."

B. S. Frost of San Francisco turned out to be Bert S. Frost from Massachusetts. The *Springfield Republican* reported: "The name of Bert S. Frost is among the lost on board the Jane Gray, which sunk when only three days out from Seattle, May 22. His friends in this city received letters stating that he was to sail on that boat on May 19. He was a young man of excellent character who made friends wherever he went, and his death is greatly lamented. Mr. Frost came to this city when quite young, and secured a position in J. R. Smith's plant, now the Springfield iron works, where he made rapid progress. He later took a position with the R. F. Hawkins iron works, and remained there for about four years. After that he was employed by Mace Moulton as foreman, and had charge of the iron work of the Besse building and the construction of the Ludlow bridge, which was his last work. He resigned his position with Mr. Moulton about six weeks ago to go to Klondike. He leaves a father, who lives in Otis, and two sisters, Mrs. John Paul of Newton Center and Miss Frost of Somersville, Ct. He was about 30 years old."

Although little was known about Charles Williams, who had taken a meager three hundred and seventy pounds of provisions for his gold-hunting expedition to Kotzebue Sound, the survivors of the disaster knew that he was born in England and had been a resident of Olympia, Washington, for a very short time. They had also heard him speak of his new wife. Accordingly, the *Seattle Post-Intelligencer* reported: "Williams Came From Olympia," with little other information about the man.

It seemed that not a single person in the entire city of Seattle was unaffected by the sinking of the schooner Jane Gray. Edmond S. Meany, the University of Washington professor, counselor and mentor to Jack Lindsay and the Schmid brothers, friend to Edward Ingraham and Clayton Packard, felt the sting of loss as keenly as if he had sailed with them on that fateful voyage. From New York, he received a letter from friends dated June 15, 1898:

"Dear Ed,

We had a most enjoyable trip across the continent and reached home on Tuesday the 7th. The weather has been very warm until this morning, but with nothing to do, and a cool brick house to live in, we have managed to get along very nicely. Last Sunday, a young man by the name of Ritter called on us and stated that he had a brother lost on the schooner 'Jane Gray,' that he had written to different parties for particulars regarding the disaster but was unable to learn the facts. MacDougall & Southwick had not answered his letter at all. I told him I would try and learn what I could regarding the affair. And as you are in a position to know from Ingraham all about it, I wish you would write me, or if Ingraham or the Captain or both have made a statement, will you kindly send me their reports and give me any other particulars you may have gathered up. Were MacDougall & Southwick in any way responsible for her going to the bottom? Was she overloaded, or badly managed? These are some of the questions he asked. Does Prince Luigi lose everything he put into the outfit? We have only had one letter from the Ward family, but are glad to have that. Thank Dickey. Arrived in Poch safely. With much love to all your family from the big and little Bushnells, I remain,

Yours Truly, Jim

#23 Washington St.

Poughkeepsie, N. Y."

The man who called on Jim Bushnell was George Ritter. He had been attempting to get information about his brother's death since learning of the wreck thirteen days prior. Along with George's interview, The *New York Times* reported from Poughkeepsie:

"Edward F. Ritter of this city was one of the thirty-five Klondike prospectors who lost their lives by the sinking of the schooner Jane Grey, which left Seattle on May 18, bound for Norton and Kotzebue Sounds, Alaska, and the Klondike. Mr. Ritter's brother, George, who is an instructor of music in this city, believes that the press reports of his brother's death are correct. He remarked that it was a great shock to him. He thought that when his brother made the dangerous passage of the Straits of Magellan and Cape Horn that his troubles were over.

Mr. Ritter, who was about thirty-five years of age, and unmarried, was one of a party of fifteen men who sailed from Lynn, Mass., on the fishing schooner Abbie M. Deering on Nov. 10 for the Klondike. Another member of the party was Louis R. Corson, a printer. They sailed down the east coast of both American continents, around Cape Horn, and up the Pacific Coast, reaching San Francisco in April. In that city the party broke up, and Mr. Ritter joined the expedition that sailed from Seattle on the Jane Gray on May 18. He was the only member of the Deering party on the lost vessel. George Ritter received a letter from his brother saying that he intended to sail on the Jane Gray."

The *New York Times* continued with more about the Gambell family in the next column:

"Great interest was aroused in the Presbyterian Building, Fifth Avenue and Twentieth Street, yesterday, by the publication in THE NEW YORK TIMES of the names of the Rev. V. G. Gambell, Mrs. Gambell, and infant, as among those drowned through the loss of the steamer Jane Gray in the North Pacific Ocean. The Rev. Mr. Gambell was a missionary sent out by the Presbyterian Home Board in this city, and he had been at St. Lawrence Island for a period of about two years. Last summer he returned for medical treatment for his wife, and was now on his way back to his station. His friends here are at a loss to understand why the family were on a steamer instead of on a revenue cutter unless it was that they were unable to get a government boat.

The Rev. Dr. Sheldon Jackson is reported to have said while at the recent General Assembly that scores of boats sailing north this Spring were totally unfit for sea service. Such may have been the case with the Jane Grey. The work on St. Lawrence Island had been most prosperous. The people are Alaskan Indians, and not so many in numbers as a few years ago, a famine one Winter three years since having wiped out nearly one-half the population. St. Lawrence is almost at the extreme end of the Alaskan peninsula and but thirty-five miles from the Siberian coast."

At Lynbrook, Long Island, New York, Emery Doxsey learned from Job Johnson that his son was a passenger on the Jane Gray. The first article published in the *Brooklyn Eagle* briefly stated: "Job Johnson of Springfield was revived after being in the water, clinging to wreckage for two hours. The two young men started for the Klondike together, several weeks ago. Doxsey was assistant station agent at this place for some time and was always very popular with patrons of the station. He was about 18 years old."

By the 18th of June, a more complete account of Job Johnson's experience appeared in the *Brooklyn Eagle*:

"LATEST LONG ISLAND NEWS.

Wilbur Doxsey Drowned in the Pacific, Saving Others.

ON HIS WAY TO THE KLONKIKE.

Letter Shown in Queens County Surrogate's Court by His Father to Prove the Death of His Son—Went Down With the Wreck of the Schooner Jane Gray, While Trying to Save a Woman and Child.

(Special to the Eagle.)

Lynbrook, L. I., June 18—At the Queens County Surrogate's Court, at Jamaica, yesterday, letters of administration were granted to Emery Doxsey of Lynbrook in the estate of his son, Wilbur Doxsey, who was drowned from the schooner Jane Gray in the Pacific Ocean on Sunday, May 22, while on a journey from Seattle to Klondike. The estate consisted of about $850 personal property. In confirmation of his son's death the petitioner exhibited in court the following letter from a companion, Job Johnson, who was saved from the wreck:

Seattle, June 3, 1898.

Mr. Charles Doxsey;

You have no doubt by this time heard of the sinking of the Jane Gray...We left Seattle Thursday, May 19...From the time we reached the ocean until we sunk Wilbur remained on deck while I was laid up in my bunk homesick. About 2 o'clock Sunday morning Wilbur came into the stateroom and said that the boat was taking water and that the captain had ordered every one on deck. I was undressed in bed at the time. I told him to get on deck as quick as he could and get into the first boat that left the ship. He left the cabin and I got up and had just time enough to pull on my pants and vest as the boat listed to one side. I picked up my hat and ran for the deck. When I arrived on deck the crew had launched a boat that belonged to a private outfit and was calling for everyone to get in. There was quite some people in the boat and I supposed Wilbur was one of the number. As I was making for the boat one of the passengers called out, 'Let the woman and child have the first chance.' The woman was the wife of a missionary who was going to St. Lawrence Island and the child was a baby of about 6 months.

When I heard the call to give the woman the first chance I and all the other men on deck stepped back to the rail and waited, thinking that they were bringing her from the cabin. She never came and in less than five minutes we were all in the water. I found a piece of wreckage and floated until daylight and was pulled into the boat half drowned. We sailed for thirty-six hours and landed at Vancouver Island—there were twenty-seven men in a 23 foot boat. I looked around and Wilbur was not among the number present. Instead of getting in the boat he must have remained on deck and refused to get into the boat until the woman and child had. This has been an awful windup to our expectations."

On Wednesday, June 22nd, the staff of the *Wichita Daily Eagle* learned that they had lost one of their former residents in the sinking. The details of the disaster were a reprint of the *Seattle Daily Times* article from three weeks prior, however, there was an additional twist:

"WAS A WICHITA MAN

How B. D. Ranney Lost His Life in the Jane Gray Disaster.

The following from the Seattle Press-Times relating to the sea tragedy in which B. D. Ranney, formerly of this city and at one time the proprietor of the Princess restaurant, on the corner of Lawrence and Douglas avenues, lost his life. The ship which went down was owned by former Wichita man, John G. Pacey, who for a number of years was a bookkeeper in the Kansas National bank. Both of the gentlemen have any number of friends here. Mr. Ben Glaze of this city, who is touring the coast, sends the story."

As more information became available, the *Seattle Post-Intelligencer* continued to publish biographies of those lost:

"Spencer W. Young, who went down with the Gray, was a veteran miner. He resided at 811 Pike street in this city, with his wife and family. His daughter, Miss Effie Young, is employed at the office of the Western Union Telegraph Company. Miss Young learned first of the death of her father in the special edition of the Post-Intelligencer...Mr. Young had lived in Washington for twenty-five years. He was an old soldier and was well known at Stanwood and Mt. Vernon. Mr. Young leaves a wife and three children, namely, Preston W., a seaman; George W., who is a clerk for John Davis, and Miss Effie Young, employed by the Western Union Telegraph Company."

"William H. Gleason lived at 820 Washington Street with his wife and family. He was an old resident of Seattle, having come here twelve years ago from Oregon. At first he engaged in the dairy business, but later followed contracting. He was the son-in-law of Paris McCain of 820 Washington Street."

"Gleason and Young were looked upon by Maj. Ingraham as two of the most reliable men. The party was to have been divided up into small squads of prospectors, which were to seek for gold, going in different directions. Young was to have led one of these parties and Gleason was to have taken command of another."

"Phil C. Little was the only son of Mr. and Mrs. Frank Little. Mr. Little is a member of the board of Public Works. Young Little was 26 years old and was a robust fellow with very steady habits. For eight years he lived in the city with his parents, attending the Denny school and later being a janitor at city hall. Two years ago, he left for Carlton, Or., where he has been engaged in farming. He was in the city only six weeks before starting on the journey north. He was a member of the Workman lodge and the Independent order of Good Templars. 'While the death of Phil C. Little will be mourned by all who knew him, it is particularly affecting to those of us in the city hall who were here while he was janitor of public buildings,' said City Comptroller Will H. Parry yesterday. 'Phil was an even-tempered, industrious and accommodating boy, and the very soul of honor. During the two years he was in the city's employ he won the confidence and respect of all the heads of departments and had the friendship of every subordinate. General regret was expressed when he resigned the janitorship, and when he returned he was a welcome visitor to every office in the hall.' The young man had prospect of an honorable and useful life, and his untimely death is a sad blow to those who hoped to see his ambitions realized."

Tales of the lost continued unabated:

"Conrad George Schmid and Victor Joseph Schmid were two well-known university boys who lost their lives on the Jane Gray. Conrad Schmid entered the university in 1895, but had only attended part of two years. He was 23 years of age. His brother, Victor Schmid, entered the varsity in 1896. He was 21 years of age. They are the sons of Vitus Schmid, one of the oldest pioneers of Seattle, who is now living on Mercer Island. Both young men were over six feet high and built in proportion. They played line positions on the varsity football team last year and went with Maj. Ingraham on the St. Elias trip."

"W. Arnot Johnston, of 823 Seneca street, Seattle, came very near missing the Kotzebue expedition. He had climbed Mount Rainier in a party under Maj. Ingraham's leadership and had made him his warm friend. He applied for a place in the party when the proposition was first started, but Maj. Ingraham could not find room for him. Two days before the Jane Gray sailed one of the men backed out and young Johnston was taken in his place. He resigned his place as collector of the Post-Intelligencer and went with the party. He leaves a mother and sister in this city. His sister, Mrs. Ella Jordan, is teaching in the Cascade school. His mother is now visiting in the East. His only brother is Rev. L. Johnston, now residing at Reynolds, Pa. He was 22 years of age."

"Horace Palmer, who perished, was one of the valuable members of Maj. Ingraham's staff and was to have charge of the engine in his launch. Mr. Palmer came from Lebanon, O., where he left a wife and two children. Dr. Lessey said, 'I slept next to Mr. Palmer and when he saw that we were undoubtedly going to our death, he said, 'I don't care so much for myself as I do for my wife and children.' He was an excellent man and was a good engineer.'"

"E. M. Taylor and F. S. Taylor, of San Francisco, were brothers of Frank Taylor and William Taylor, connected with the paper house known all over the Coast as successors to the S. P. Taylor Paper Company. E. M. Taylor was in the mercantile business in this city for six months prior to his departure for the north. He went to San Francisco and induced his brother, F. S. Taylor, to go north with him. E. M. Taylor leaves a wife and F. S. Taylor leaves a wife and two children. The Taylors formerly owned the resort known as Camp Taylor, situated about forty-five miles from San Francisco, and where the mother still resides. B. F. Spencer was a single man and was an attorney-at-law at San Francisco. Charles W. Wilkinson, one of the survivors, was with this party and was formerly connected with the Valeau & Spencer job printing establishment at San Francisco."

"A. G. Kingsbury, of Boston, and B. D. Ranney, of Kalamazoo, Mich., were partners on the Jane Gray. Ranney was lost, and Kingsbury has before him the unwelcome task of sending word to the dead man's family of his tragic end."

On June 25th more incredible reports arrived from Vancouver Island. Apparently, the Jane Gray had not yet used up her nine lives because she surfaced again. The *Victoria Daily Columnist* printed another startling revelation:

"JANE GREY DID NOT SINK

Indians Report That the Wrecked Vessel Floated Ashore Above Clayoquot

The Schooner Jane Gray, of Seattle, did not sink in mid-ocean as claimed by her captain, officers and surviving passengers, who arrived here on the schooner Favorite after the disaster which caused the death of thirty-four men, a woman and a child, unless she was built of material which after sinking would again come to the surface and drift for at least a hundred miles, and schooners are not built of such stuff.

For the schooner Jane Gray is ashore just above Kyuquot, according to a story brought by the steamer Willapa, which arrived yesterday afternoon from the West Coast. Capt. Foot and the officers did not see the schooner themselves, but they received reliable information from Indians at Clayoquot that she had drifted ashore above Kyuquot and that the Indians were looting her cargo. Beyond the fact that two planks in her starboard bow had been sprung, the Indians knew nothing of the condition of the vessel. They said there were no bodies on board, but it is probable that the schooner was waterlogged and that they were unable to reach the cabins.

According to the position of the vessel given by the Indians she must have been carried by the wind in the exactly same direction as was the launch in which the survivors reached shore. She must soon break up, Capt. Foot says, as the coast in that vicinity is very rocky.

It will be remembered that when the survivors reached Victoria, two of them reported that they left the schooner as she went down. The probability is that a wave swept over her and they thought she was sinking.

The Quadra will leave for the West Coast early next week and will probably visit the wreck."

Adding observations to the story, the *Seattle Daily Times* reported:

"The Willapa will leave again for Vancouver Island in a few days and will investigate the matter more thoroughly than opportunity afforded on the present trip.

It is thought probable that many bodies will be found in the hull and it is possible that a tug boat will be immediately dispatched to the scene to recover the bodies of any of the victims and such of their effects as may be still in the hold or cabin of the boat.

The fact that the hull of the Jane Grey has drifted ashore would appear to confirm the strongly expressed opinion of The Times' inspector that she was sound, but overloaded, especially on deck, and that this heavy deckload had simply rolled her over, or capsized her, with the terribly fatal consequences which resulted.

Others, however, have insisted that she was rotten and the opportunity now had for an investigation will enable those interested to determine who was right.

It would be a very remarkable thing for a rotten vessel to hold together as the Jane Grey appears to have done and the result of the investigations that will now follow will be watched with much interest."

Late in the month of June, the Quadra did visit the West Coast of Vancouver Island and their voyage became a bit of a salvage mission. Between their regular duties that included being the floating courthouse and law enforcement agency, they collected items that the natives had scavenged from the wreck of the Jane Gray. When Captain John T. Walbran, commander of the Canadian vessel, filed his report, he stated, "During the cruise revenue work was also attended to, the wreckage from a vessel recently wrecked, the 'Jane Grey,' being taken charge of at each place where it had been picked up and sold by myself as acting receiver of the wreck, at public auction on the spot, the proceeds of the sale being handed over to the receiver of the wreck on the return of the 'Quadra' to Victoria."

The most valuable item of the wreckage, the Italian's steam launch, fetched $175. Neither the ship, a single body, nor signs of other survivors had yet to be found.

CHAPTER 18 - THE COMMITTEE

James Eustace Blackwell, image courtesy of the Blackwell family.

While the search for survivors was under way, James Blackwell took charge of the committee seeking financial compensation for those who were left most destitute by the wreck.

The publicity and speculation had things heating up at the MacDougall and Southwick outfitting firm. Initially somewhat sympathetic to the plight of those who had escaped the sinking schooner, the company paid for their passage on the Favorite and the freight to return Ingraham's launch to Seattle, then put the men from out of town up at the Hotel Brunswick. They even provided clothing and meals to a few. Less than twenty-four hours later, the firm had changed its tune.

En route home to Seattle, several of the survivors agreed that they would present the company with a fair demand for one suit of clothing and the $100 for baggage that was guaranteed on their ticket stubs - since the disclaimer seemed to rule out any other compensation. James

Blackwell was appointed spokesman for the group. In addition to his military and civil engineering experience, he had served on the city counsel and been the mayor of Bremerton, Washington, where he was also in charge of construction of the dry dock. And although he claimed that he was not "a seafaring man," he was neither a novice at maritime matters, nor a stranger to the laws of the maritime world.

Wednesday, the afternoon of their arrival on the steamship City of Kingston, James Blackwell and the committee of survivors visited the MacDougall and Southwick store at the corner of 1st and Cherry, presenting their claim to John MacDougall. After listening to their request, MacDougall went to the upstairs office, presumably to consult his partners, and returned, telling the men that he would honor their claims.

As the men began browsing the racks and shelves in search of new clothing, Blackwell said, "Mr. MacDougall, we have agreed among ourselves that no man shall exceed $20 or $25 in his selections."

To this, MacDougall replied, "Oh. That makes no difference. We are to deduct it from the $100."

"No." Blackwell responded, "This is to be in addition to the $100."

Somewhat taken aback, MacDougall exclaimed, "Oh, well. Go ahead and we will arrange that all satisfactorily."

The following day, Henry Southwick, vice president of the company, had blown into town on the fastest train he could catch from New York. Now acting as the company spokesman, he refused to make good on the $100 baggage insurance or any part of the agreement that MacDougall had made with the committee the prior evening, saying that the company did not own the boat and that the survivors should look to John Pacey for the payment of any claims they might have. He went even further by making the statement, "We will not recognize any committee, but if each one of you men will come to us and show that he is absolutely without means we will try to assist him in getting a job or give him enough money to get out of town."

Henry had seemingly not inherited his grandfather's generosity of spirit. To the committee members, Southwick had a parting shot. With a sarcastic curl to his lips that was familiar to many of the residents of Seattle, he stated, "The MacDougall-Southwick Company are only doing this because you are our friends and we are doing it out of charity, just as we pay pew rent or do missionary work at home instead of abroad."

Struggling to maintain his cool, James Blackwell replied, "I do not wish you to do any missionary work for me. Whether you are legally responsible or not, I do not know, but I do know that you are morally. However, I will pay you now for the goods I have received."

Before word of this incident made it around town, The *Seattle Daily Times* printed a somewhat forgiving story, allowing MacDougall and Southwick an opportunity to correct their position in the matter:

"JANE GREY SURVIVORS

Make Informal Demand on MacDougall, Southwick Co.

WHO OWNED THE SCHOONER?

Large amount of Litigation Liable to Result From Alleged Refusal of Reputed Owners to Provide for Survivors as Per Agreement.

The story of the Jane Grey disaster is the all-absorbing topic of conversation throughout the city today, and wherever one of the survivors is recognized he is made to repeat that terrible tale of the sea.

The more the matter is discussed the greater becomes the mystery and the final solution, or the general drift of opinion, is that the vessel was overloaded and carried too much freight on deck.

The condition of the survivors is attracting some attention, now that the first shock and excitement in the public mind are giving place to thoughts concerning the destitution of those who lost everything they possessed on the ill-fated schooner.

A statement was made in the morning organ that the MacDougall-Southwick Company had provided clothing for the survivors. That is a mistake, for while several have been given clothing by the concern in accordance with the agreement which they made with the committee, that they would give each man a full outfit of clothing and $100 on account of their liability for baggage, which is shown by a clause on the face of the tickets and which makes them liable for baggage to the extent of $100, yet it is known that Major E. S. Ingraham, Dr. L. M. Lessey, George Pennington and C. H. Packard did not go to the store to be outfitted for a single thing. J. E. Blackwell went with a majority of them and got his clothing under the belief that the agreement made with Mr. MacDougall in person would be carried out, yet when the firm backed down from their agreement on Thursday morning and claimed to be doing this for 'charity and in the manner of paying pew rent,' Mr. Blackwell became so indignant that he declared he would not place himself under obligations to such men under any consideration and he thereupon obtained sufficient money from some friends to pay the firm for the articles furnished to him, taking a receipt for the $18.50 paid.

One of the remarks that incensed the survivors was Southwick's statement: 'We will not recognize any committee, but if each one of you men will come to us and show that he is absolutely without means we will try to assist him in getting a job or give him enough money to get out of town.'

This appears to put the men on the level with street beggars and was resented by all of the survivors whose manhood had not been crushed out of them by the weight of their terrible experience."

While failing to delve any further into why not a single member of the Ingraham party nor any of the families of their lost men had sought compensation from MacDougall and Southwick, the article continued with more speculation about who actually owned the Jane Gray:

"Although J. G. Pacey is the reputed owner of the vessel, yet for reasons not known the actual owners are alleged to have been MacDougall-Southwick Co., and much criticism is now being passed upon this method of doing business, it being alleged that Mr. Pacey is merely a clerk in the company's employ and that his financial responsibility is a question not fully settled in the minds of those most deeply interested. And it is further alleged that the company simply used him in the matter in anticipation of just such a contingency as has now arisen.

However this may be, it should be stated that they are responsible to have considered the request made by the survivors and to have refused it, but it is possible that the firm may even yet assume all responsibility and make good at least the $100 specified in the tickets as the limit of the owner's liability—the moving spirit toward this assumption being a court of justice."

Once full details of the incident made it's way around the streets, alleys and brothels, the *Seattle Daily Times* got wind of Southwick's deplorable behavior and printed another column the following day:

"JANE GREY SURVIVORS

Are Indignant at the MacDougall, Southwick Co.

WERE TREATED LIKE DOGS

After Courteously Requesting the Owners of the Jane Grey to Pay Them the $100, They are Subjected to Insult and Abuse.

The survivors of the Jane Grey have been here since Wednesday afternoon, and have been endeavoring in a courteous manner to secure from the owners of the schooner some amicable settlement of their claims for lost baggage. In order not to jeopardize their efforts to obtain pecuniary satisfaction in a purely friendly way, The Times has refrained from publishing the sequel to the Jane Grey wreck, as far as that sequel has been unfolded up to date; but in view of the shameful manner in which the MacDougall-Southwick Company have treated their unfortunate victims the time has come when the public should know the contemptible spirit of greed and avarice that has characterized the way in which the men composing that company have treated these survivors.

In the first place the public must understand that those men, whose lives have been so miraculously saved, are not beggars or hoboes who had sought some cheap means of reaching the land of gold, but are gentlemen in every sense of the word, and, in many instances, highly educated and cultivated—some following professions requiring the highest skill, and others trades requiring more than ordinary intelligence.

This, therefore, is the class of men who had sought to better their financial condition by a voyage to Alaska. Many of them have families and all of them were prominently known in their respective localities. But they have now lost everything and are practically destitute, many still wearing the water-stained clothing in which they escaped from the wreck; but this fact does not detract from their manhood nor lessen the respect in which they are held by all who know or have met them. Under these circumstances, therefore, the treatment accorded them by the MacDougall-Southwick Company merits the severest condemnation by every self-respecting man in this community."

Meanwhile, MacDougall contended that it was all a simple misunderstanding, that the company gave the surviving men clothing on the condition that if the company decided to recognize the claims for baggage, the amount of their goods would be deducted from the $100. Otherwise, the men would owe a debt on their individual accounts.

The *Times* reporter recounted the conversation that occurred between James Blackwell and George Southwick on Thursday, noting that MacDougall never made mention of Pacey at the time the original conversation took place, nor did he consult Pacey before making the agreement with the committee on Wednesday.

"All the other promises, which were made by Mr. MacDougall personally on Wednesday, are alleged by the survivors to have been repudiated in their entirety through Mr. Southwick. The passengers contracts or tickets are signed by J. G. Pacey, who claims that MacDougall, Southwick & Co. have no interest whatever in the vessel, but merely acted as his agents in advertising and receipting for money received for passengers and freight.

However this may be, there are many tradesmen around town who furnished supplies to the Jane Grey upon the order of the MacDougall-Southwick Company, and neither the order nor the checks given in payment bore the word 'Agents' after the company's signature. This and other matters not necessary to mention now have come to the knowledge of the attorneys engaged by the survivors, and have created an impression almost amounting to a conviction that the real owners of the Jane Grey are the MacDougall-Southwick Company, and that Mr. Pacey is simply their stool-pigeon, working one of the side schemes either of the company itself or of the individuals composing it."

When some of the men of the committee, desperate for money, arrived at the store as had been suggested by Southwick, he seemed incensed by the news coverage and continued to rant with his customary arrogance, "You fellows have talked about the ship and said she was a rotten old hulk and if you were down on the wharf now in your overalls and wet clothes, I would let you lay there. The owners of the Corona said we were fools to do anything for you and I am sorry we did."

James Blackwell was steaming mad when he learned how the survivors were treated on their last visit to the store. Wise to the workings of MacDougall and Southwick, with the stool pigeon John Pacey aiding and abetting them, Blackwell and the committee began duplicating their document trail. Retracing the path the party made during the first two weeks of May, James Blackwell, Charles

Chard, and George Boak visited every store that had sold them anything larger than a sewing needle. Splitting up, Blackwell went up the hill to Seattle Grocery at 900 Second Avenue, while Chard visited Louch, Augustine & Company on First between Columbia and Marion. Between June 6th and June 11th, the three of them called on no less than nine stores, picking up copies of receipts for their purchases.

Reconvening at the Hotel Brunswick at First and Columbia, the committee tallied their invoices. Blackwell wrote on the hotel stationary:

"Party for Port Clarence = 8

Jas. E. Blackwell

Silas Livengood

Wm. S. Weaver

Geo. R. Boak

Wm. F. Deterling}Drowned

Wm. Otten}Drowned

Chas. E. Chard

Jas. K. Livengood

Chard purchased his outfit separately. Jas. K. Livengood did not leave on the Jane Gray, but purchased outfit. So 7 have interest in the following not including Chas. E. Chard.

Seattle Grocery Co. $443.49

Seattle Hardware Co. $115.67

V. R. Pierson 2 boats $53.00

Gold Washer and leather

Last of purchased by Deterling $4.95

Medicine case, towels, etc $2.90

$620.01"

The men of "the Committee" were ready to go to war with MacDougall and Southwick.

CHAPTER 19 - FROM "HOO-DOO" TO LAWSUIT

"Sailor's superstition" or "hoo-doo" was a term often applied to a vessel that had a history of bad luck. Besides being named after the "Nine Days' Queen" of England (who was beheaded at the age of seventeen), the Jane Gray had numerous incidents in her relatively short life. After the first capsizing, a mate had been convicted of cruelty and fined $1500 in San Francisco for beating crewmembers. A couple of years later, several of her sailors were abandoned in a dory off of the coast of Japan (miraculously, they survived). And that was before she was impounded for the illegal hunting of seals.

Further inciting questions as to whether John Pacey, Henry Southwick or John MacDougall were at any time aware of the past incidents involving the schooner, on June 20th, the *Seattle Post-Intelligencer* published yet another column about the questionable history of the Jane Gray:

"JANE GRAY IS A HOODOO.

STORY OF THE ILL-FATED SCHOONER'S ARCTIC EXPERIENCES.

Thirteen Years Ago, While Cruising Off the Coast of Siberia, Her Crew Was Attacked by Natives and Killed—Some Other Experiences.

The ill-fated schooner Jane Gray, which drowned so many prospective miners off Cape Flattery a few weeks ago, will not down, as is shown by meager reports of the finding of her hull on the shores of Vancouver Island. This is not the first time that the schooner has to all appearances been lost only to bob up again to the great surprise of mariners. The Jane Gray's other trouble occurred years ago in the Bering sea, but did not cost the lives of the whalers who manned her.

The story of the Arctic romance of the "hoodooed" schooner was well told yesterday to a Post-Intelligencer reporter by an old sailor now stationed on the United States steamer Perry, who was in the Arctic on the war vessel that saved the Jane Gray—that eventually she might drown the men who trusted in her.

"I first heard of the Jane Gray," said the old sailor, "In 1885, when she was attacked by natives while cruising off the north coast of Siberia. The captain, first mate and ten of her crew were killed in the fight that followed. A few survivors managed to escape with the vessel, and among them the captain's daughter, Kate, a lass of 17 years. She was the only one aboard who had a knowledge of navigation, and the command naturally fell on her shoulders. The whaling season was not over and the girl decided to continue the cruise, making the best of the misfortune that had overtaken them. For months she continued the work with her short crew, steering the little schooner from one place to another through the ice-dotted Arctic sea. When the long winter night began to cast its gloom over the whaling grounds she set sail for San Francisco, coming out past Dutch Harbor and finally going into the Golden Gate without difficulty. She then turned the vessel over to the owner along with a fair catch.

On Another Cruise.

"At the beginning of the next season the Jane Gray again started out whaling with provisions for three months. The pretty commander was again on board, but this time as wife of the owner, Capt. Watterson. Two years later the old United States steamer Thetis, while cruising with the whaling fleet in the Arctic, was informed that the wreck of an unknown schooner had been sighted among the ice floes far to the north, the captain decided to investigate and, if possible, relieve the crew of the castaway vessel.

"It took a week to find the vessel, which at first appeared to be a total wreck, lying on her port beam's end and firmly embedded in the ice pack. Her masts and rigging were sheathed with ice and the hull had a coating of white. Through the icicles hanging from her stern the relief party made out her name, Jane Gray, of San Francisco. On boarding her the fact developed from the log book that her officers and crew had deserted her more than a month before. A previous entry in her log read thus:

"'Died on shipboard, Kate, the beloved wife of Capt. Paul Watterson, August 2. Buried at sea August 4, 1888'

"There was pathos wonderfully deep in that simple inscription, which told many things to those of the Thetis' crew who had heard of the daring whaling trip of the pretty girl. What had become of the crew was a mystery.

Thetis to the Rescue.

"Commander Emory, of the Thetis, now on the auxillary cruiser Yosemite, determined to attempt the rescue of the imprisoned schooner after making an examination of the hull, which proved to be practically uninjured. Accordingly, all hands were ordered out to cut away the ice from her hull and rigging. When that was completed the ice floe in which she was imbedded was blown up with dynamite. By reason of the ice which had formed in her hold the vessel still lay on her beam's end. A purchase was made rigged from her mainmast to that of the Thetis, with which she was pulled on an even keel. It took fourteen days to get the schooner out of the ice, but at the end of that time she was in as good shape as she had been before.

"Ensign Robert Lopez, with ten men, was sent aboard the craft with instructions to proceed to Point Barrow in search of the missing crew, and on not finding them, to head for San Francisco. The Jane Gray arrived at Barrow just after Capt. Watterson and his crew had sailed for Sitka on another vessel, so Lopez squared away for his 3,000-mile voyage to the southward. She had fair weather and in six weeks was at anchor inside the Golden Gate.

"The arrival of the Jane Gray was a nine-day wonder in the maritime world, which had been apprised of her loss by a letter written by Capt. Watterson from Sitka. The skipper arrived a few days after the Gray, on a passenger boat from the north, and was, of course, more than surprised on seeing his schooner at anchor. On going aboard he was pleasantly greeted by the young officer, who tendered him the ship with the compliments of Commander Emory.""

Although based largely upon speculation and rumor, the story was half true. The Jane Gray had indeed been capsized and frozen in the Arctic ice in 1888. However, no lives were lost. She was under the command, or at least the ownership of, Captain William H. Kelley at the time, and since she was not built until 1887, the tale of young Kate seems to be romantic lore of the times. Perhaps the old seaman had the dates and names confused with another Jane Gray - because there were other vessels of the same name (in various spellings). Regardless of the actual veracity of the story, two days after this article was published, it had become apparent that neither John G. Pacey nor the MacDougall and Southwick Company had any intention of reimbursing the survivors a single penny for their losses. And the survivors were thoroughly convinced that the outfitting firm new of the vessel's history.

Assuming that the dispute could only be resolved in a court of law, five members of the committee engaged the legal services of Bausman, Kelleher & Emory, Metcalfe & Jurey. On the behalf of Blackwell, Boak, Chard, Livengood and Weaver, Frederick Bausman filed suit in King County Superior court on June 22nd. In addition to filing a civil suit, the action was duplicated by a filing in the criminal court.

Their suits each alleged that the MacDougall and Southwick Company, a corporation, along with John G. Pacey, were jointly responsible for the disaster, stating that the defendants were the agents and owners of the Jane Gray who "had the sole and exclusive possession, management, operation, use and control" of the vessel. Citing the advertisements that the outfitting firm had taken out, soliciting passengers and freight, the plaintiffs alleged that MacDougall and Southwick were engaged "in the business as carriers and common carriers, of transporting passengers and freight, for hire, by means of the said schooner and other vessels, from the said port of Seattle to diverse ports and places in Alaska."

By naming them "common carriers," Bausman, the attorney for the plaintiffs, hoped to eliminate the question of who owned the boat. Under common law, common carriers were absolutely liable for goods carried, the only exceptions being: "acts of God or nature, acts of a public enemy, fault or fraud of the shipper, an inherent defect in the goods, fire on board the ship, or navigational errors committed by the ship's captain or members of her crew."

Striking the same vein that had so thoroughly infuriated Henry Southwick just three weeks prior, each action went on to say: "The schooner 'Jane Gray' was during all the time aforesaid, old, weak, defective, and rotten, in bad repair and condition, and wholly unseaworthy, all of which, during all said time, was well known to the defendants, and wholly unknown to the plaintiff, although he exercised due diligence, care and caution to ascertain the condition of said vessel."

Frederick Bausman sought to prove the outfitting firm's culpability, calling all of their actions negligent, careless and unskillful:

"That prior to the sailing of the said schooner, as aforesaid, and, to-wit, on or about the 18th day of May, 1898, the libellants so negligently, carelessly and unskillfully constructed and placed cabins and other structures for passengers, freight and baggage, on the deck of the said schooner, for said voyage, and so carelessly and negligently suffered and permitted the same so to remain during said voyage; and also, prior to the sailing of said schooner, as aforesaid, and to-wit, about the time last mentioned, the libellants so negligently, carelessly and unskillfully raised and adjusted the main-mast boom of said schooner, and made various other changes and alterations in her structure, tackle, apparel and equipment, for said voyage, and so negligently and carelessly suffered and permitted the same so to remain during said voyage; and also so negligently, carelessly and greatly overloaded said schooner for said voyage; and so negligently and carelessly suffered and permitted the same so to proceed upon and pursue said voyage; and also so negligently, carelessly and unskillfully loaded, placed, stowed, and disposed of the cargo of freight and baggage placed on board said schooner for said voyage, and so negligently and carelessly selected and placed in charge of said schooner for said voyage an unskillful and incompetent master and crew, well known by the libellants to be such, and so negligently and carelessly suffered and permitted the same to remain in charge and control of the sailing and navigation of said schooner on said voyage; and so negligently and carelessly suffered and permitted and caused the said schooner to sail from the said port of Seattle and proceeded upon the high seas on her said voyage, in the condition and under the circumstances aforesaid; and the said schooner was by reason of her unseaworthy condition aforesaid and of the wrongful, negligent, careless and unskillful acts aforesaid, foundered and lost upon the high seas off the coast of Vancouver Island on or about the 22nd day of May, 1898, while pursuing said voyage with the plaintiff..." He went on, detailing injuries and the damages, both physical and financial, that his clients had suffered.

In the courtroom of the streets of Seattle, the case had already been tried - MacDougall and Southwick, as well as their "stool-pigeon," John Pacey, were guilty as charged.

Defending the outfitting firm, the attorneys at White, Munday & Fulton, Stratton & Powell tossed in every conceivable legal delay, requesting revisions to the language in documents submitted by Frederick Bausman, pointing out statements that they contended were "irrelevant, immaterial, and redundant." Once the phrases in question were corrected and filed with the court, they denied that their clients had any knowledge of injury or the losses alleged by the plaintiffs, demanding further proof that any and all were indeed passengers on the Jane Gray when she went down.

MacDougall and Southwick's lawyers were biding their time with the knowledge that they had six months from the date that the original suit was filed to enter a counter suit in admiralty law, where special rules apply. Their greatest advantage in admiralty was that there was no right to a jury trial.

On behalf of the survivors of the wreck of the Jane Gray, Frederick Bausman needed to prove that the owners were knowingly negligent, beyond the shadow of a doubt. And his argument needed to withstand the scrutiny of Judge Cornelius Holgate Hanford.

Finally quelling the persistent speculation that perhaps wreckage of the Jane Gray would be found, on Friday, July 8, 1898, the *Victoria Daily Colonist* printed the column:

"HAS NOT BEEN FOUND.

Story of the Jane Gray Wreck Drifting Ashore a Fairy Tale."

"After all, only the launch from the wreck of the Jane Gray drifted ashore at Kyuquot, and this, minus the boiler, was sold to Messrs. Chas. Spring and Mill on Monday last. The Jane Gray has never been seen since the day her seams opened and she became a floating coffin. The story that she had floated ashore, it will be remembered, was told by Indians."

CHAPTER 20 - THE NON-LITIGANTS

While the men of the committee of survivors became deeply embroiled in the legal proceedings against MacDougall and Southwick, the search for bodies and more survivors ended. Sadly, no others were found and all those who were not fortunate enough to gain their escape in Major Ingraham's launch appeared to have been devoured by the waves of the Pacific Ocean.

The lack of physical evidence caused challenges for those who sought to redeem life insurance policies and manage the financial matters of the missing. Needing proof of his actual death, the family of one of the lost San Francisco men went so far as to take out an advertisement in the *Victoria Daily Columnist*:

"$200.00 REWARD

A reward of TWO HUNDRED DOLLARS will be paid for the recovery, dead or alive, of the body of B. S. SPENCER, of San Francisco, who was lost on the Jane Gray off Cape Flattery, May 22, 1898.

Said Spencer weighed 185 pounds, was 5 feet 7 inches high, had very full smooth face, with marked dimple in chin, thick black hair, gray eyes, and heavy brow."

Charles Wilkinson, who had been traveling with Burrey Spencer and the missing Taylor brothers, chose not to stick around Seattle and took Henry Southwick up on the offer to pay his fare home. After returning to San Francisco, he joined Blackwell, Livengood, Boak, Chard, and Weaver in the lawsuit against MacDougall and Southwick.

A. G. Kingsbury, originally a member of the committee, disappeared from the litigation. The man who had so valiantly attempted to save baby Margaret and the Gambell family never mentioned, in any of his interviews, that he had sustained a shoulder fracture in his struggle to swim through the debris field of the Jane Gray. After visiting the MacDougall and Southwick store with James Blackwell and C. J. Reilly on the day that they arrived from Vancouver Island, Kingsbury underwent surgery and spent fifteen days quietly recovering enough to continue his expedition to Alaska. He only had a nickel in his pocket and had lost all of his gear in the wreck, but unlike many of the other survivors, was able to wire home to Boston for additional funds. By June 16, 1898, Kingsbury had purchased a new outfit and caught another ship, the steamer Grace Dollar, for Kotzebue Sound.

Other survivors needed time to regroup. C. J. Reilly, who remained a witness for the survivors, withdrew from the lawsuit for unknown reasons. His partner, J. H. Conture, disappeared, as did Manuel Roberts, neither of whom ever participated in the legal proceedings against Pacey, MacDougall, and Southwick. George Hiller and Percy Davenport returned home to Harrisburg, Pennsylvania, to wait out the winter and make another try for the Klondike in the spring of 1899.

~~~

It was well into the month of July when someone in Eau Claire, Wisconsin connected the dots and concluded that O. F. McKelvey, who had reportedly been the last man to purchase passage on the Jane Gray, was his brother-in-law. The *Eau Claire Leader* printed his letter to the editor under the headline:
~~~

"THE ILL-FATED JANE GRAY

AN EAU CLAIRE BOY ON THE WAY TO KLONDIKE THOUGHT TO HAVE BEEN LOST.

PATRICK McKELVEY TOOK PASSAGE ON THE JANE GRAY AND HAS NEVER BEEN HEARD FROM SINCE.

Eau Claire, July 9, 1898.

'To the Editor:

On May 22, 1898, an account of the loss of the vessel "Jane Gray" on route from Seattle to the Yukon appeared in the Leader. You will remember that 35 passengers were reported drowned in the wreck. Among the names of the missing was that of Patrick McKelvey, an old and highly respected Eau Claire boy. Mr. McKelvey was 43 years of age and was on his way to the Klondike gold regions. His mother, Mrs. Ellen McKelvey resides in this city at 223 Bellinger street. Mr. McKelvey's two sisters also reside here; they are: Mrs. John McMahon, 416 Beach street, and Mrs. P. H. McCreash, 223 Bellinger street. He has two brothers living in Rhinelander, Wi., one at Wolfstown, Canada, and another sister, Mrs. John Todd, residing in Johnsbury, Vt.

Yours respectively,

JOHN McMAHON,

416 Beach street.'"

~~~

By August of 1898, another shipwreck made the headlines. Nobody died. And somewhat ironically, C. W. Thornton, the same man who had climbed Mount St. Elias with Major Ingraham and Prince Luigi, and bet on which ship would
~~~

make Kotzebue Sound first, reported on the fate of the schooner Moonlight:

"The first news received from many vessels that left here early in the summer with gold seekers for Kotzebue sound, Alaska, came today in a letter form Charles Thornton announcing the wreck of the schooner Moonlight, July 2, at the entrance of the Kawayk river. Her passengers and their outfits were saved. The vessel was wrecked on one of the many small islands that lie in the entrance to Kotzebue sound. The skipper, who was unfamiliar with the coast, refused to take on Indian pilots. The Moonlight was one of the first vessels to sail from here this season for Kotzebue sound. She sailed May 19. It is a noteworthy coincidence that she sailed on the same night that the schooner Jane Grey, also bound for Kotzebue sound. The Jane Grey was wrecked May 22 a few hundred miles off Cape Flattery with a loss of 36 lives. The Moonlight succeeded in getting within 25 miles of her destination. The Moonlight carried from here 55 passengers. On the Moonlight was a large amount of lumber. This was saved and will be used by the shipwrecked passengers in the construction of boats to ascend the Kawayk river and continue their exploration."

~~~

From *A Family Paper*, a memorial to W. Arnot Johnston was published December on 28, 1898:

"Death of William Arnot Johnston, son of Rev. N. M. Johnston, deceased, and brother of Rev. S. Dell Johnston, was drowned in the Pacific Ocean, off the coast of Vancouver Island, May 22, 1898, aged 22 years.

A party had been formed for the purpose of exploring the territory bordering on Kotzebue Sound, in the north of Alaska. The leader of the expedition had selected Mr.
~~~

Johnston to be one of the party, knowing him to possess the physical powers necessary to withstand the hardships incident to such an undertaking; to be a young man of strict morals and sterling character, and one to be relied upon under all circumstances. On May 19 the party sailed from Seattle on the schooner "Jane Gray," and when but three days out, at 2 o'clock in the morning, from some unknown cause, the vessel suddenly foundered. Twenty-seven survivors reached land, after drifting for some time in an open boat, and reported that all the other passengers had gone down with the ship.

William Arnot Johnston was born in New Galilee, Pa., Jan. 24, 1876. While young, his parents removed to Kansas, and he received his education in the Topeka schools. In 1892, after the death of his father, he located with his mother and sister in Seattle, where he resided until he started on his fatal voyage. He united with the church when 18 years old, and was ever since an active worker in the Sabbath school, young people's society, and the Y. M. C. A. His was a noble disposition. He carried sunshine everywhere he went. He knew not how to be unkind. He was dutiful and affectionate as son and brother; faithful and generous to his friends; trustworthy and capable in business. A host of friends mourn his loss, but their sorrow is not hopeless, for they have the assurance that he is with his Saviour, and will be found clothed in the robe of white on that day when the sea gives up its dead.—United Presbyterian."

~~~

The sinking of the Jane Gray was so well publicized that even the President of the United States recognized the importance of acknowledging the event. When William McKinley awarded the captain of the schooner Favorite an honor for his role in saving the shipwrecked survivors of
~~~

the Jane Gray, on January 30, 1899, newspapers in Canada and the U. S. told of the honor: "As an illustration of the amity existing between the two great English-speaking nations of this continent, a ceremony took place this afternoon..." Captain McLean of the Favorite was awarded a commemorative pair of binoculars as a token of appreciation for his services rendered in the rescue. In the midst of other conflicts, particularly the Spanish-American War, the gesture was one of thanks to the maritime brotherhood that was being formed along the border of the two countries.

CHAPTER 21 - ERMINIO AND THE MAJOR

Erminio Sella, image courtesy of the Sella Foundation, Biella, Italy.

Events were particularly difficult for the party of Italians and their Austrian friend. Erminio Sella had lost his brother-in-law, Edoardo Gaia. Secondo Bianchetto had lost his cousin, Secondo Bissetta. The other two survivors of the Sella party were Abele Ceria and Hans Wachter (Waechter or Wacker). None of them spoke or understood English well. And to complicate communication matters, most were from a northern region of Italy near the French-German border. As is the case in many ancient European villages, the community has its own dialect - in Biella, the language is a combination of Italian, French, and German, with peculiarities that are almost unique to that area. A simple English word such as "say" could easily be misunderstood - since the Italian word "sei" sounds exactly the same, but is the familiar form of the verb meaning "you are."

With little English between the remaining four members of Erminio's group, the nearly penniless men were stranded in a foreign country. The *Seattle Post-Intelligencer* reported on their plight within days of the sinking:

"SONS OF ITALY.

Those Who Escaped Will Not Again Risk Their Lives in Local Waters.

Six sons of sunny Italy, lured to the Northwest by the tales of the wonderful Yukon, made up a party on the Jane Gray. Four of them came back...determined never again to risk their lives in the search for gold. The other two are probably floating around on the bottom of the Pacific, near where the Jane Gray went to the bottom.

E. Gaia, a lawyer, and Erminio Sella, a civil and mechanical engineer, were the leaders of the party. They purchased their outfits in Seattle and were well supplied with provisions, etc. They are almost destitute of immediate funds.

The four remaining subjects of King Humbert gathered together in a corner of the lobby of a downtown hotel...and chattered in their own language with a friend who lives here, and who had come to console them. They told and retold their adventures with their own peculiar gestures and in tones that often spoke volumes for the sorrow they felt for the loss of their comrades."

In the face of overwhelming sadness, finding money to get home was a first priority for the stranded Europeans. Frank Little, superintendant of Seattle streets and a father of one of the missing, helped them find employment through his contacts at the board of public works: "Among the applicants for assistance at the public employment office on Saturday were four Austrians, who were among the survivors of the Jane Gray. They were left absolutely penniless by the loss of the schooner. Commissioner Grout referred them to the contractors who are cleaning the army post site. One of the foremen employed on this work is an Italian, with which language the Austrians are conversant. One of the party, however, speaks German also, and through him as a spokesman the four unfortunates are able to make themselves fairly well understood. The Austrians lost their leader by the wreck. All the money in the party, $500 in gold, was strapped about his waist when he was drowned."

For Erminio Sella, the grief and the sense of failure could have easily consumed him while he was stranded in America. This youngest son of a wealthy Italian family had intended for the expedition to Alaska to be an opportunity to achieve his own success. According to his descendants, his life had been filled with obstacles and he felt some sort of inferiority that constantly concerned his mother. He idolized his older brother, climbing the Alps with him while learning the art of mountaineering photography that their father had pioneered and that Vittorio had already become famous for. The emotional statement that he made that afternoon on the dock in Seattle - the day that the survivors landed after the wreck, "The welcome I received today somewhat alleviates the immense pain I feel; it is one of those spontaneous demonstrations that is very good and that I will never forget," was very prophetic. He would not forget it. And although not the turning point that he had imagined, the disaster erased much of his self-doubt and propelled him into a destiny that had previously eluded him.

Erminio's ascent from the guilt of losing his brother-in-law, Edoardo Gaia, and the family employee, Secondo Bissetta, was as arduous as any ascent of a soaring Alpine peak. During those thirty-six hours, bobbing around in the launch Kennorma on the Pacific Ocean, he was keenly aware that Edoardo and Secondo were absent. Thoughts of his sister, his parents, and the disgrace at his abject failure likely tortured this sensitive soul. After the wreck, he returned to Vancouver Island with Dr. Lessey, hoping beyond hope that he would find them. If not able to find them alive, at least, perhaps, he could have brought their bodies home for a proper Catholic burial. When that proved impossible, he returned to the reality of going home. And to his sister, who was now a widow raising a one year old son.

Sending a telegram requesting money from his family at the "Banca Sella" could not have been an easy thing. Clearing brush at the army base in Seattle was probably preferable. However, Erminio knew that only by swallowing his pride and asking for money from the family financial institution would he be able to help his friends and employees return home. He did. After their return to Seattle, nearly a month would elapse before the money arrived.

On June 15, 1898, Erminio summoned the courage to write a letter to his sister in Italy, explaining the events that led to the death of her husband.

[Translated]:

"My dear Giuseppina,

I would prefer to wait to Biella to voice the painful story. But the things here go a bit too long and for twenty days I have had no hope of getting rid of it. Then you can imagine my pain when I think of you, the impression that these lines will have on you and the infinite evil to you which is partly my fault.

I do not know what I would not do to find something of an idea that could somehow bring comfort to you. Why this disaster occurred, for which no essential reason is known, and perhaps you will know precisely. The rapidity with which it occurred suggests that all of the sudden a large opening formed in the right side of the ship. This was loaded, over-loaded, (and this is the main point that will dissolve the dispute brought against the owner of the Jane Gray) but this does not seem to be a good enough reason because at the time of the sinking the sea had already tended to decrease. Not unless you suddenly bump into a rock; we were 50 miles from the coast with 270 fathoms deep. The Jane Gray had only ten years since it was launched in San Francisco in '87 and was considered strong and safe ship. Some intelligent men said that it was one of the best that were in the bay of Seattle. Among them was the brother of Ingraham, who had long been a sea captain and he examined her as thoroughly as possible; for more security for us we had a visit conducted by a certain Captain Schiaffino Genovese who was passing through Seattle with his vessel. Below the waterline no one had been able to inspect but it was judged of this part by the others that were examinable; the trouble of the Jane Gray was that she hit an iceberg and was capsized and she had been a year in the waters of the Bering Sea. But no one knows this before the disaster.

In the decision for the Jane Gray we left to be guided by Ingraham because we had never had the opportunity to do with our own hands that which we intended. Because of the steamboat, we could not start off on the ship 'Guardian' of 2000 tons, almost twenty times bigger than the Jane Gray. Ingraham advised against it, to him it did not seem safe, but to us it was regretted because it seemed to be. But Ingraham had reasons and the Guardian made just thirty miles and had to retreat in great haste to the port of Porthansen to be put in the dockyard. It was from this port that we made to the shipwreck. So here is how things happened or better as I saw them.

As you know we left from Seattle the evening of the 19th (Thursday) around five, beautiful weather, not even the shadow of wind so that we had to be towed up to Porthansen until around midnight. During all of Friday the wind was felt from time to time and always very weak so that we arrived in the evening and we were still at the beginning of the channel of Juan de Fuca. The location was wonderfully beautiful and after the tremendous work of the last few days we cared little that the wind was lacking, we rested and could finally surrender to the delights of the travel. It is true that the meat and food smelled of oil, but we were in an unusually good mood and the day that was the most beautiful that we had spent together was also one of the last. We spent the day fastening our boat better with ropes and props and with the boards removed from our cabin we had made inside a very comfortable private home envied by those who did not have a launch. The men played cards and the poor Bissetta was forced to teach me the game tressette. Towards evening Secondino told us the story of Palo di Ferro and Edoardo was very surprised by the epic instructions of Secondino. At dusk the story was interrupted by the passage near the Jane Gray of a schooner on the return from the Copper River. It gave news on good weather in the Pacific and the Jane Gray the news of the Spaniards seized in the war and the latest victories. When that was finished a fresh breeze came up and the history of Palo di Ferro no one spoke more of.

Going down to the cabin I think: who knows how long it will take to resume! The breeze became more and more strong; poor Edoardo began to suffer, and like this all the others one after the other retreated into the cabin whence they came up almost no more until the last. It was very fortunate that I do not suffer like this at the time of the disaster I could still be able to do something for myself and for others. The Jane Gray began to dance strongly and since we left Seattle with some apprehension because the Jane Gray was too full and essentially overloaded too high; on the bridge I noticed with pleasure that when she danced well I did not hear any of those creaking noises that had worried me so much on the Champagne. But this near the day (Saturday) just out in the Pacific water enters the cabins constructed on the deck.

The south wind blows from the left side of the ship, the sails are swollen, we bend to the right and water enters the cabins...of the right and in the outer part gets to a height of 60-70 centimeters. It is an indescribable scuffle, because all of the first bunks are under water and when the vessel for a stronger wave or the wind lessens, she straightens up a little.

Then the water floods the whole dining room and then trunks, chests, bags, everything floats in and out of the cabins. But our stuff in our cabin we already saved. I heard that the Captain had the intention to go back into the channel to check what is the reason for this and doing this the right side of the ship would be exposed to the wind and then we would bend on the left to balance out our downward cabin; here all are suffering and I pray, fingers crossed, to rise up and make room for the stuff lying on the ground, no one moves; so that you understand to get everyone out of the cabin to do any one thing you need to know what the total size of our cabin and berths including for 6 people were 1.70 x 1.80 x 1.80 [meters]. *Since the intermediate space was only fifty centimeters wide so you have to go to bed one at a time, and not without difficulty. So before I can move someone turns the ship on the left side and since to extract the stuff we put away with such care to conserve space it takes time, the wave comes to cover everything before we can move it. Like this two cameras were ruined. As I can finally take out my dear camera on which laid the foundations of my first hopes of the voyage it is already soaked with water and when I open the boot lid, everything comes off and the shutters and stereoscopics simply will not work any more. This misfortune of not knowing the future seemed extraordinary. The men finally saw what was done, in that moment of weakness, I had brought it up and they helped to carry all of our things to our launch. It was fortunate because with the stuff they also took the sack of lifesavers and not being able to immediately pull it from the cabin, I began to open it with the idea of extracting some lifesavers when the waves decrease in volume; after I also succeeded but in the meantime having made a small opening in the bag of lifesavers, this thing was of the utmost importance when the ship sank. During the day Saturday, the men did not move from their bunks any more. I worked almost continuously to dry the bellows, with fresh water I rinsed the shutters, disassemble and reassemble, but ended up giving up all hope of saving anything, so rapidly had the oxidation progressed. After I remembered the big tin box containing our pharmacy, I descended to the cabin to get the key from Edoardo. And when I opened it I found it nearly full of water, I took everything out to dry; a map, phenolized wadding, packs of salts, and everything was ruined.*

This was the second to last time that I spoke with poor Edoardo.

Not to make you wait any longer, I start to send you this part; tomorrow I will continue. In the meantime your loving courage Erminio."

~~~

What Erminio probably never knew, and Ingraham did know, was that the Guardian had been virtually branded a shipwreck and had been tied up in San Francisco, rotting for years, before it was "refitted" and brought to Seattle to transport gold-seekers. Passengers later reported being able to pick the caulking from between the planks with their fingernails. Once the steamer miraculously made it to Alaska, it was in such horrible condition that it was again abandoned, this time on the shore near Kotzebue Sound.
~~~

One of the other things that he may not have known was that Ingraham had penned the contract with John Pacey for transport on the Jane Gray more than a month before his party arrived in Seattle.

Six days passed before Erminio was able to continue his letter to Giuseppina. Although some of his perceptions were likely due to the language barrier and cultural differences, others were not and seem to confirm that Major Ingraham was more involved in the operation of the Jane Gray than anyone ever cared to admit.

Erminio Sella (left) and Edoardo Gaia (right), image courtesy of the Sella Foundation, Biella, Italy.

[Translated with caveat: Some phrases within this letter are loosely translated from the Biellese dialect, others are translated from the way Erminio likely heard them. Some text is missing due to water damage and is replaced by...]

~~~
~~~

"June 21, 98 Seattle

Dear Giuseppina,

I ask you a thousand pardons for this new delay to tell you the rest of the painful event. But this week was one of the most stormy and most laborious of my life. Before Gaudenzio's telegram that struck me very much and after which I decided to resume the expedition to the Bay of Kotzebue. How much strength of mind this decision cost me is difficult to imagine. First of all there was to overcome the desire to return home to see all of the rest of you again and continue a little of our tranquil life, that desire after the great misfortune would be immense.

Then the repugnance to start the long and tiresome work to put together another 'outfit' with the prospect of not being able to do so complete as the other and to do everything alone, no longer supported by the hope of a fortunate voyage done with intimate friends and the harmony of the group and of many other resources that I can now no longer have. I started from Biella with a brother Edoardo who had become a true friend, with the men for whom I had deep affection and the most blind trust, with my guns, camera, tools, etc. and here we have prepared to go to Kotzebue with an absolute superiority to the other miners. Now everything was lost; and apart from all the pain I will be forced to start with an 'outfit' almost modest, with new faces and without even the shadow of the hope of success on the adventures that awaited me before. I was in Tacoma to find the men in the Italian garden where they work and of course I did not say a word to persuade them to accompany me; their rejection for all of the disappointment that I produced on their loyalty caused me a pain that their crude minds are never going to understand.

When I returned to Seattle I finally decided on these two: M. Roberts and H. Wachker both survivors of the Jane Gray, the first is a Portugese and one that of all the companions in misfortune seemed less wild to me, and the second was already in our group and he seems a good man; of course the information that I could gather about them is very very limited.

But back to what interests you most strongly:

Saturday morning, half an hour after the captain had to turn back the Jane Gray, we once again reached the mouth of the channel Juca and through the murky air we could distinguish the two sides.

I was standing on the bridge near Ingraham, and was extremely astonished to hear the second mate ask Ingraham if the water was really entering the cabins, only the holes of the anchor chains had now been stopped up with bags; Ingraham was sure of it, and then gave the command to turn the sails back to the direction of N. W. to the endless Pacific. The fact that the master of a ship asks the advice of a passenger on a fact so important was exceedingly astonishing to me. I tried to persuade Ingraham to the contrary but to no avail. The ship was already turned bending on her right side and after some time seeing that despite the continuous work of two sailors with buckets emptying water from the cabins did not make it lessen, I think it is already much higher, I asked the older of the two (expert after all) if this thing did not seem dangerous and uncertain - all of the water. The sailor affirmed this and that the passengers would do well to agree and pray to the captain to return. Hearing that I went on the bridge and found Ingraham at our boat, I told him the opinion of the sailor; I also tried to make him see apart from the serious drawback of having five or six cubic meters of water in the cabins, we could really be in danger since it was not entirely clear which side the water had entered; the holes of the anchor chains were stopped up they continually worked to remove the water that did not decrease. Upon hearing that I could not persuade him I told him that since all of the passengers were prostrate to death by seasickness, it was up to us to decide on the return, and I said then that in my group were four married men and there were certainly also in his, and that the responsibility which we were getting into was incalculable. We absolutely needed to tell the captain to return; return to the channel when we could be able to see, make repairs and with a small loss of time of two or three days return on the voyage. I did everything to persuade him but simply by him saying that he did not believe it dangerous certainly, I left it to the American.

If Ingraham was a man of conscience, which I doubt very much, he should no longer forget our conversation on the morning of May 21, 98.

Then I spoke with the second mate and the captain who by their irony at my inexperience in matters of the sea they nearly ended up persuading me to stay calm.

The evening arrived and I could not go down to my bunk because it was occupied by all of the pieces of my cameras placed on the mattress to dry; I decided to spend the night in our launch. About eleven o'clock Secondino (Bianchi) came to tell me that if I wanted to go down to the bunk they would have thought to have made me a place. I sent him back to sleep, telling him that I would stay there; in fact, I had placed the bags of our stuff below, I was wrapped in a wool blanket and one of our yellow tarpaulins was over me for shelter from the wind and the chance of rain.

At two after midnight, I woke to an excited voice and I grab the phrase 'all sails down' shouted from the captain. All of the sudden I throw off the covers and erect in the launch I see the Jane Gray tilted to the right side; they drop the sails but the Jane Gray did not straighten. I turn to an individual near me (the attorney Spencer of S. Francisco lost then also was he) and I say to him: siamo perduti [are we lost]*? and he responds to me with the calm of terror: Jes J quest so* [That's the question]. *The captain shouts then Every hody on dech! Then with one bound I am again in our launch where I had left to better see what was happening, I freed the heavy sheath of the sheet metal of the boiler from the ligaments and the props which we had fixed in the launch with such care, with spunk I moved it a little to enter and take the sack of life preservers, this becomes entangled in the nails of the furnace, but finally I can tear the outside, I widen the opening some, I pull out a life preserver which is taken by the one nearby and that moves away in the dark. I pull the other ones and adapt one to me, I take another and go in search of poor Edoardo who after many calls had then responded; just then I heard the voice of Edoardo, I shouted to him to climb above, he replied that he can not (perhaps prevented by the crowding, but soon after I see him climb on the high bridge where the launch is) I hand him the life preserver and adjust it to him. He says to me only one word: grazie [thank you], and it was the last! I go back to the bottom of the launch to help Abele and Secondino with the life preservers, which instead of acting, they hugged and burst into tears remembering their families. I fitted their life preservers for them. The Tyrolean served himself to a life jacket. Bissetta is not healthy and...certainly not out of the cabins because I heard his voice when I call to Edoardo.*

From the time I awoke to this point I do not believe that more than three minutes passed. In between this time almost all of the passengers came out of the cabins and instinctively took to the left side of the Jane Gray - almost straightens up, but she bends always more and the right edge is already in the water. But when after a command of the captain (which I do not understand) I saw in the darkness people rush toward the point where the launch had disappeared - I turned to Edoardo who was there on my left perhaps a meter and a half leaning, supported like all of us by our launch, I cried: Andumo [Let's go]*! this was the last* *time that I saw him. I said to jump across our boat because to go around would take too long; since the bridge of the Jane Gray was already very steep and the ropes had been cut off, our boat had already slipped sideways down the deck, for about a meter. Jumping again outside the other part I reach the right side of the Jane Gray and put my feet and balance on the edge and jump into the sea which receives me with an enveloping wave of white foam. With the energy of desperation I try not to let it overwhelm me and reach after about ten meters I put a hand on the launch of Ingraham. The first sensation was surprise to feel her floating.*

At that moment the cross shaft of the main shaft of the Jane Gray passed over our launch and sweeps the three that were in her with water. Then again another surge it passes two times always lower but finally all of the hands of those who had taken to the launch which almost instinctively try to push it finally away from the launch. The third time it passed very near to the point of the launch and I was still outside and had to lower my head below the wave to not be knocked into. This was a moment of great danger over the launch and a moment of extreme terror. That black specter that passed over our heads was always more dangerous and a quick little hit the launch would have capsized and everything would be finished.

After a fight to climb into the boat; while I was stretched out trying in vain to climb in the launch I was prevented by the life preserver...outside of the launch one time I felt to catch a part and of the other two that used me like a limb of support, another I felt the barefoot on the neck of one near who was trying to climb in I made the effort to not become disconnected so that for more than a week the fingers of my right hand remained an ache. Finally after much unnecessary imploring those that were already trying to help me I was trapped by the belt of the lifesaver to take me up two of the men above take me and pull me in.

I fall to the bottom of the boat exhausted like I have never found and stayed there briefly unconscious. I raised myself to see Abele and Secondino attached to the launch also impeded from climbing by the lifesavers. Abele told me Sur Erminio c'em salva [here Erminio I am saved]*! and Secondino: Suma chi* [I am here]*! with indescribable expressions. I started to help Abele closest and then Secondino; then we all fell into the launch exhausted with chills and fear to the bottom of the boat. My torment was that while I was struggling to climb into the launch, Edoardo called me and I could not hear. I had heard Secondino. The noise of the wind and the sea was now such that to speak with those in the bottom of the boat you needed to scream when you could. It is an opinion that Edoardo called to me, and was the misfortune for me to get back to our launch on which he had as a ship for the sea far more confidence than for that of Ingraham. But our launch is to be found whether you go with the Jane Gray in the sea or takes on water or by a collision with the mast in a way that it filled quickly with the crashing of the waves. How it is that after the first moment no one saw her any more can only be explained with the height of the waves there were immense valleys. Of course it does surprise like this how so little protruding from the water was able to then be pushed from the sea up to Kyuquot it is about 80 miles away.*

As I became myself again and I found no answer in the launch, I began to call Edoardo. The Jane Gray did not appear for more than the tip of the trees, then began to get light and before we could cut the boards that were located to make oars for the launch, the wind had brought us a little farther away. When we returned with great difficulty, we fished out two castaways attached to two boards and with them was one of our bags of clothes (Secondino's) that were shared with all (except us) to dress and change: but for those greenish bumps and those valleys we see nothing more than some boards and capsized boats. I had lost my glasses and communication in the launch was difficult for many reasons, it was only after a time that I came to know that our boat had been seen the first time with four people inside but nearly full of water. Of course if we had been warned, before the accident and had time to drop our boat well when the Jane Gray was sinking it would have been a good thing to tell us; to throw a launch of thirty feet would take some time and I believe that the sinking of the Jane Gray did not last more than five minutes.

When we saw nothing more of the Jane Gray the captain and the sailors who were saved with us considered our position as we were almost desperate they fixed a small drag and made a small sail and we went off a long direction North in the launch...the 'Kennorma' the launch named for the sons and the wife of Ingraham seemed safe...in immense waves. After the first fear came equally that we would be lost because we were about 45 miles from Vancouver Island and the wind seemed to bring us parallel to it. The rudder with that sail so small and imperfect had absolutely no reason. After...the sea grew, it began to rain and the wind seemed to turn even more to the East, but in reality these things were better than we had imagined. The island of Vancouver does not run N. S. like they were sure of but rather N. W. - S. E. and those who watched the compass forgot the derivation of 23 degrees so instead of running parallel and away from the island, we approached it at an angle of about 45 degrees. This ignorance on the part of two men from the ship made me learn always to save ourselves. If we had clear weather from the evening of the first day we could see the mountains of Vancouver but the air was foggy. Towards evening we saw a duck that made us hope that it is not very far from the land as we had believed before and the captain when the night since that the coasts of Vancouver Island are very famous for their crowns of rock cliffs, it did wash the sails in the waves of the sea and the breakers.

The thirty-six hours in the launch without a name for a thousand reasons. In addition to all the rest, we felt from them an Italian race hatred of which I never dreamed before existed. I am assured that someone came out with the proposal to throw us into the waves of the sea in order to increase the probability of rescuing others. The moment perhaps more terrible for everyone that was around noon on Monday when all of the sudden appeared the beautiful land illuminated by the sun very close! It was then that there was finally hope and we would almost certainly be saved, racing in the mind of everyone the thought far more painful the mistrust of the first poor fellows lost. It is so then the sail was bigger and after many dangerous passes we crossed the line of the surf, the sea entered a calm bay and little by little, at two we landed in a small cove, silent, calm and wonderful. It was almost from the day of our departure from Seattle that we did not eat again, because the food on the Jane Gray smelled of oil and on the launch we had nothing but a few slices of turnip and some prunes, and we were 36 hours in the clothes dripping wet now; and beyond having fallen in the water, all the time we were forced by the immobility in uncomfortable positions, the one man above, the other man below to always lower more our center of gravity in the launch. When we put our feet on the ground we could barely steady ourselves on our feet and Secondino had until Victoria very sharp pain and acute swelling in the knees. For that night I ate without appetite the seafood and the next day an Indian accompanied us to Kyuquot a small Indian village where I still had no appetite, after a long time we tried to eat.

Although there was no hope for our companions, if we wanted to undertake a search, it had to be done soon; but this would have to be in a small steamer because a similar search on the dangerous coast of Vancouver Island was impossible for a sailing ship. But even if we had been able to find a small steamer, shipwrecked without a cent as I was, it would not have been possible. It was only by engaging the launch that had saved us that we stumbled *upon the schooner 'Favourite' in Kuyoquot - they decided to take us to Victoria. The wind was calm and after having very slowly passed the scene of the disaster, we arrived eight days later in Victoria. I thought then that it was best to go up to Seattle where I had many relationships, but these were not sufficient to allow me to find $1,500 to hire a tugboat for a trip that I intended to do on the coast of Vancouver. Then I thought of calling on the families of the poor shipwreck survivors for the cost of an expedition, but here I found an inordinate and inexcusable apathy and it was not until when the news came (false) of the seven victims fished out by the Indians of the coast that there was a meeting in City Hall for us to combine to finally do something. In this meeting, in which I could not keep myself from getting up and insulting the assembly in unspeakable meanness, then finally it was decided that it would be convenient to go to Victoria to request information!!!*

Like this, I left with six others who were either brothers or fathers of some of the castaways, but the mood of the party could give the impression that they were on a picnic.

In Victoria we stopped for a few days...to wait for the return of a tug sent away for a search. The English government gave us no particular interest they gave us like this a good lesson, and we should be ready to go on fire in order to do something while also futile!

Never again would I have dreamed that I would resume my trip to Kotzebue but now that the telegram of Gaudenzio incites me, I will go. Of all of the moments that have existed before not one remains. I go there just to do something.

In early October I will be however again in Seattle where I will take care of your interests in the litigation brought against the owner of the Jane Gray and then I will come to Biella.

Many greetings from your aff.mo Erminio."

Of the other three men in the Sella party; Abele Ceria, Secondo Bianchetto, and Hans Wachter, it remains unknown who stayed in America with Erminio. From his letters and other documents, it seems likely that he parted ways with Abele and Secondo. What is known is that sometime in late June or early July of 1898, instead of continuing north to Kotzebue Sound, he wandered out to the Olympic Peninsula, taking a camera and at least one of his friends. Along the way, photographic images began to emerge that surpassed all of his prior work. To describe the light through the towering pines as Erminio stood on a rutted, muddy trail, seems as inadequate as he must have felt on that day.

After the Olympic Mountains, he scaled Mount Rainier, snapping images, each one more introspective and majestic than the last. Toting his equipment, Erminio left coastal Washington, traveled around the arid interior of the state, headed south through Oregon and Northern California to Yosemite National Park, then northeast to Yellowstone, photographing his experiences along the way. The pictures seemed cathartic - he was a man in search of himself, in search of meaning in the thing that he could most relate to, the unpredictable nature of nature. Perhaps these natural wonders helped provide an explanation, or at least a point of reference, for the disaster that claimed two beloved men, while his life was spared. Perhaps after witnessing an eruption of Old Faithful, her steam billowing from the ground, as she had for thousands of years, Erminio's guilt finally began to melt away. Somewhere between Seattle and New York, he made peace with his grief and made a pact with himself.

A Sella family member would eventually write of Erminio's travels in America that (translated), it was "A chance to assimilate within himself the difficult event that he had endured."

~~~

While Erminio was battling his personal demons, Major Ingraham organized another trip to Kotzebue Sound. Although once again funded by Prince Luigi, this expedition was less publicized. The loss of so many beloved citizens remained fresh in the minds of those affected and Ingraham had no desire to remind those who had lost loved ones, or all of their worldly possessions, of the fact that he was continuing with the expedition. This was a business venture. He had investors who counted on his expertise to bring them profits. And he had personal collateral in the game.

On the 18th of June 1898 (one month after their first departure), way back on page 11 of the *Seattle Post-Intelligencer,* a small column detailed their next attempt at the gold fields:

"LUIGI EXPEDTION.

Maj. Ingraham stated yesterday that he would leave Seattle on the Del Norte today for St. Michael with Dr. L. M. Lessey, of Seattle, and C. H. Packard and George H. Pennington, of Snohomish, three other survivors of the Jane Gray disaster. The other members of Maj. Ingrahams's party are: Charles E. Chard, Ralph Sheafe, J. D. Whitney, Gus Shaser, C. W. Brandon, C. H. Leedy, and Harold Post, all of Seattle, and Coney Weston, of Skowhegan, Me., who expects to be able to start for St. Michael today on the Louise E. Kenney. They will be joined at St. Michael by Maj. Ingraham and the other two members, who leave on the Del Norte.
~~~

Maj. Ingraham also stated that Seattle men were interested with Prince Luigi in sending this expedition to Kotzebue sound.

The party will remain at St. Michael only a short time, and will start almost at once for Kotzebue sound."

What the *Seattle Post-Intelligencer* reporter failed to realize was that there were not just four survivors of the Jane Gray disaster, but six in the Ingraham party. Charles Chard, who had been a member of the Blackwell party; and Coney Weston, who lost his partner, Edward Ritter, in the sinking; had accepted positions on the Major's new team of gold prospectors.

CHAPTER 22 – IN ADMIRALTY LAW

When Frederick Bausman filed his motion on January 3, 1899, for the cause to be heard in the civil department of King County Superior Court, other claimants were lining up to join the suit against Pacey, MacDougall, and Southwick. The widows of Frank Ginther, William Gleason, Ed and Fred Taylor, and Spencer Young, as well as one other survivor, Charles Wilkinson, were poised to file their own petitions for compensation. The five claims thus far filed totaled over $30,000. The case was scheduled to be heard in front of a jury in four days.

The firm representing MacDougall, Southwick, and Pacey had a plan that would further stall the litigation. In admiralty cases, special rules apply, most notably that there is no right to a jury trial. Word on the streets was that few felt any sympathy toward the outfitting firm, making an impartial jury unlikely to be found anywhere in the entire country, let alone in King County. If the judge approved their counter-suit, the judge, and only the judge, would be responsible for the final ruling.

On the same day that Bausman filed the motion for the cause to be heard in civil court, the attorneys for Pacey, MacDougall, and Southwick climbed the six steep blocks up "profanity hill" to the courthouse at 7th and Jefferson where they filed a libel suit against Chard, Weaver, Livengood, Blackwell and Boak.

In addition to the libel suit, MacDougall and Southwick petitioned for a limitation of liability, citing an act of Congress that limits the liability of an owner or operator of a vessel to the amount of freight pending (prepaid cargo fees) and the value of the vessel, if anything remains of her, after a maritime accident.

The "Shipowner's Limitation of Liability Act," was enacted in 1851, largely in order to stimulate the shipping business. At the time, it was thought that by limiting the liability of vessel owners, growth would naturally occur within the industry. Under this act, the owner or owners only need prove that they had no "privity or knowledge" of the act or condition that caused the marine casualty.

The "Harter Act," which for the most part applies to the limitation of liability for freight, was cited as their second grounds for being granted limitation. If the attorneys representing Pacey, MacDougall and Southwick could prove that they exercised "due diligence prior to the voyage to make the vessel seaworthy and to properly man, equip, and supply it," then it was probable that none of them would be held liable for loss or damages caused by errors of navigation or management of the vessel; perils of the sea; acts of God; inherent defects, qualities, or vices of the cargo; insufficient packaging; or loss resulting from any act or omission on the shipper or owner of the cargo. All that the law required was that they needed to prove that they had exercised "due diligence" in order to gain the right to this limitation of liability.

If the judge agreed with either plea, that they exercised "due dilligence" and did not have prior knowledge of problems with the vessel, then actual ownership became irrelevant. All that would remain to be decided was whether any of them could be held liable in any way, and if they were, for how much.

Pursuing this course of action, Mr. Mundy entered the plea:

"That your petitioner, the MacDougall & Southwick Company is and was during all the times herein mentioned a corporation organized under the laws of the state of Washington, with its principal place of business at the city of Seattle, King county, Washington, within said district, and within the jurisdiction of this court. That during said times and now, your petitioners John B. MacDougall and John G. Pacey were and are now the president and secretary of said corporation, respectively, each and both residing at said city of Seattle; and your petitioner Henry C. Southwick was, and is, vice president and treasurer of said corporation."

Using the "acts of God" defense, they argued that the schooner encountered heavy storms off the Northwest Coast of Vancouver Island and "was so broken and torn by the extraordinary severity of the winds and waves that she filled with water, sank, and was completely lost with all her tackle, apparel, boats and appurtenances, and cargo," and that the accident happened without their knowledge, by no fault of their own, and "was solely due to the perils of the sea."

This defense could present its own set of problems since multiple witnesses had already stated that the storm they encountered was a "moderate gale" of no extraordinary consequence. Under the "Harter Act," carriers are expected to anticipate unexpected weather conditions and take appropriate precautions. Failing to demonstrate that they had taken adequate steps to deal with a storm, particularly a storm that was not considered out of the ordinary for Cape Flattery in May, might lead the judge to rule that it was not the storm, but their lack of preparation that was the real cause of the disaster.

In their petition, the attorneys for Pacey, MacDougall, and Southwick acknowledged that the Jane Gray carried fifty-six passengers, of whom thirty-four, as well as three crewmembers were lost, and countered allegations that the captain and crew were in any way at fault by stating that the vessel was "fully manned with a full and competent crew under command of an experienced officer."

And while it was common knowledge that the Canadian vessel Quadra collected and sold at auction salvaged portions of the Jane Gray, as well as the Italian launch, the attorneys for Pacey, MacDougall and Southwick contended "That no portion of said schooner, her tackle, apparel, boats, or furniture has ever been recovered or found. That no freight moneys have been earned, paid, or received there from, except the sum of two thousand one hundred eighty two and 47/100 dollars."

$2,182.47 - That was the sum that they claimed remained from the Jane Gray venture.

There was no mention of the $5,000.00 insurance policy that John G. Pacey had already collected. Nor was there mention of the clause within the policy that provided for reimbursement of wages paid to the crew while the vessel was being repaired or between ports awaiting repair. That is because the Limitation of Liability Act, while limiting claims against a vessel's owners to the amount of freight and passage money pending, inclusive of her total value at the time of the last incident on the voyage where the accident occurred, excludes any moneys received by the owners from insurance compensation. (That's right, the owners were, and are, allowed to keep all of the insurance money received from their claim of loss of the vessel. At the time, there appears not to have been a clause for coverage of uninsured passengers.)

Wrapping up their plea for a limitation of liability, the petitioners detailed the claims of those involved in the impending litigation: "Nevertheless, certain persons claiming to have been passengers on said vessel, and claiming to have lost certain freight as a portion of said cargo, and to have suffered bodily injuries by the loss of said vessel have already, each, separately for himself, brought suits against all of your petitioners, jointly, in the superior court of the state of Washington, for King county, to recover damages for alleged loss of freight, and for personal injuries, and for recovery of freight and passage money paid."

With the exception of James Blackwell, who received a discounted rate as the organizer of his party, the five men paid $60.00 each for passage on the Jane Gray. Including the price of their tickets, all of them asked for compensation "and damages for loss of freight and personal injuries, and other damages alleged to have been suffered through the loss of said vessel." Charles E. Chard was suing for $5,834.98; William S. Weaver - $6,858.82; Silas Livengood - $5,831.72; George R. Boak - $6,155.57; and James E. Blackwell sought $6,155.57 as well.

Reiterating that they were in no way liable for the wreck, and that "each and all, desire to contest their liability for the loss, destruction, damage and injury occasioned by said accident, and also to claim the benefit of the limitation of liability…and to that end desire an appraisement to be had of the value of said schooner in condition in which she was after said accident, (which condition petitioners state was that of a total loss) on the 22nd day of May, 1898, and the amount and value of her freight then pending; and for that purpose your petitioners ask that such appraisement be made by a commissioner of this court, or by such other means as the court may direct; and your petitioners are ready and willing to give a stipulation with sureties for the payment of the amount of said appraisement into court whenever the same shall be ordered by court; or to pay the same into court."

As is allowed by the "Harter Act," John Pacey, under the direction of MacDougall and Southwick, had inserted the appropriate disclaimer on the ticket stubs issued to each and every passenger. Their attorneys stated that all of those who paid for passage on the Jane Gray were fully advised and cited this clause in their plea for limitation: "That, in the contract, or ticket, issued to each of the persons who took passage on said schooner, and which was accepted by each of them, it was provided that in case of the loss of said schooner her owners should not be held responsible for damage resulting from accidents of navigation or dangers of the seas, nor be under obligation to refund the amount of passage money paid."

In spite of overwhelming evidence to the contrary, the suit alleged that "John B. MacDougall, Henry C. Southwick, and the MacDougall & Southwick Company, a corporation, claim that they are each and all exempt from all liability for any loss or damage arising out of said accident, for the reason that, neither they nor any of them was ever at any time in any manner interested, as owners, or otherwise, in said vessel or said voyage."

John Pacey was well aware of the names of every person who purchased passage for the trip to Kotzebue Sound on the Jane Gray. He retained the ticket stubs, as well as the contract with Major Ingraham. Many of the survivors visited the store at First and Columbia immediately after returning from Victoria on the City of Kingston. Widows and family members called on MacDougall and Southwick, searching for their relatives, desperate for any information as to their whereabouts. The *Seattle Daily Times,* the *Seattle Post-Intelligencer,* the *San Francisco Call,* the *New York Times* and a dozen other newspapers had published information about many of the identities of the lost. Suffering from greed-induced amnesia, they pled: "That, your petitioners are each and all ignorant of the amount of injuries and losses suffered by the several freighters, passengers, and others claiming to have suffered loss and damage by said accident, and are each and all ignorant of the names and addresses of all persons claiming loss and damage occasioned by said accident, save and except of the said Charles E. Chard, Silas Livengood, James E. Blackwell, George R. Boak, and William S. Weaver, the address of all of whom is Seattle, Washington, except that the address of William S. Weaver is unknown to each and every of your petitioners. That the amount of the claims for loss and damage occasioned by said accident greatly exceeds the amount and value of said schooner, after said accident, and her freight then pending, earned and to accrue on said voyage."

While stating that "your petitioners will contest their liability, independently of the limitation of liability claimed under the act and statute aforesaid," they requested that Judge Hanford issue a motion (or monition) against anyone who could conceivably have a claim against them for the accident, "citing them to appear before this court and make due proof of their respective claims" at a time to be determined by the court.

If indeed the court should find any of them financially liable for claims arising from the loss of the schooner, they further pled that all claims should be limited to whatever the appraiser determined her after-accident value to be. And "that this Court will, by its decree, limit the liability of each and every one of your petitioners so found liable, to the amount of the value of their respective interests in said vessel."

While waiting for the court to make a final judgment, they also requested "an order restraining the further prosecution of all and any suit or suits against the petitioners, or any of them, in respect to any such claim or claims, particularly by said Charles E. Chard, Silas Livengood, James E. Blackwell, George R. Boak, and William S. Weaver, who brought suit in the superior court of the state of Washington, in and for King county and here in before specified."

In Superior Court Judge Cornelius Holgate Hanford, Pacey, MacDougall and Southwick had perhaps found the only sympathetic ears in all of Seattle. His father and uncle were early Pacific Northwest settlers, so his connections in the Seattle business community ran deep. Hanford's brother, Clarence, owned an outfitting business with a similar vessel service to the Klondike and Alaska gold fields. In addition, Clarence had a printing and photography company operating out of the same storefront at 616 First Avenue. Clarence's partner at Lowman and Hanford was James Lowman, a cousin of Henry Yesler, the notorious Seattle pioneer. And Lowman was a partner with Bernard Pelly, specializing in estate management and insurance. One of Judge Hanford's other brothers, Frank, was a partner in Hanford and Stewart, general insurance agents at 207 Pioneer Building, with a secondary company, Western Marine Insurance in the same offices. A fourth brother, Arthur Elwood Hanford, was employed as a lawyer in the city.

Through an appointment by President William Harrison, Hanford had first come to the bench as a chief justice in the Washington Territory. Through hard work and connections he was appointed Washington State's first federal district court judge in 1890. With every year that he served, the conviction in his own superior intellect grew, as did his ego. He would later write of himself and his work on the bench: "...it is safe to say that during the fifteen years that he has presided as Judge of the United States District Court for the State of Washington he has performed an amount of judicial labor not equalled, certainly not surpassed, by that done by any other judge in this country."

While devoting the vast majority of his time to "that zealous mistress - the law" who, he said, "has never had one occasion to complain that he neglected her," the esteemed Judge Hanford was neglecting his own family and had little-publicized problems at home. He and his wife, Clara, had built a lordly mansion, large enough to accommodate eight children, at the corner of Madison and Boren. Everyone who was anyone had a view from the heights of First Hill. In 1896, the sparkle of the mansion began to fade when their twelve year-old son, Ralph, died at home from meningitis. The prestige of the Hanford house apparently could not provide a salve to a mother's grief, for some time after her little boy's death, Clara receded from public view and was quietly admitted to the Eastern Washington Hospital for the Insane.

Although Cornelius (by his own admission) was probably not the most attentive husband, it seems likely that Clara's mental health was more a manifestation of her physical health than from the neglect of her spouse. Seattle was a veritable petri dish for infectious diseases of the times. The city was struggling with the problem of high tides forcing sewage back up the hill (through the wooden plumbing that entered directly into Puget Sound) into the water-closets of affluent homes, where lids were put on toilets, not as a gentlemanly courtesy, but to prevent sewage from blowing all over the bathroom when the tide came in. The moist climate, with few days of frost, contributed to the incubation of bacteria. Tuberculosis was so rampant that spitting in the streets was banned and made an offense worthy of a hefty fine. The disease was spread through shared handkerchiefs, sneezes, dairy products, and in a gamut of other ways. This respiratory ailment made breathing difficult, caused extreme weight loss, and was highly contagious. And if you came down with tuberculosis, the best place to recover (or die) was in a dry climate, confined to a facility where the risk of infecting more citizens was minimized. In Washington State, that meant being sent to the dry side of the Cascade Mountains - as an "inmate" at the Eastern Washington State Hospital for the Insane. (This disease is still alive and just as deadly. See the Center for Disease Control for complete information.)

While never publicly acknowledged, Judge Hanford's wife never returned to Seattle. During the Jane Gray court proceedings, Cornelius was supporting six children. And their African-American housekeeper, Lotta Smith, spent more time with his family than he did.

On the day that John G. Pacey, MacDougall and Southwick filed their petition, the judge issued a stay prohibiting any further legal action against them, or any entity they might do business under with the stipulation that they, and those representing the committee of survivors, must provide a $250.00 surety, or bond, to cover the legal costs of whichever party who won a ruling in their favor.

As Pacey's had requested, and as was required by law, Judge Hanford appointed an appraiser, one John P. Hoyt, to determine the value of the Jane Gray, as she would have been valued "immediately after the said accident and her loss above referred to and of her freight then pending for said voyage."

A final stipulation was ordered "against all persons claiming damages for any loss, destruction, damage or injury occasioned by said accident, citing them to appear before this court and make due proof of their respective claims, at a time to be therein named; as to all which claims your petitioners will contest their liability, independently of the limitation of liability claimed under the act and statute aforesaid."

The date set for any persons claiming damages to provide proof was May 4, 1899 - almost one full year after the Jane Gray went down ninety miles off of Cape Flattery.

CHAPTER 23 - C. J. REILLY

Reilly, the thespian and survivor who had been found floating on a pile of boards after witnessing the death of William Gleason, was the first to enter his deposition. Just one day after Judge Hanford issued the order to appear with a proof of claim, C. J. testified as a witness for James E. Blackwell, giving his deposition in the presence of counsel for both parties. The date was January 4th, 1899. Pacey, MacDougall and Southwick were represented by the firm White, Munday, and Fulton, Stratton and Powell. Frederick Bausman represented James Blackwell.

"What is your name?"

"C. J. Reilly."

"You live in Seattle?"

"No sir; my home is in the East."

"When did you first come to Seattle?

"I got here last May; the first week of last May."

"After coming to Seattle last May, did you form any acquaintances of any schooner by the name of Jane Gray?"

"I did."

"What connection did you have with that schooner?"

"I secured my passage on the schooner Jane Gray, in addition to buying my outfit from the same firm, MacDougall and Southwick."

"You have stated you secured passage on the Jane Gray. What voyage did you secure passage on the Jane Gray?"

"From Seattle to Kotzebue Sound."

"From whom did you secure passage?"

"For myself and freight. For myself and partner; I am only speaking for myself."

"In what manner did you secure your passage and from whom?"

"I secured my passage from Mr. Pacey."

"Did you purchase a ticket from anybody?"

"From Mr. Pacey."

"Did you purchase a ticket for any else besides yourself?"

"My partner."

"How many persons did you secure passage for besides yourself?"

"Just my partner."

"What did you pay for your passage as a passenger, excluding freight?"

The attorneys for MacDougall and Southwick interject, "Objection. Defendant objects to the question on the grounds the question calls for testimony incompetent, irrevolent and immaterial."

Reilly's answer remains on record. "One hundred ($100.00) Dollars. That is One Hundred ($100.00) Dollars each; I am speaking as an individual, not as a partner."

"Do you know the Corporation, known as the MacDougall and Southwick Company?"

"I do."

"Do you know what connection, if any, Mr. Pacey has with that company?"

"I understand he is the secretary."

"State whether or not you had any conversation with the MacDougall and Southwick Company, or any of its officers, with regard to what should or should not be paid by you for freight and you friend's freight upon your completed voyage."

"Objection. Defendant objects to the question and giving any answer to the same, for the reason the question calls for testimony which is incompetent, irrelevant and immaterial."

Reilly's response was allowed. "When my partner and myself found we had bought three and one-half tons of freight, and as our understanding with Mr. Pacey was that we were to be allowed only one ton with each ticket, when we spoke to Mr. Pacey in regard to the additional ton and a half, he said he would have to consult Mr. MacDougall in reference to allowing it to go free."

"Did you make any request of the MacDougall and Southwick Company with regard to the payment or non-payment of freight?"

"Objection. Defendants object to the question and giving any answer to the same, on the ground that the question calls for testimony that is incompetent, irrelevant, and leading."

"Question withdrawn."

"What request, if any, did you make with regard to this payment of freight for your outfit upon the voyage to any officer of the MacDougall and Southwick Company?"

"Objection. Defendants object to the question and giving any answer to the same, on the ground that the question calls for testimony incompetent, irrelevant, or immaterial and on the further ground that question is leading."

"When it came to make the arrangement in reference to our excessive freight, over the stipulated amount, Mr. Pacey claimed he would have to see Mr. MacDougall relative to the matter. After seeing Mr. MacDougall, as he claimed, he said in view of the fact, that we had bought our entire outfit, or most of the outfit from the firm, amounting to between seven and eight hundred dollars he would waive all further demand for freight money."

"Did you mention what firm your outfit had been bought from?"

"I bought the entire outfit, not the entire outfit, but the bulk of the outfit from MacDougall and Southwick."

"Did you have any conversation with Mr. MacDougall with reference to that arrangement?"

"None whatever. All my arrangements had been made with Mr. Pacey."

"From whom had you bought the greater part of your outfit?"

"From the clerks in he employ of MacDougall and Southwick."

"In what store?"

"The MacDougall Store."

"Where is that store situated?"

"Corner First Avenue and Columbia Street."

"In this city?"

"Yes sir."

"Was the fact of those purchases made to Mr. Pacey?"

"They were."

"Where was Mr. Pacey at the time you had this conversation with him?"

"In the store. At least in the outfitting department of the MacDougall and Southwick Store."

"Did you see the Jane Gray prior for her departure for Kotzebue Sound?"

"I did."

"Where was she lying?"

"At the foot of Columbia Street."

"Do you know when the Jane Gray sailed upon her voyage?"

"The 19th of May, 1898."

"Are you familiar with her condition as to the manner in which she was loaded immediately prior to her voyage?"

"Yes."

"How long a vessel was the Jane Gray?"

"I could not say."

"Describe the structure which she had upon her deck at the time?"

"She had built on her forward deck a cabin to accommodate fifty odd people."

"How long, how broad and how high, in approximate figures was that structure?"

"As to the figures, I could not give the exact figures. It was high enough to give free headway."

"About how high was the roof of that forward cabin from the deck amidship?"

"About six foot, I should judge."

"Describe the after cabin as it appeared above the deck of the Jane Gray?"

"The after cabin –the roof of the after cabin was about three feet above the deck—the deck proper."

"Were both, or only one of these structures new?"

"Only one."

"Which?"

"The forward cabin."

"How many hatches did you observe in the deck of the Jane Gray?"

"She had a middle hatch, as well as the hatch forward."

"Did you look into the hold of the vessel through these hatches immediately prior to her departure?"

"I did."

"State the condition of the hold of the vessel as to its being filled or unfilled with freight?"

"The hold was entirely filled."

"State in a general way the condition of the deck of the ship with regard to being loaded with cargo of any kind?"

"Well, on the roof of the after cabin, she had two steam launches. On the deck amidships, between forward and after cabin, there were forty sacks of coal and barrels of beef, pork and water, which took up the entire deck space. On the roof of the forward cabin, there was the beef which was to be used on the voyage for passengers, as well as a skiff and knocked down boat."

"How about that portion of the deck that lay on either side of the cabins to its condition of being loaded with any cargo or freight?"

"The forward cabin extended from rail to rail. The after cabin as well."

"Did you state whether or not there was any lumber contained in the deck load?"

"There was no lumber on the deck load, as far as I can remember, outside of the "knocked down" boat."

"State in a general way Mr. Reilly the condition of the roofs of the two cabins and the space between them as to its being covered or uncovered with the deckload?"

"The condition of between decks, as well as roofs of forward and after cabins was such that there was practically no space to exercise in."

"After your conversation with Mr. Pacey which you have described, when did you next have any talk concerning business matters with the corporation of the MacDougall and Southwick Company, or any of its officers?"

"On my return after the wreck."

"On you return to the city of Seattle?"

"On my return to Seattle."

"About what was that date?"

"About the first of June."

"Do you remember the day of the week?"

"I do not remember the day of the week."

"In what capacity and in whose company did you see the corporation of the MacDougall and Southwick Company, and what particular officer did you see and talk with?"

"I was one member of a Committee of three appointed by the survivors of the Jane Gray wreck to wait upon the firm of MacDougall and Southwick, relative to damage indemnity and to see what could be done for the destitute members of the wreck."

"Who were the other members of the Committee?"

"Mr. Blackwell and Kingsbury."

"Who was in your company at the time of this interview?"

"Mr. Kingsbury and Blackwell."

"To whom did you come to have your talk?"

"On entering the store on that day we had an interview with Mr. MacDougall."

"Do you know what relationship Mr. MacDougall bears to MacDougall and Southwick Company?"

"I understand he is one of the firm."

"State what conversation you had as between all of you with Mr. MacDougall on that occasion."

"In the presence of Mr. MacDougall our demands for baggage indemnity to the extent of one hundred dollars and also requested suitable clothing to the extent of twenty-five dollars to cover us for our incidental loss. After we had put this before Mr. MacDougall he hesitated for a while and finally told us he would have to consult his partners. He left us and went up stairs, as we thought to his office, as we understood, and came back presently and said to us 'All right, go ahead.'"

"Against whom did the committee make this demand, if any they expressed against who they made it?"

"Defendants object to the question on the ground that it calls for testimony incompetent, irrelevant, immaterial and on the ground that it is leading. And that it calls for the conclusion of the witness and not for what was said."

"Against the firm MacDougall and Southwick."

"After Mr. MacDougall said, 'All right, go ahead' what did the Committee do?"

"We then informed the survivors to go up stairs and get their necessary outfit and that the MacDougall and Southwick Company agreed."

"Objection. The defendants object to the witness in answer to the question detailing conversations between witnesses from three parties such conversation not being in the presence of any of the defendants."

"Were any of the officers of the corporation of the MacDougall and Southwick Company present at the time you made these statements to the survivors as to what the Company had agreed to?"

"Objection. Defendants object to the question on the ground that it is incompetent, irrevolent and immaterial, and leading and not appearing that the witness made any statements."

"As near as I can remember both Mr. MacDougall and Mr. Pacey were there at the time."

"Go ahead and tell what was said in the presence of these people if anything was said, by the committee and the survivors. That was how soon after your arrival in Seattle?"

"In the course of two hours."

"Is the Mr. Blackwell, who was the member of the Committee you have testified, the same James E. Blackwell who has commenced this action?"

"The same party."

"What was then done by the Committee and by the survivors?"

"Objection. Defendants object to the question on the grounds that it calls for evidence which is incompetent, irrelevant and immaterial and not being material as to what the other survivors did."

"They then went to the up stairs department of the MacDougall and Southwick and got what miscellaneous clothing they required."

"Did you go also?"

"I did the next morning; not that evening."

"Do you know whether any of the officers of the corporation of the MacDougall and Southwick Company were present while selection of clothing were being made by any of the survivors?"

"Mr. Southwick was there."

"You say you went the next morning?"

"I went next morning, yes sir."

"What further was done or said between the parties in reference to this settlement, if you know?"

"Objection. Defendants object to the witness in answering the question giving any conversation."

"On the following day the Committee again saw the MacDougall and Southwick Company and during their interview Mr. MacDougall claimed that he made no such agreement with the Committee, Mr. Southwick, in a very flippant manner, stated that what had been done, had been done in the light of charity, upon which Mr. Blackwell asked the firm to make out a bill for what clothing he had got and paid them for same. At this interview, there was present Mr. MacDougall, Mr. Southwick and Mr. Pacey, in addition to the three members of the Committee."

"Did Mr. MacDougall at that time say what it was that he had agreed to?"

"Objection. Defendants object to the question for it calls for testimony incompetent, irrevelant, and immaterial and calls for conclusion of the witness and not for what was said."

"Mr. MacDougall simply repudiated the agreement that was made with the committee the previous day."

CHAPTER 24 - APPRAISAL AND PUBLIC NOTICE

After Reilly's deposition, the ship's appraisal came in. And Pacey did not like it.

Judge Hanford had appointed John P. Hoyt, Esquire, to fulfill the task of appraising the value of the Jane Gray, including the "freight pending" on the date of her loss. In addition, he issued an order stating that all of the claimants must be notified so that they would have the opportunity to be present at the appraisal. Since Pacey maintained that neither he, nor MacDougall or Southwick, had any knowledge of other potential claimants, only the five named in the original order were aware of the date and time of appraisement. With the exception of William Weaver and Charles Chard, all of the claimants showed up. Silas Livengood, James Blackwell, George Boak, and G. Mead Emory (representing Chard and Weaver), arrived at the courthouse at 2 o'clock on January 5, 1899.

John Pacey had introduced expenses that he felt should be deducted from the fares and freight money collected in advance of the sailing of the Jane Gray, in spite of the fact that Fireman's Fund Insurance Company had already issued him a check for $5000.00 and partially reimbursed him for crew wages paid. However, Mr. Hoyt denied the allowance and set the value of the schooner at $4,392.18 - well over the amount of $2157.21 that Pacey claimed she was worth.

Without in any way waiving their objection to Hoyt's appraisement, the attorneys for Pacey, MacDougall, and Southwick agreed to pay, or supply a bond ensuring the same, the amount of $4392.18 until Judge Hanford decided if any of them were liable for damages.

Meanwhile, as is the normal practice in lawsuits where there is the potential for a group of unknown claimants to crawl out of the woodwork, the judge issued a formal warning, a "monition," that had to be publicly published: "Now, therefore, upon the application of the said libellants and petitioners it is hereby ordered that a monition issue herein against all persons claiming damages for any loss, destruction, damage or injury done, occasioned or incurred by reason of the loss and destruction of the said schooner Jane Grey on or about the 22nd day of May, 1898, citing them to appear before this court and make due proof of their respective claims on or before the 4th day of May, 1899. That public notice of said monition shall be given by the publication thereof in The Weekly Post Intelligencer, a weekly newspaper published in the City of Seattle, state of Washington, for eight weeks, and that publication of said notice therein shall be completed at least thirty days before the said 4th day of May, 1899; and that service of the said monition shall be made upon all of such persons whose address, after diligent search and inquiry, shall become known to the petitioners and libellants herein, or any of them; and that due personal service of said monition shall be had upon all such claimants who can be found within the district."

Once again, the order also restrained anyone, even unknown parties, from "commencing or prosecuting any suits or actions against said petitioners, or any of them, in respect to any such claim or claims." Weaver, Livengood,

Chard, Blackwell, and Boak were separately admonished and restrained from prosecuting their pending claims against John Pacey, John MacDougall and Henry Southwick – or any other names that they might have done business under.

"Within the district," where the sheriff was required to post the notice of loss, can be defined as King County, Washington State. At least three members of Ingraham's party were known residents of Snohomish County – in Washington State, but to the north and out of "the district." Six of the passengers were from Pennsylvania, one of the deceased hailed from New Jersey, and two were from Connecticut. Still others came form Ohio, Michigan, New York, Maine, Minnesota, Illinois, California, and Iowa. Not to mention the six men from Italy. It was now January 7th of 1899. More than six months had elapsed since the Jane Gray went down. Few, if any, of the survivors or their heirs remained within King County. Pacey, MacDougall, and Southwick were counting on this.

The action in Admiralty law had swapped the roles of the plaintiffs and the defendants, forcing anyone who might have had a claim against Pacey, MacDougall, and Southwick to prove their right for compensation and defend their position. All of those who had presented claims against the outfitting firm were now "cross-libellants." And anyone else who might have come forward would have needed to provide substantial evidence to support their claim as well.

On March 6, 1899, James E. Blackwell arrived at the desk of A. C. Bowman, the commissioner appointed by Judge Hanford to record the testimony of each claimant. His version of the Jane Gray disaster was common knowledge and his presence in the courthouse was by now commonplace.

Not only did James Blackwell work as an engineer on the Bremerton dry dock, he was also one of the architects who completed the construction of the Bailey Building at Second and Cherry. However, he was more than mere mortar in public structures around Puget Sound. During those fifteen or twenty minutes between the alarm of "all hands on deck!" and abandoning the Jane Gray, most of the men in his party made it into the Kennorma. Soaking wet, frozen and seasick, he shared his clothing with his fellow survivors while battling heavy seas in an overcrowded launch, almost one hundred miles from land. He never spoke of his own heroism, but others did, and there were very few residents of Seattle who remained unaware of Blackwell's admirable character.

His claim against Pacey, MacDougall and Southwick was entered in court records: $6212.44 - it seemed a pittance in comparison to all of the hardships he had endured - and the generosity of spirit that he steadfastly displayed.

After James Blackwell, one of the Livengoods provided testimony on behalf of "the committee" of survivors.

CHAPTER 25 – LIVENGOOD TESTIMONY

Silas Livengood, a member of the Blackwell party, had already entered his proof of loss, stating the amount of money he paid for passage, the value of his "baggage and effects," and the cash that he had in his pocket when the ship went down. In his claim for further compensation, he testified that he endured "exposure and hardship, and suffered great pain and anguish of body and mind and was greatly and permanently injured in health and body," the value of which was stated at $5,000.00. For lost wages, Silas asked for $500.00. His total claim, including the $10.00 he paid for passage on the City of Kingston for a return ticket to Seattle, was $5949.00.

On March 14, 1899, G. Mead Emory, representing James E. Blackwell entered an affidavit requesting the testimony of the witness, James K. Livengood, a brother of Silas Livengood. Although he negotiated the price of passage on the Jane Gray with James Blackwell, James did not join his brother or any of the Blackwell party on the ill-fated journey.

Mr. Emory supported his request with the statement:

"I am one of the proctors for the cross-libelant James E. Blackwell; that said cross-libelant expects to prove by J. K. Livingood, the witness referred to in the annexed motion, and who is a resident of Lincoln, Nebraska, the following facts: That in the early part of the second week of May, 1898, said Livingood and said Blackwell went together to J. G. Pacey, who was at that time Secretary of the MacDougall & Southwick Company, to get rates for transportation upon the "Jane Gray" upon her voyage to Kotzebue Sound, on which she was subsequently lost; that Livingood and Blackwell stated to Pacey that they wished twelve tickets for a party of twelve, at sixty dollars ($60.00) each, with a bonus of one and one-half tickets free; that Pacey then stated that he would have to see J. B. MacDougall, the President of the MacDougall & Southwick Company, and made an appointment with his callers for five o'clock the same day; that they went to Pacey's office at the time named but MacDougall was not there; Mr. Pacey then said: "I will go up and see if he is in his office". Just then MacDougall came down stairs and took a seat. Pacey told him the proposal made and MacDougall asked him what he thought of it. Pacey said, "Well, we want to fill our boat and this will just fill it", to which MacDougall replied, "Well, let it go." Later in the same week, Livingood and Blackwell met MacDougall in front of the MacDougall & Southwick Company's store and asked him if the "Jane Gray" had not been pulled off the ice in the Arctic Ocean by the Revenue Cutter "Grant", to which MacDougall replied: "That cannot be so, or we would have heard of it when we bought her, and I have heard nothing. Another boat I own had an accident in the Bering Sea." On the same occasion Livingood asked MacDougall if the bottom of the "Jane Gray" had been inspected or repaired, to which MacDougall answered that before he bought and paid for the "Jane Gray" he had had her inspected by one of the best inspectors or judges in the country. That said deposition may be taken and returned within 2 weeks after the issuance of a commission."

Seven weeks later, as a witness for James Blackwell and the other claimants in the case against John G. Pacey and the MacDougall and Southwick Company, James K.

Livengood entered his deposition on May 6, 1899 in Lincoln, Nebraska.

"J. K. Livingood of lawful age being by me first duly examined, cautioned and solemnly sworn, as hereinafter certified deposes and saith as follows to the interrogatries propounded:"

"What is your name, age and residence?"

"James K. Livingood, age 47, residence at the present time Lincoln, Nebraska."

"Where were you in the month of May 1898, from the 1st to the 16th of that month?"

"I was in Seattle, Washington."

"Do you know James E. Blackwell, John G. Pacey and John B. MacDougall?"

"Yes Sir."

"If you answer the last question in the affirmative, state when and where you first met the men named and in connection with what business."

"I met them in Seattle, Washington in connection with transportation to Alaska on the Schooner 'Jane Gray', some time in the second week of May, in the fore part of the week as I remember, in 1898."

"Were you acquainted with the Schooner 'Jane Gray' during the month of May, 1898?"

"Yes Sir."

"Did you have any conversation with James E. Blackwell, John G. Pacey and John B. MacDougall at any time during the month of May, 1898, on business pertaining to the 'Jane Gray'? If so, state in detail, as exactly as possible what it was, giving the language where you can and the substance where you cannot, and when and where the conversation occurred."

"Yes Sir. Along about the fore part of the second week of May, 1898, Mr. James E. Blackwell and myself called on Mr. Pacey in reference to transportation on the Schooner 'Jane Gray' to Kotzebue Sound, Alaska, for a party of twelve. He said that number would fill the boat, and I told him I would give him sixty dollars a ticket, provided he would furnish me with one and a half tickets free. He said he couldn't give me a definite answer until he consulted with Mr. MacDougall. This conversation occurred in the forenoon and he requested us to call at Pacey's office in the MacDougall and Southwick Building, Seattle, Washington. I returned in company with Mr. Blackwell at the appointed hour, and Mr. Pacey said that he had not consulted with Mr. MacDougall in reference to the matter, but he would go and call him down, but just as he started to call MacDougall, he looked up and said, 'There he comes now,' and as Mr. MacDougall stepped up Mr. Pacey submitted our proposition to him and Mr. MacDougall said, 'I can't stand that price.' Mr. Pacey then said that that would fill the boat, and that they were waiting to fill the boat so that they could sail as advertised which was on the 18th day of May, 1898. I told him that that was the best that we would do. After a few more remarks that I do not remember, Mr. MacDougall said, 'Let her go. We will do it.' And accepted our proposition."

"Did you and Mr. Blackwell have any conversation with Mr. MacDougall alone, about business concerning the 'Jane Gray?' If so, detail what it was and when and where it happened.

"Yes Sir. A few days afterwards, Mr. Blackwell and I met Mr. MacDougall in front of his store. Mr. Blackwell said, 'Mr. MacDougall, I heard that the Jane Gray had gone down in the Bering Sea last year and was pulled out by the schooner Granada'. MacDougall remarked, 'That could not have been as I would have heard of it when I purchased the Jane Gray'. He answered that he had the Jane Gray inspected before he purchased her."

CHAPTER 26 - THE WIDOWS, HEIRS, AND OTHERS

For the women who had been left widows, this was a particularly painful time. Their relationships with their husbands were called into question. Dissatisfied men disappeared every day. Many changed their names and had no desire to be found. Others simply vanished without a trace and any whisper of marital discontent fueled public gossip. Now the court was demanding proof that that their husbands had not voluntarily fled the marriage.

Emma Ginther's claim arrived from Harrisburg, Pennsylvania on May 1st. She stated that she had been married to Frank since August 3rd, 1882, "and that the said F. W. Ginther died without issue, and leaving surviving him, his widow the said Emma C. Ginther, this cross libellant as his sole heir at law."

Frank's widow had been left destitute. "That said F. W. Ginther at the time of said death was not possessed of any property or income except such as was derived from his own labor and personal earnings, and was wholly dependent upon his personal earnings for his support and the support and maintenance of his said wife, the cross libellant hereafter, that he was at all times preceding his death a young man of sober and industrious habits, and was then of the age of forty two years and vigorous health of body and mind, and of good ability for and capable of earning and did earn high wages for himself and wife, that besides, he was a prudent, kind and affectionate husband, and this cross libellant was wholly dependent for her maintenance and support upon him; that by reason of his death, this cross libellant was and is deprived of his support, maintenance, protection, and has lost his earnings…" The counter suit concluded with Emma seeking $30,000 in compensation.

All of the other answers and cross-libels arrived at the commissioner's desk on May 3rd. Each and every one contended that the schooner Jane Gray was at all times "old, weak, defective," rotten and badly managed, manned by an incompetent captain and crew, and that Pacey, MacDougall and Southwick knowingly sent the passengers to their detriment and deaths in an overloaded, unseaworthy vessel. While acknowledging that the vessel was a complete loss, all contended that the wreck was not an "accident."

However, during this portion of the proceedings, the number of passengers and crew who were actually on board the vessel was still unresolved. In each "cross-libellant" claim, it was stated that the schooner carried on board " a general cargo and fifty-one passengers" when she left Seattle. And that "thirty-four passengers and three of her crew were lost." If there were indeed eight crewmembers and fifty-one passengers, the head count would have been fifty-nine, yet it was known that twenty-seven survived. So, if thirty-seven were lost, who were the missing five in this equation? This question may never be fully answered.

Fred Taylor: Image courtesy of California State Parks.

The claim of Kate Taylor, widow of Frederick Taylor, and their two minor daughters began with the establishment of their relationship to the deceased. "That the said respondent and cross libellant Kate E. Taylor was married to the said Frederick Taylor at San Francisco in the State of California on or about the second day of September, 1890, and ever since was, up to the time of the death of said Frederick Taylor, as hereinafter stated, the lawful wife of said Frederick Taylor, and lived with and was supported by him as such; that there are two children by said marriage, the cross-libelants above mentioned, Edna M. Taylor, aged seven years and Frances M. Taylor, aged four years, who reside with their mother."

"Deprived of the maintenance and society their husband and father," Kate's attorney outlined Frederick's fine character, setting the stage for justification of their claim for monetary damages: "That the said Frederick Taylor during all his said married life was a kind and indulgent husband and father and supported his family in comfort; that he was capable of earning and did earn during his married life and annual sum averaging $1800.00 Dollars; that his age at the time of his death was thirty years, and that his natural and reasonable expectancy of life was the period of 35 years." Asking the judge to dismiss the request for a limitation of liability, Kate and the children demanded $6,000 and "further relief as in law and justice they may be entitled to receive."

The widow of Spencer Young did the same: "...that the said respondent and cross-libelant Cordelia A. Young was married to said Spencer W. Young at Rostook County Maine in the State of Maine on or about the 10th day of April, 1869." From this marriage there was one minor child, "Effie Young, aged 18 years, who resides with her mother." Like Frank Ginther and Fred Taylor, Spencer Young was a "kind and indulgent husband and father." He too supported his family "in comfort," but certainly more so than some of the other men: "he was capable of earning and did earn during his said life an annual sum of twenty five hundred dollars." At the time of his death, Spencer was sixty-two years old. Cordelia and Effie decreed and demanded $5000 for the loss of their husband and father.

Nellie Taylor, Ed's widow, filed her claim in the same manner as the others: "That the said respondent and cross-libellant Nellie M. Taylor was married to the said Edwin M. Taylor at San Francisco in the State of California on or about the 13th day of March, 1883, and ever since was up to the time of the death of said Edwin M. Taylor, as herein after stated, the lawful wife of the said Edwin M. Taylor and lived with and was supported by him as such." There were no children from the marriage, but the forty year-old Edwin Taylor made a good living as an agent for the family paper business, earning on average $4000 per year. Nellie's claim was for a mere $6000.

Ed Taylor: Image courtesy of California State Parks.

The last of the widows to present her case was Ollie Gleason. She was the wife of William Gleason, who young C. J. Reilly witnessed sinking beneath the waves after clinging to a pile of boards on that stormy night. Establishing her relationship with the deceased, Ollie stated that she was married to "W. H. Gleason at Sheridan, in the State of Oregon, on or about the 4th day of April, 1882." She had one minor child at home, Bessie, who was twelve years old by the time of her testimony. Like the other women, Ollie relied entirely on her husband for support. Although the forty-seven year-old William was a well-paid and respected contractor in Seattle, earning $2000 per year, Ollie's claim only amounted to $5000.

Charles Wilkinson, Silas Livengood, George Boak, William Weaver, Charles Chard, and James Blackwell had already entered their proof of claim. Most did so again, submitting the same lengthy statements to the commissioner.

As a condition of this type of legal action, the petitioners for a limitation of liability swore before the court that they had "made diligent search and inquiry for any persons claiming damages for any loss, destruction, damage or injury done, occasioned or incurred by reason of the loss and destruction of the said schooner Jane Gray." MacDougall, Pacey, and Southwick each entered separate, yet identical statements, deposing that they had "not been able to find and there has not come to his knowledge any such person save and except the following; Emma C. Ginther, James E. Blackwell, William S. Weaver, Charles E. Chard, Silas Livengood, George R. Boak, Nellie M. Taylor, Kate E. Taylor, Frances M. Taylor, Edna M. Taylor, Ollie Gleason, Bessie Gleason, Cordelia A. Young, Effie Young and Charles Wilkinson, and C. J. Reilly."

Pacey went so far as to swear that he "has diligently searched for any survivors or heirs who might be claimants, to no avail…none others than those already found could be located."

The law was specific in defining the measures that needed to be taken to contact potential claimants. Notice was to be posted and the United States Marshall had to personally serve those involved in an action such as this – provided that the Marshall could find the claimants. And talk about putting the fox in charge of the henhouse - the records at MacDougall and Southwick were his primary source of information.

However that may be, the Marshall reported back to the court on June 8th, having fulfilled his duty: "In obedience to the within monition I duly cited and admonished all persons claiming damages for any loss...to appear on or before the aforesaid date before A. C. Bowman, commissioner of said court at the office of the said A. C. Bowman in the Burke Block in the said City of Seattle, and make due proof of their respective claims for any such damage."

The Marshall stated that he personally served Reilly, Livengood, Boak, Blackwell, and the attorneys for Emma Ginther and that "No other claimants after diligent search and inquiry could be found by me in this district, and no other claimants in this district or elsewhere have come to my knowledge except William S. Weaver, Charles E. Chard, Nellie M. Taylor, Kate E. Taylor, Frances M. Taylor, Edna M. Taylor, Ollie Gleason, Bessie Gleason, Cordelia A. Young, Effie Young and Charles Wilkinson."

In addition, he had placed public notice in the "Weekly Post Intelligencer, a newspaper printed and published during all the said times in this district in the city of Seattle. The date of the first publication of said monition and citation was on the19th day of January, 1899, and the date of the last publication thereof was the 16th day of March, 1899." Notice of the action was also conspicuously placed at the Seattle Post Office, one in the King County Courthouse, and another in the building where the sessions of the district court were held at the corner of Marion and Fourth Avenue.

As part of the process, the attorney's for Pacey, MacDougall, and Southwick received copies of all of the claims and file another round of objections.

CHAPTER 27 - CAPTAIN CROCKETT

Captain Ezekial E. Crockett's account of the night of the sinking had been inconsistent in every single interview. Why he went to bed and didn't make it up on deck until the ship was already half under water had been called into question. His statements about the condition on deck varied as well.

On June 1, 1898, in his first post-wreck interview with the *Seattle Post-Intelligencer* - in the private offices at MacDougall and Southwick - he was quoted as stating, "My opinion is that a butt in the Gray sprung open during Saturday night and let in enough water to sink her…There was no heavy storm; that is, sufficient to wreck such a staunch vessel as the Gray. We were carrying practically no sail and were hove-to when I was called on deck at 2 o'clock on Sunday morning. It was my watch, but the mate and one seaman were on the deck at the time, while I was down below."

When further questioned by the same publication, the Captain said, "The plight of the ship grew quickly worse. Indeed there was no time for anything. At the same time there was no excitement."

His account changed in a second interview, this time with a reporter from the *New York Times* - on the same day as his interview with the *P. I.*: "We were lying to, to mend our foresail. A moderate gale was blowing and the seas were running high. I had gone to bed and was sound asleep when the watchman awakened me with the announcement that something was wrong. I arose at once and found the vessel was leaking." Further contradicting his earlier statement, he says, "A scene of great confusion then took place, and it is impossible to give any detailed account of the events that followed. The darkness added to the confusion."

In this second interview, he also said, "At this time the Jane Grey was almost under water. A heavy sea struck her, throwing her on her beams. There was no time to launch other boats. The water was over the hatches and every one below was certainly drowned. Those on deck, however, got in the launch."

When he went to bed was also questionable. In one statement, he said that he "turned in near midnight," while others, corroborated by the testimony of survivors, said that he went below at nine. Where was he during those three hours?

Further adding to the confusion of what actually happened in those final ten minutes, he added, "As the launch drifted away from the almost submerged schooner we saw eight or ten men standing on the lee rail clinging to the rigging. Soon they disappeared from sight. Two of them John Johnson and C. Reilly kept afloat by clinging to bundles of boat lumber." Was he referring to Job Johnson of Long Island, New York? And not just three or four men, but eight or ten were left on the sinking hull?

In another interview, Captain Crockett recounted how they caught water in a tarp during a driving rain, while in another he stated that they had no water to drink until they reached the shores of Vancouver Island.

Could he possibly have any true recollection of the events a full twelve months later? Or would he say whatever

Pacey wanted him to say in order to protect his reputation as a loyal and capable captain?

After all of the potential claimants entered their answers and cross-libel pleas with the commissioner at Seattle, the attorneys for Pacey, MacDougall, and Southwick requested that the court issue an order for the deposition of Captain Crockett.

On May 6, 1899, John G. Pacey entered the motion based on his own deposition:

"John G. Pacey being first duly sworn, upon oath deposes and says that the said petitioners and libellants expect to prove by E. E. Crockett, for the taking of whose deposition the foregoing and annexed motion is made, that the said E. E. Crockett now residing at Rampart City in the Territory of Alaska. That he was master of the schooner Jane Grey at the time of her loss, and during all the time of her voyage upon which she was lost, and during all the time said schooner was lying at the port of Seattle and being prepared and loaded for said voyage."

"That the said schooner was at the time when she started upon her said voyage, sound, staunch and seaworthy in all respects. That the repairs made upon said schooner were all made under the direct supervision of the said Crockett. That the repairs consisted in a general overhauling of the said vessel, extending about 18 feet in length, and extending athwart the bow of said schooner and in small repairs to the mast of said vessel."

No mention was made of the construction of the forward cabin – only "repairs."

Further attempting to distance John MacDougall and Henry Southwick from any liability, the deposition of John Pacey continued: "That the said Crockett was hired as the

Master of said schooner by John G. Pacey, and by none other."

Where, exactly, the one hundred twenty to one hundred fifty tons of freight was stowed on the Jane Gray was never fully resolved. Pacey steadfastly contended that the vessel was not overloaded and "that the deck load of said vessel consisted only of the following freight: Two launches. Two knocked down boats. Two canvass boats. Two tons of coal. Eighteen barrels of water. About seven hundred pounds of meat. Two ships boats. One dory. Certain machinery, about five hundred pounds in weight. One small launch boiler. Two small sleds. That the entire deck load amounted to not more than four tons in weight." The eighteen barrels of water alone, if each barrel contained twenty-five gallons, would have weighed in at nearly two tons. And invoices supported other witness testimony that there were forty sacks of coal stacked on the deck amid ship - their total weight being over two tons, which could have more than doubled in weight when waterlogged.

Speaking for Captain Crockett, Pacey continued: "That the witness did not at any time on board the schooner Favorite when proceeding to Victoria, after the loss of said schooner, state to James E. Blackwell that there was no sea to cause the loss of said vessel, and that he hated to lose his vessel in a hatful of wind; and that he did not make at that said time and place, nor at any other time and place such a statement in substance to said Blackwell. That the said Crockett did not at the port of Seattle, while the said schooner was loading, state to said Blackwell or to any other person, that the said schooner would take no deck load upon said voyage. That the said vessel was lost because of the fact that she filled with water from below because of an opening in her hull caused by straining in the cross seas in which she was laboring at the time of her loss."

Once Pacey's deposition was entered, he stated that the shortest time within which an actual deposition from Captain Crockett could be taken would be eighty days.

It was May 11, 1899 when the claimants received notice that Crockett's testimony would take nearly three more months. Conceding that the captain's version of the facts would likely mirror John Pacey's deposition, they chose to avoid the delay and accepted Pacey's testimony as though he had been in command of the Jane Gray.

John G. Pacey was allowed to answer questions at the trial in the place of Captain Crockett. And his responses were allowed as valid testimony – for all of the details involving command of the ship and the events that occurred before, during, and after the night of the sinking.

CHAPTER 28 - THE SURVEYOR

Seeking to prove that they had fulfilled the responsibility of "due diligence," the attorneys for Pacey, MacDougall, and Southwick ordered the testimony of the surveyor who examined the ship before they took ownership of her. In spite of the fact that the survey occurred before construction of the forward cabin, it was entered into the records.

"BE IT REMEMBERED, that pursuant to the notice hereunto annexed and on the 31st day of May, 1899, at the hour of 11 o'clock A. M. of said day, at my office in the Mills Building in the City and County of San Francisco, State of California, before me ALFRED A. ENQUIST, a Notary Public in and for the City and County of San Francisco, State of California, personally appeared A. M. BURNS, a witness produced on behalf of the libellants and petitioners in the above-entitled matter, who, being by me first duly sworn, was then and there examined and interrogated by John H. Powell Esq., of counsel for libellants and petitioners--no other counsel being present,--and thereupon deposed and testified as follows; to wit,"

"What is your name?"

"A. M. Burns."

"What is your age?"

"Seventy-three years."

"Where do you live?"

"1506 Washington Street, San Francisco."

"And where is your place of business?"

"At 306 Sansome Street, San Francisco."

"What is your business, Captain?"

"Marine Surveyor."

"How long have you been in that business?"

"Thirty-odd years—thirty years, about."

"At the port of San Francisco?"

"Yes sir, at the port of San Francisco."

"Do you know the schooner Jane Gray?"

"I do. I did."

"Did you ever survey her or examine her?"

"I did."

"Where was she when you surveyed her?"

"On the dock, at the foot of Spear Street."

"At this port?"

"Yes sir."

"Port of San Francisco?"

"Port of San Francisco."

"Was she on the ways?"

"On the dock."

"Was her hull fully exposed?"

"Entirely so. Out of the water altogether."

"In what condition did you find her?"

"Found her in good condition."

"And her timbers?"

"Good. Hull was all good,--frames, planking, decks."

"Of what material was her planking, do you know?"

"Oak."

"What was the date of the survey made by you?"

"In March, 1898."

"At whose request was it made?"

"Mann & Wilson's."

"Who are Mann & Wilson?"

"Agents of the La Fonciere Insurance Company."

"What is the difference, Captain, between a crank vessel and a stiff vessel?"

"One don't stand up as well as the other; one requires more ballast than the other."

"That is, a stiff vessel will stand up better under sail than a crank vessel?"

"Yes, and a stiff vessel would stand up without ballast at all, where a sharp vessel or crank vessel would not. All sharp vessels or crank vessels require ballast."

"What kind of vessel was the Jane Gray, on account of her model?"

"Well, she was naturally crank, on account of her model. She was sharp underneath, but she wasn't so very sharp on her water line. Some people would call her a sharp vessel; I would not. She was not a particularly bluff vessel at the bow, but she was not what I call sharp. Under her bottom she had a good deal of dead rise, she didn't come out level on the bottom, as some do. She had a good deal of dead-rise; she was pretty sharp."

"By dead-rise, you mean the slope up from her keel?"

"The slope up of her frame. As the frame goes up more towards the perpendicular, we say she has more dead-rise."

"The amount of dead-rise is indicated by the angle which the timbers of the ship make with the keel?"

"Yes, from the keel."

"Did you, at the time of your survey, make a memorandum of it or report of it?"

"Yes sir, I made a report of it."

"(Showing witness instrument) Is that a copy of the report made by you?"

"That is a copy of the report made by me, which is now on file in my book in the office,--an exact copy."

"Was the report made at the time of the survey by you?"

"Made at the time. That is, within a day or so. It may have been a day after, or two days after,--but right away afterwards."

"I notice on this report, after the word "Model," the letter M,--For what does that stand?"

"That stands for 'Medium,' her model was medium."

CHAPTER 29 - THE TAYLOR FAMILY

In San Francisco on June 24, 1899, Nellie Taylor, widow of Edwin, entered her deposition, providing proof of her relationship to the missing man. A woman who had grown accustomed to living the rather pampered life of a paper company executive, she had to give up her home and move to a hotel after her husband's death. Her brother-in-law, James Taylor, accompanied her and entered his deposition as well.

Nellie Taylor responded to the list of questions:

"What is your name, age and residence?"

"My name is Nellie M. Taylor, my age is 38 years, my residence is Hotel 'Bella Vista', San Francisco, California."

"What relation did Edwin M. Taylor bear to you in his lifetime?"

"Edwin M. Taylor was my husband."

"When were you married to Edwin M. Taylor?"

"On March 13th, 1883."

"When did you last see your husband? And what was his age at that time?"

"I saw him on May 4th, 1898. At that time he was 39 years old."

"When did you last hear from your husband and from what place?"

"The last I heard from my husband was the 19th of May, 1898 from Seattle, Washington."

"If you have any letter from him received from Seattle prior to the sailing of the 'Jane Gray', please attach the envelope to your deposition as an exhibit, after identifying his handwriting."

"I have two letters from Edwin M. Taylor my husband received from Seattle, Washington prior to the sailing of the 'Jane Gray.' The envelopes containing said letters are attached hereto, marked respectively Exhibits A. and B. The handwriting on said envelopes I recognize and know to be the handwriting of my said husband Edwin M. Taylor."

Image courtesy of the National Archives and Records Administration, Seattle, Washington.

"What business had Edwin M. Taylor been engaged in during your married life up to the sailing of the 'Jane Gray'?"

"He had been engaged in the wholesale paper business and special agent."

"On the average, how much did your husband earn per annum during your married life?"

"About four thousand dollars per annum."

"State your husband's conduct towards you during your married life as to his treatment of you and manner of supporting you."

"Most indulgent and liberal in ever way."

"Are there any children of the marriage between you and your husband?"

"No."

"What means of support have you at present?"

"None, except what my brother does for me."

"Did you know Frederick Taylor during his lifetime? If so, what relation did he bear towards Edwin M. Taylor and Mrs. Kate E. Taylor?"

"I knew Frederick Taylor during his lifetime. He was Edwin M. Taylor's brother and Mrs. Kate E. Taylor's husband."

"Give the date and place of the marriage of Frederick Taylor and Mrs. Kate E. Taylor."

"They were married in San Francisco, California sometime in the year 1890.

"Are there any children of the marriage between Frederick and Kate E. Taylor? If so, give their names, sexes and approximate ages."

"Two girls, Edna about 7 years of age and Frances M. about four years of age."

"What was the age of Frederick Taylor at the time of his death?"

"Frederick Taylor's age at the time of his death was 31 years."

"Where do his wife and children reside at present?"

"At Mt. Vernon, New York."

"When did you last see Frederick Taylor?"

"About the 1st of May, 1898."

"What was the average amount earned by Frederick Taylor during his married life?"

"About twenty-four hundred dollars a year."

"What was Frederick Taylor's business during his married life?"

"Wholesale paper business and special agent."

"What was his conduct towards his wife and children, with reference to his treatment of them as a husband and father in supporting them and education the children?"

"Kind, indulgent and liberal."

"What means of support has Mrs. Kate E. Taylor at present for herself and children?"

"None except that given by her brothers."

~~~

Once Nellie finished her deposition, the same questions were asked of her brother-in-law, James I. Taylor:

"What is your name, age and residence?"

"My name is James I. Taylor, my age is 43 years, residence San Anselmo, Marin County, California, occupation Agent – Manufacturers' Agent."
~~~

"Did you know Edwin M. Taylor and Frederick Taylor during their lifetime? And what relation did they bear to you?"

"I did: They were brothers of mine."

"What was the age of each in May, 1898?"

"Edwin M. Taylor's age was 39 years, nearly 40: Frederick Taylor's age was 31 years."

"When did you last see either of them?"

"I saw each of them the last time May 4th, 1898, in San Francisco, California."

"If you have in your possession letters from either or both of them received from Seattle, attach such letter or letters, with the envelopes, to this deposition as exhibits."

"I have none such."

"Give the dates as nearly as possible of the marriages of your brother Edwin and Frederick Taylor, and the names of their respective wives."

"The date of the marriage of Edwin Taylor was March 13, 1883, his wife's name is Nellie M. Taylor. Her maiden name is Nellie M. Martell. The date of Frederick Taylor's marriage was 1890, about September. His wife's name was and is Kate E. Taylor, maiden name Kate E. Eagleson."

"Give the names of the children, if any, of each of your brothers by their said marriages, and their ages."

"The wife of E. M. Taylor had no children. To the wife of Frederick S. Taylor, two girls, Edna about seven years of age and Frances M. about four years of age."

"What respective occupations did your said brothers engage in during their married lives?"

"They were respectively engaged in the wholesale paper business and special agents."

"What was the manner of treatment and support accorded by each of you said brothers towards his family during his married life?"

"E. M. Taylor earned about $4000.00 per year: F. S. Taylor about $2400.00 per annum. Both were kind, liberal and indulgent."

"What means of support have the respective widows of your two said brothers at present?"

"None, except such as they received from their respective brothers."

"Where do the widows of your said brothers reside at present?"

"Mrs. E. M. Taylor resides in San Francisco, California at the Hotel "Bella Vista". Mrs. Frederick S. Taylor resides with her children at Mt. Vernon, New York."

CHAPTER 30 - WEAVER SPEAKS

From Muncy, Pennsylvania, Williams Weaver, a witness for the cross-libellants, entered his deposition on June 27, 1899:

"What is your name, age and present residence?"

"William S. Weaver. 36 years. Muncy, Pennsylvania."

"Were you one of the passengers on the 'Jane Gray' which left Seattle for Kotzebue Sound on May 18, 1898?"

"I was one of the passengers on the 'Jane Gray' which left Seattle for Kotzeue Sound on May 19, 1898."

"Describe the voyage briefly from its beginning, giving particular attention to what constituted the deck load of the 'Jane Gray,' whether there was any water on the main deck in the forward cabin on the day before she was lost, and the full details of what you personally observed of the catastrophe as it happened."

"We left Seattle on the evening of May 19th, 1898, with the "Moonlight," a small vessel, both vessels being towed out by a tugboat which left us in the straight about 4 a.m. Friday. We were all day in the straight of San Juan De Fuca. Some time about midnight of Friday we ran into the ocean off Cape Flattery; about 5 o'clock I went on deck feeling very sea sick, I noticed passengers carrying water out of the front deck house, and they told me that it was more than two feet deep in there, and that people in the lower berths had to crawl out during the night on account of the water coming in on them. I helped place some of the deck load and gear and can tell there was from eighteen to twenty knock down boats, two launches, the Ingram and Italian, about three dories besides a great many barrel of water, pork and bags of coal, and in all entirely too much load on deck. As stated before I went on deck about 5 o'clock Saturday morning and sat down near the pump in or about the middle of the vessel between the two deck houses, the ocean was washing over on the vessel between these two deck houses faster than the scuttle holes could clean it out. During the day we had to place boards at the cabin steps to keep it from washing down them. Feeling very sick I did not remain long on deck, but retired to the cabin and remained there all day excepting a few visits to the top of the steps where I found things in the same condition or getting worse. About ten o'clock Saturday night I was so sick that I could not sit in my chair and was thrown across the cabin several times by the violent lurching of the vessel. I was asked to go to my berth many times but could not do it, being so ill and weak, finally, Charles E. Chard helped me to it and then lifted me into the upper berth leaving the state room door propped open by a sack of salt so that I could see the steps, as I could not sleep, and wanted to see what was going on, near about 2 o'clock I noticed a splash of water come down the steps - soon another one or two and then I asked my berth mate, George R. Boak, whether he had strength enough to alarm the others, he said he did not have much, however we made someone understand what was going on and they roused the mate who went on deck at once, and as soon as he saw the situation came running down the steps, hammered on the captains door - telling him there was something wrong on deck and that he should come up at once, the captain ran up on deck, looking upon the scene presented, called for every body to come on deck."

"Describe how you got into the 'Kennorma' and by what means she finally reached land."

"Charles E. Chard helped me on deck from the top of the cabin step, I held to the side of the Italian launch, with both hands while they were trying to get it loose, in the mean time the Kennorma was cut loose and the captain calling for all to get into this launch, but no one got in about that time for a wave came along and washed it over board. She then came back against the vessel knocking a hole in her side. The mate and captain then both got in to protect her and commenced to throw the boiler and what all they could overboard assisted by some others. I was still clinging to the Italian launch, on deck thinking it the last launch of the two and made up my mind to stick to her, although in the meantime I was watching the direction the Kennorma was going, it was dark but I could see figures of people standing on deck of the 'Jane Gray', in a moment or two they would disappear - supposed to have been washed over board. I still clung to the Italian launch until I could not see any one on board excepting three or four who were working at it. All at once I decided to make the Kennorma if I was to be saved and at the same instant I went overboard striking in among some light wreckage sticking me in the right side of the chin and right shoulder, pushing it away with my left hand I swam on until I struck the bow of the Kennorma, one man in the bow, an Italian, who finally helped me in after quite a quarrel, when I got on there were perhaps eight people aboard. We held the launch by a boat hook to the end of one of the masts of the Jane Gray, which had turned 'Turtle' and picked up enough to make our load 25, as we could not have or see anyone anymore, and thinking the vessel would soon sink we decided to get away. We floated around until daylight, in the meantime bailing hard, about that time we heard a voice, going toward it we picked up a man by the name of Johnson, we soon heard another voice and picked up a man by the name of Riley. We had a terrible time in reaching land which we finally did about 3 o'clock p.m. on Monday by the assistance of a sail which we rigged up out of canvas which was in the launch.

"Did you see anything of the launch known as the Italian launch? Did you see any persons aboard of her at the time of the sinking of the 'Jane Gray?' If so, who were they? And what was the condition of the Italian launch when you saw her?"

"Don't remember of seeing her after I left the Jane Gray."

"What was your condition of health when you became a passenger on the 'Jane Gray?'"

"Good."

"Did you undergo any suffering either of mind or body during the voyage to land on the 'Kennorma?' If so describe the same."

"I suffered terribly from being cold and wet. My mental agony cannot be described."

"Did you experience any bad results from the voyage in the 'Kennorma?' If so, describe them."

"I do feel some evil effects of the exposure and hardship we endured, and think that I notice it quite plainly at times."

"Did you lose any freight, baggage or other personal effects in the 'Jane Gray?' If so, name them as nearly as possible, and state their value. State also the cost in gross of all your personal belongings lost on the 'Jane Gray.'"

"I lost everything I had on board, which consisted of my complete outfit and personal effects, which I valued at about $500. And a gold machine on which a line value cannot be placed as it was made a present to me when I left Pennsylvania, but undoubtably would have been very valuable to me in the gold field."

"At what hour and in what part of the 'Jane Gray' did you last see the following passengers: Edwin M. Taylor, Frederick Taylor, W. H. Gleason, Spencer W. Young, James C. Ginther?"

"The last I saw of any of them was on Saturday, May 21, to the best of my knowledge."

CHAPTER 31 - GEORGE BOAK

From Hughesville, Pennsylvania, George's testimony was entered on June 29, 1899:

"What is you name, age and present residence?"

"George Rupley Boak; 23 1/3 years; at Seattle, Washington. Am visiting relatives at Hughesville, Pennsylvania and Pine Glen, Pennsylvania, at present."

"Were you one of the passengers on the 'Jane Gray' which left Seattle for Kotzebue Sound on May 18, 1898?"

"Yes."

"Describe the voyage briefly from its beginning, giving particular attention to what constituted the deck load of the 'Jane Gray,' whether there was any water on the main deck in the forward cabin on the day before she was lost, and the full details of what you personally observed of the catastrophe as it happened."

"The 'Jane Gray' left port in such a condition of disorder that the cook refused to give the passengers any supper the first night out. It seemed that a great many things had been thrown on the ship and not put away where they belonged. The next day some of the passengers had to pile a great deal of the top cargo in shape and lash it down, especially that on the forward house. Mr. James E. Blackwell and myself took an inventory of the goods on the deck. The list was made out by Mr. Blackwell in his own handwriting and is now in his possession. I am only able to state generally the contents of the deck as follows:"

"Two launches; two ships boats, one on davits behind; the ships boats were nothing but small row-boats, a dory and a number of knock down boats; a quantity of iron; a quantity of lumber; coal in sacks; barrels of water, salt beef, etc."

"As soon as the 'Jane Gray' got out to sea, she began to roll. This was on the night before the wreck, and it was not long afterwards that the water began to come over the main deck. I was sick and did not go out on Saturday before the wreck; but could hear the waves washing the deck almost continually, and quite often there was so much water on deck that it came down the companionway into the after cabin. From where I lay I could see it come in, and as the entrance to the companionway was so much higher than the entrance to the forward house the water was running in and out of the forward house, for the water must have been six inches higher than the boards at the bottom of the door off the main deck. Every one that came into the after-cabin said something about the water in the forward house being knee deep and no way to keep it out, and a great many of the fellows said they would have to sleep out of the forward house as they could not sleep in the lower berths and only a few of the middle berths, for when the ship rocked the water would come up into many of the middle berths. Just before the wreck, we, in our state room got to talking about the water coming down the companionway. There were five in our room. Chard in the lower berth; Reilley and his partner in the middle berth; Weaver and I on top. The water was at this time running down in a stream, and Chard got up and called the mate's attention to it. The mate hurried on deck. He came down almost at once and called the captain, who, in a minute, went out on deck. I then heard some sails rustling, and very soon the captain called everybody on deck. I jumped and grabbed some clothes and rushed for the deck. I found the ship had listed so to starboard by this time that about five or six inches deep of water was running down the companionway. When I had made my way over the galley to the port side and had gotten what clothes I had on, I found the ship listed so that the water was over the starboard rail. Soon I saw the 'Kennorma' go into the sea. The fellows crowded into her and tried to get her so the ropes would not catch her. I had started for the ships boat on the davits in the rear which some one started to lower when I saw the rope on the one end break and when the other end was let down, she flooded with water. By this time the 'Kennorma' was behind the ship."

"Describe how you got into the 'Kennorma' and by what means she finally reached land?"

"I crawled out on the boom which must have been lashed in place and when I found the Kennorma under me I dropped and fell into the boat. People were being helped in over the sides of the boat at this time. We then took anything we could get to paddle the boat away from the sinking ship. We drifted awhile and finally a sail was fixed out of a canvas blanket. The wind was so that it blew us towards land. Then the awning was nailed over the boat to keep the water out, and so when any water would get on we would rise it up and the water would run off. On Sunday night the sail was taken down and put out behind with the other things that could be spared to steady the boat and break the waves. The sail was raised again on Monday morning, when at last land was sighted, and we slipped in after much difficulty in finding a place to land."

"Did you see anything of the launch known as the Italian launch? Did you see any persons aboard of her at the time of the sinking of the 'Jane Gray?' If so, who were they?

And what was the condition of the Italian launch when you saw her?"

"I saw the Italian launch in the water with four people in her. She set low in the water as if she had considerable water in her. I could not recognize the people in her, and did not see her after the ship went down."

"What was your condition of health when you became a passenger on the 'Jane Gray?'"

"I was feeling well, but had had a cold."

"Did you undergo any suffering either of mind or body during the voyage to land on the 'Kennorma?' If so, describe the same."

"The agony of my mind can never be described, but it was something terrible, as we knew not what minute would be our last, and if we did not drown, we did not know if we would ever reach land. And, again, I often thought I could not stand the cold, as I had only a gauze undershirt, an ordinary coat and a pair of light weight corduroy trousers. This was everything I had on. The boat was so crowded that I would be in one position until I would give up and think I could endure it no longer, and almost always when I tried to move I was so cold and stiff I had not strength to move until the person next on top would move when it suited them or give me a helping hand, and when the boat struck the sand and we started for the dry sand I had to crawl through the water part of the way. I was so cold, weak and stiff that it was impossible for me to walk more than a step or two at a time."

"Did you experience any bad results from the voyage in the 'Kennorma?' If so, describe them."

"The first night at Seattle I retired early and soon a fever came on me. At midnight I got Dr. Bories. My temperature was over 104 and my pulse was very high. The doctor said my lungs were affected, and it was only calling him at once that saved me from pneumonia."

"Did you lose any freight, baggage or other personal effects in the 'Jane Gray?' If so, name them as nearly as possible and state their value. State also the cost in gross of all your personal belongings lost on the 'Jane Gray.'"

"Yes. My freight consisted of groceries, hardware, etc. See list of Blackwell's party; I own one full share. Bausman, Kelleher and Emery have a list of baggage and personal effects made out by me, which consisted of clothing, gun, tent, etc. The cost of all I lost on the 'Jane Gray' amounts to $774 and some odd cents."

"At what hour and in what part of the 'Jane Gray' did you last see the following passengers: Edwin M. Taylor, Frederick Taylor, W. H. Gleason, Spencer W. Young, James C. Ginther?"

"The Taylor Brothers were in the after cabin of the ship on Saturday, but I don't think I saw Gleason, Spencer Young since the Friday before. I saw Ginther when I was rushing out of the cabin after the captain had ordered every one on deck."

"I, Agnes B. McCabe, a notary public in and for said county, do hereby certify that the above deposition was taken before me, and reduced to writing by myself, at Lock Haven, in said county, on the 29th day of June, 1899, at two o'clock a. m. in pursuance of the stipulation hereto annexed; that the above named witness, before examination, was sworn to testify the truth, the whole truth, and nothing but the truth, and that the said deposition was carefully read by said witness, and then subscribed by him."

Dated at Lock Haven, Pa. the 29th day of June, 1899.

Agnes B. McCabe

Notary Public in and for the county of Clinton, state of Pennsylvania.

CHAPTER 32 - EXCEPTIONS OVERRULED AND OTHER DRAMA

John Pacey just could not seem to catch a break when it came to his life as a ship owner. In the midst of the Jane Gray proceedings, one of his other schooners encountered trouble on July 14, 1899. The schooner Una struck his vessel, the Nellie G. Thurston, while she was anchored off Anvil City, about ten miles from Cape Nome, Alaska. Apparently, Captain Thomas Harkin, in command of the Una, attempted to cross the bow of the Thurston, couldn't control his ship and tore the entire bowsprit and half of the rigging off of John's schooner, which then had to be towed into St. Michael where $750 worth of repairs were performed before she could get back to business again.

While John was still processing the fact that he had one more ship down, and yet another dam in the cash flow, Judge Hanford filed his first opinion and issued a ruling as to whether the widows and orphans had a right to claim damages from the loss of the Jane Gray.

Providing a synopsis of the entire case, he began: "In this proceeding, John G. Pacey, as owner of the American schooner Jane Grey late of the port of Seattle, and others, have petitioned the court for the benefit of the act of congress limiting the liability of the owners of vessels for damages resulting from marine disasters. The petition avers as the reason for uniting in seeking relief that a number of actions to recover damages have been commenced in which all the petitioners are charged as being joint owners of the Jane Grey, and jointly liable for the damages alleged to have been sustained. It appears that in the month of May, 1898, said schooner, left the port of Seattle on a voyage to Kotzebue Sound in the District of Alaska, having on board a large number of passengers with their equipments and supplies, who were going in search of gold and to explore that country, and while proceeding on said voyage the Jane Grey filled with water and sank in the Pacific Ocean, and with all her tackle, apparel, boats, appurtenances and cargo, was completely lost, and 34 of the passengers and three of the crew then on board were drowned. Other persons who were on board were successful in making their escape in a small launch owned by some of the passengers. The petition avers that "said accident happened and the loss, damage, injury and destruction above set forth, were occasioned, done and incurred, without fault, or privity, or knowledge of your petitioners, or any of them, and was due solely to the perils of the sea."

"According to the practice in such cases, an injunction was issued restraining all persons from commencing or prosecuting suits and actions for the recovery of damages resulting from said casualty pending the determination of the rights of the parties in this proceeding. The widows and heirs of several of the passengers who were drowned, have entered appearances herein and filed answers and cross libels in which they each respectively plead their relationship to the deceased, and charge that the disaster and loss of life were occasioned by the neglect and wrong of the petitioners, in knowingly sending the Jane Grey on said voyage when she was rotten, weak and unseaworthy, and without boats and equipments necessary for the safety of her passengers, and very much overloaded, and each of the said cross libellants prays for a decree against the petitioners jointly for full damages and costs. The case has been argued and submitted upon exceptions to each of said cross libels raising the question as to the right of the heirs or persona representatives of deceased persons to recover damages for tortuis injuries taking effect upon the high seas, and resulting in death."

"In the light of the numerous decisions in different courts, in this country and Europe, which have been cited upon the argument, the question is not only interesting, but perplexing; I shall, however, leave out of view all cases other than the decisions of the Supreme Court of the United States, and my endeavor will be to decide the case in accordance with the principles which I regard as being established by the announced determinations of the highest court in the country."

Citing cases, laws, and rulings Judge Hanford explored every possible outcome in both civil and maritime law, eventually concluding with:

"Since the maritime law is not inconsistent with the right to recover damages for the death of a person caused by a wrongful or negligent act, the decision in the case of Stewart v. Railroad Co. is an authority fully supporting the proposition that the law of the forum must control in determining the question as to the liability of the owners of a vessel, who are citizens of the United States, for damages caused by their negligence resulting in death. The rule of the common law is not now a barrier to the right to recover damages for the death of a person, because in this state and in all the states of the Union the common law has been changed by statutory enactments. 5 Enc. PI. & Prac. 849. The statutes of this state provide:

"When the death of a person is caused by the wrongful act or negligence of another, his heirs or personal representatives may maintain an action for damages against the person causing the death. In every such action the jury may give such damages, pecuniary or exemplary, as under all the circumstances of the case may to them seem just." 2 Ballinger's Ann. Codes & St. Wash. § 4828 (2 Hill's Code. § 138).

"All steamers, vessels, and boats, their tackle, apparel, and furniture, are liable for injuries committed by them to persons or property within this state, or while transporting such persons or property to or from this state. Demands for these several causes constitute liens upon all steamers, vessels, and boats, and their tackle, apparel, and furniture, and have priority in their order herein enumerated, and have preference over all other demands; but such liens only continue in force for the period of three years from the time of cause of action accrued." 2 Ballinger's Ann. Codes & St. Wash! ,§ 5953 (1 ,Hill's Code, § 1678). See, also, The Willamette, 59 Fed. 797; Id., 18 C. C. A. 366; 70 Fed. 874.

If the facts pleaded by the widows and orphans who have appeared as cross libelants in this case are true, the law of the land entitles them to damages, and the law of the sea is not inconsistent with the rights which they seek to enforce. Exceptions overruled.""

~~~

It was July 17, 1899, when Judge Hanford ruled that the widows and heirs of the deceased were entitled to sue for compensation. MacDougall and Southwick's plea for a limitation of liability was yet to be addressed.

By the end of the month, Hanford was also involved in Pacey's suit against the schooner Una. John had received word that the vessel was moored in Port Townsend. The
~~~

judge entered a lien against her in the amount of $1800 and ordered that both the ship and the captain must appear before the court to answer charges no later than August 31st, 1899. Would Pacey's troubles never end?

CHAPTER 33 - EMMA GINTHER

For nearly a year, Emma had endured questions surrounding her husband's disappearance. Although Frank had a life insurance policy and left clear directions to ensure that it remained in effect during his absence, his plans went awry. On September 20, 1898, the details of the dispute made the second page of The *Evening News* in Keokuk, Iowa:

"WAS HE DELINQUENT?

Insurance Case in Court That Turns on the Question of Delinquency.

INSURED MAN GOES HUNTING GOLD.

Leaving the Payment of His Assessments in the Hands of His Father—En Route to the Klondike He is in a Shipwreck and is Never Seen Afterward—No Body Ever Found and the Society Refuses to Pay the Policy.

Charlston, Ills., Sept. 20.—A missing railway postal clerk, a policy for $2,000 and the question of delinquency at the time of disappearance are involved in one of the most interesting insurance cases on record. The parents and beneficiaries reside in this city, where efforts are being made to collect the amount of the policy. The insured is supposed to have gone to the bottom of the Pacific while on his way to the Klondike last May. Prior to April 3 F. W. Ginther was for twenty years a railway postal clerk running out of Harrisburg, Pa., where he had resided sixteen years. In December, 1890, he took a policy in the United States Railway Mail Service Mutual Benefit association, an organization to which only railway postal clerks or other persons identified with the service are admitted, the amount of the policy being $2,000.

Ginther Starts for the Klondike.

April 3 he left Harrisburg, giving notice to L. H. Tyson, local secretary of the association, to have notices of assessments sent to Charleston, where his father would receive them and make payments. Early in April he went to Seattle and May 19 sailed on the schooner Jane Grey for the Klondike. May 23 the Grey foundered at sea and went down with all on board save those who had taken refuge in a single launch which, after thirty-seven hours, reached shore. On the Grey were George Hiller and William S. Weare, the former being Ginther's room-mate and the latter occupying the next stateroom. They say that at 2 'clock that fateful morning Ginther was seen to leave his stateroom and go on deck, but that he was never seen afterward. He was not taken into the launch in which the survivors reached shore. Captain J. C. Pacey, master of the schooner, corroborates this testimony, which is in the form of affidavits.

Assessments Go to the Wrong Place.

The reader is now taken back to the day when Ginther instructed Secretary Tyson to have his assessment notices sent to his father at Charleston. Tyson makes affidavit that he then notified the general secretary and treasurer of the association at Quincy, Ills., so to address the notices. That was April 3. There was an assessment, but it went to the old address at Harrisburg and Ginther having left at his hotel no direction to forward it, it failed to reach W. E. Ginther, the father. According to the rules of the association, if any assessment is not paid in thirty days the policy lapses, though there is an additional thirty days in which the insured may pay and be reinstated. W. E. Ginther got notice June 2 that assessments Nos. 198 and 199 were due.

REFUSED TO RECEIVE THE MONEY.

After It Was Found That the Insured Man Was Lost.

The amount was $4. The money was sent at once to J. V. Henry, secretary and treasurer, at Quincy, and Henry forwarded a receipt for the amount. Immediately afterward it was reported that the Jane Grey had gone to the bottom and that Ginther was among the lost. Secretary Henry at once sent the $4 which he had received from W. E. Ginther back to him. Ginther sent it back to Henry, who returned it to Ginther, and the latter, after it passed back and forth between Quincy and Charleston a dozen times or more, refused to take it out of the post office and it is now in possession of postal authorities.

Ginther claims that not having received the assessment notices after the insured had served notice on the legal agent of the association to send them to him at Charleston, he cannot be considered delinquent and that it was because the association missent them to Harrisburg that they were not paid. Secretary Henry says he did not receive Tyson's order to send the notices to Charleston until April 26. In receiving the $4 June 2 he was acting according to the rules permitting the insured to reinstate himself providing he is in good health. But the day after he had sent the receipt he got a letter from W. E. Ginther saying; "I presume you have noticed in the metropolitan press that the Jane Grey went down and my son is dead." This showed that the money had been paid after the insured was said then be made, it is declared.

The executive committee of the association at Chicago directed that the $4 be sent back and in passing on the claim decided to refer the case to the convention of railway postal clerks at Atlanta, Ga., Sept. 6. H. A. Neal, an attorney of this city, representing the beneficiary, the mother of the insured, went to Atlanta and presented his claim to the clerks, who voted to refer the case back to the executive committee with instructions to pay the claim on satisfactory proof of death. This takes the case back to Chicago, where the committee will insist that the body be produced before payment is made.

The committee now claims to have evidence that a second launch of the Jane Grey was found beached; that in this boat were evidences that it had reached shore with human occupants, and that it contained a number of articles which identified it and which articles could not have remained in the boat had it been capsized. From this the committee contends that Ginther may yet be alive. The Ginthers offer to furnish bond that, the policy being paid, should the insured turn up alive the amount will be repaid to the association."

~~~

Why Frank's widow was not named the beneficiary of his life insurance policy is unknown. Regardless, based on her testimony, he left her penniless. On July 18, 1899, Emma Ginther entered her deposition in front of the Notary Public, Frank J. Roth, Esquire, in Harrisburg, Pennsylvania:

"EMMA C. GINTHER, respondent, being first duly sworn, deposes and says, in answer to interrogatories propounded to her, as follows":

"State your name, age and residence, and how long you lived at your present residence."
~~~

"Emma C. Ginther, maiden name Abbott. I was born December 7, 1860, in Harrisburg, Pa., and have always resided here."

"Were you acquainted with F. W. Ginther in his lifetime? If so, how long did you know him, and what was your relation to him at the time of his death? If you answer that you were his wife, state when and where you were married to him, and whether any children were born as the issue of said marriage, and if any such were born, were they living at the time of death of the said F. W. Ginther, and are they living now?"

"I knew F. W. Ginther twenty-two years. I was the wife of F. W. Ginther, and was married to him August 3, 1882. We never had any children."

"State when said F. W. Ginther left Harrisburg, Penna. For his trip to Alaska, and in whose company he went."

"The first Monday in April 1898. He was accompanied by Percy Davenport and George Hiller."

"State the age of said F. W. Ginther on the 22nd day of May, 1898; state the condition of his health previous thereto, was he strong or not, what was his earning capacity, and his attention to business, habits of industry."

"F. W. Ginther was between forty-two and forty-three years of age; he was born September 20, 1855. He always enjoyed good health, was strong and hearty, industrious; earned $95 per month as Postal Clerk."

"State the means of your support previous to May 22, 1898, and did you come by or receive any property through the death of F. W. Ginther."

"I depended entirely on my husband. I never received any property through his death."

"Have you received directly or indirectly from the petitioners herein any compensation or payment for the loss of the said F. W. Ginther?"

"None whatever."

"What property if any did F.W. Ginther have at the time of his death on May 22, 1898. Have you any property of means of support now?"

"He had no property except his clothing. He had a diamond stud and ring and a gold watch, which he had with him when he went away."

"What was the nationality of said F. W. Ginther?"

"He was of German decent, but born in the United States. He always used to say he was a 'true born American citizen.'"

"State anything further occurring to you material to the issue involved here."

"I don't know that I can say anything more."

CHAPTER 34 - MORE DENIAL

After Judge Hanford's ruling allowing the testimony of the witnesses to be entered into evidence, the attorneys for Pacey, MacDougall, and Southwick launched their next counter-offensive.

With all of the men and women heading for the Klondike, Seattle had become a city plagued by reports of missing people. The police department fielded inquiries from wives, mothers, and orphaned children on a daily basis. The attorney's for the outfitting firm continued to use this to their advantage, implying that the men who had gone missing on the Jane Gray were simply that - missing. And perhaps, like so many others, they did not want to be found.

Although John Pacey had provided an affidavit in the Ginther insurance claim, Frank's widow became their first quarry. While denying every allegation against them, they admitted, "that said schooner did not have as a part of her equipment any life preservers except two life buoys at the wheel, and that said schooner was lost upon the high seas off the coast of Vancouver Island on the 22nd day of May, 1898; and except further, that these petitioners are each and all ignorant as to the truth of the allegations in said article that the said F. W. Ginther drowned."

Rubbing salt into Emma's open wound, they denied that Frank died on the ship, stating: "That the wreck, loss and destruction of said schooner occurred upon the high seas without the jurisdiction of the state of Washington and not within the jurisdiction of any other state of the United

States, or of any nation; and that the cross libellant has not any claim for damages by reason of the death of the said passenger F. W. Ginther if it shall appear that the said passenger met his death by reason of said wreck, nor any right of action therefore."

For James Blackwell, William Weaver, George Boak, Silas Livengood, and Charles Chard, their tactics differed. "By no means waiving the objection to said cross libel" they acknowledged the amount that each of the men paid for passage on the Jane Gray with an additional, unexplained concession, that each man's "said freight was of the value of $350.00," while denying that any one of them were damaged in any amount "greater than the sum of $350.00 for loss of baggage, freight and personal effects."

Every other original argument presented on behalf of Pacey, MacDougall, and Southwick remained. They still contended that no part of the boat had ever been found or recovered and that the total value of all freight money received was no more than $2,152.47. They had no knowledge of any defects in the vessel, they properly manned and equipped her, and the accident was "wholly due to the perils of the sea."

In this same objection, they once again added the argument: "That in the contract, or ticket, issued to each of the persons who took passage on said schooner, and which was accepted by each of them it was provided that in case of the loss of said schooner her owner should not be held responsible for damage resulting from accidents of navigation or dangers of the seas, nor be under any obligation to refund the amount of passage money paid, nor be liable for the loss of any freight or baggage of said passenger in excess of the sum of one hundred dollars."

Why the offer of $350 followed by the denial of any claim in excess of $100?

Reiterating that the outfitting firm had nothing to do with the boat, that they contended was solely owned by John G. Pacey, they concluded with: "And petitioners John B. MacDougall, Henry C. Southwick, and the MacDougall & Southwick Company, a corporation, claims that they are each and all exempt from all liability for any loss or damage arising out of said accident for the reason that neither they nor any of them was ever at any time in any manner interested as owners or otherwise, in said vessel or said voyage."

Now they took a swing at Nellie Taylor, Ed's widow, demanding that she prove her relationship to him. While admitting that Edwin Taylor purchased a ticket for passage on the Jane Gray, John Pacey stated again that neither he, nor MacDougall and Southwick, was under any obligation to refund the ticket or any other damages in excess of the $100 for baggage. Throwing the final punch, they applied reasoning similar to that given to Emma Ginther: "The cross libellant has not any claim for damages by reason of the death of said passenger Edwin M. Taylor if it shall appear that the said passenger met his death by reason of said wreck, nor any right of action therefore."

Cordelia Young, Kate Taylor, and Ollie Gleason all received the same objections to their claims against Pacey, MacDougall, and Southwick: Prove that you were indeed married. Prove that he didn't leave you of his own accord. If you had children with the alleged victim, prove it. Prove that he provided for you and your family. And, since no bodies have ever been found, prove that your husband actually died during the last voyage of the Jane Gray.

There was one other widow who had not been acknowledged. Yet.

CHAPTER 35 - MARY WILLIAMS

Charles and Mary Williams moved to Olympia, Washington at the beginning of May, 1898, where the newlywed couple had made arrangements for Mary to stay with her brother and his wife, Mr. and Mrs. T. J. McDonald, while Charles was seeking "his fortune in the Klondike country." When Charles left for Alaska later that month, T. J. had come down with a case of pneumonia, but since he was "in the full vigor of sturdy manhood," it was expected that he would be well soon.

Mary anticipated receiving word of her husband's arrival in Alaska no later than the end of June. He told her that the trip north on a fast schooner would put him on the shores of Kotzebue Sound in less than four weeks. Within two years, they would be wealthy and he could take care of her in the manner she deserved.

Things did not go well for Mary. Three day after the Jane Gray capsized, her forty-five year old brother died, and on May 27, 1898, she was attending the funeral and consoling her sister-in-law, without knowing that she herself was already a widow.

On June 3, 1898, the *Morning Olympian* reported Mary's sorrow:

"Mrs. Charles Williams is prostrate grief at the home of her sister-in-law in this city, Mrs. T. J. McDonald. Just a week ago today she was called to the sad duty of attending the funeral of her brother, T. J. McDonald, whose leave-taking, it will be remembered, was remarkably sudden. The news yesterday imposed upon her a second grief, as it was found that her husband was among the lost in the awful wreck of the Jane Gray, enroute to Kotzebue Sound. She telegraphed to Seattle, only to get a confirmation of the awful truth that had been conveyed in the dispatches. Charles Williams, whose name is included in the list, with residence unknown, proves to have been none other Mrs. Williams husband, and he is one of the thirty-six who certainly perished in the open sea."

Nearly a year later, Mary almost missed the opportunity for an award in the case against MacDougall and Southwick. Judge Hanford set the date for all claimants to appear before the commissioner no later than May 4, 1899. By the time she learned of the court proceedings, the month of August was in full swing.

However, this was not due to a lack of effort on her part. In July of 1898, she had made the sixty-mile trip on the muddy, rut-ridden trail from Olympia to Seattle, Washington, in search of answers. Upon questioning the men at the outfitting firm, it was once again confirmed that her husband had indeed been on board the Jane Gray and was one of the missing. Lawsuits had already been filed by five of the survivors, but the boys at MacDougall and Southwick didn't want any more grief, so they told Mary that they were sorry; there would be no financial compensation for the survivors, widows or heirs.

With that, Mary Williams returned to Olympia and set about finding some means of supporting herself. She soon found work as a laundress in the basement of the Olympia Hotel, washing and pressing the garments of those well off enough to afford such services.

A full year later, in August of 1899, one of Mary's clients, a young lawyer who until recently had not been aware that her husband was one of those lost in the sinking of the Jane Gray, told her of the court proceedings against MacDougall and Southwick in King County Superior Court. He had seen the notice in the Seattle Post-Intelligencer and was following the case as it looked to possibly set a precedent in maritime law. No life preservers, inadequate lifeboats, the ownership of the vessel being in question and a handful of other citations made the wreck and the outcome of the case significant.

On August 10th, after agreeing to represent her, the proctor for Mary Williams made his first appearance, pleading her case for an exception that would allow her claim after the May 4th deadline: "James A. Haight being first duly sworn on his oath saith; that he is proctor for Mary Williams named in application, motion and action herein to attached; that he was on the 5th day of August 1899, requested by the said Mary Williams to investigate the matter of her husband Charles Williams in and by reason of the loss and foundering of the schooner Jane Grey and damage done to her by the death of her husband; that on the following Monday the 7th day of August 1899 deponent went to Seattle to make said investigation and for the first time found that the above entitled cause and proceeding was pending; that on the following day he returned to Olympia Washington and on Wednesday the 9th day of August 1899 deponent notified said Mary Williams of the pendency of this said action and proceedings."

Four days later, Mr. Haight entered two more documents on Mary's behalf. The first was an application to open default, which would allow her to make a proof of claim against Pacey, MacDougall, and Southwick, "all on such terms as to the court may seem just, the undersigned Mary Williams being without money or property or other means to prosecute her said actions."

The second was her affidavit: "Mary Williams being first duly sworn on her oath saith that she is the widow of the late Charles Williams, one of the passengers lost in the foundering of the Jane Grey referred to in the libel and petition herein; that by reason thereof she has and claims to have a claim and cause of action for damages against the libellants and original petitioners; that she has fully and fairly stated the case to James A. Haight her counsel and proctor who resides at Olympia in said state of Washington and that she has a good and substantial defense to said libel and has a cause of action arising from said loss of said schooner Jane Grey and said loss and death of her said husband Charles Williams, as she is advised by her said counsel and proctor, after such statement, and verily believes; that subsequently to said loss and foundering of said schooner Jane Grey and in the month of July 1898 deponent being then a resident of Olympia in said County of Thurston and State of Washington went to Seattle in said state and made personal inquiries of libellants and petitioners the MacDougal & Southwick Company as to the facts connected with the loss of said schooner Jane Grey and the loss in the wreck thereof her said husband Charles Williams; that she was informed by said company that her said husband was a passenger on said Jane Grey at the time the same was wrecked and lost and she was then and there notified that it would be useless and idle for her to bring action on account of the loss and death of her said husband because there would be no recovery thereof; that deponent received no personal notice of this cause and the pendency thereof and as deponent is informed and believes no process has been issued direct to said deponent or served personally on deponent and no attempt has been made to procure issuance of process direct to deponent or to be served upon deponent in said cause and no actual or personal notice to deponent of the pendency of this cause has been given or attempted to be given and that deponent was and has been in utter ignorance of the pendency of this cause until Wednesday the 9th day of August 1899 when she was informed by her counsel and proctor James A. Haight of the pendency of said cause; that deponents leaning of the pendency of this cause due to the fact that on the preceding Saturday the 5th day of August 1899 she requested said James A. Haight to investigate the matters of the loss and death of her husband Charles Williams and advise her whether she had any cause of action by reason thereof; that she read the copy of libel and petition of John G. Pacey, John B. MacDougall, and Henry C. Southwick and MacDougall & Southwick…deponent further says that she was married to said Charles Williams at St. Louis Missouri in May 1897..."

Similar to the widows who had pleaded their cases before her, Mary's affidavit said of her husband and her current circumstances: "during all of his said married life was a kind and indulgent husband and supported his wife in comfort; that he was capable of and did earn during is married life an annual income of one thousand dollars and upwards; that his age at the time of his death was fifty six years…that the deponent has no property save wearing apparel and personal effects and said cause of action; and has no means of support save her own manual labor as laundress and has no property with which to prosecute her said cause of action or furnish security for costs otherwise herein."

Mary and Charles had just celebrated their first wedding anniversary when he departed for Alaska and had no children. She was his only heir, and for damages "including the loss of society and support from the death of her husband," Mary Williams claimed $6000.

Judge Hanford, showing that perhaps compassion still resided within his heart, overruled the objection filed on behalf of Pacey, MacDougall, and Southwick, allowing Mary's claim to be entered against the libellants.

CHAPTER 36 – BAUSMAN'S SCATHING REPORT

Image courtesy of the Seattle Public Library.

Frederick Bausman was a savvy little man. The wit packed into all of his 5′ 3 1/2″ could have filled the body of a man twice his height. Later in his career, it would be said of him that he possessed "enough brain and legal ability to supply three or four ordinary lawyers." During the Jane Gray proceedings, his keen intellect was on full parade.

After conducting his own investigation, the attorney for the claimants, Frederick Bausman, presented his findings to the court on August 26, 1899:

""UNITED STATES DISTRICT COURT

District of Washington

In Re "JANE GRAY"

General Narrative and Statement of the Issues.

Frederick Bausman,

Of Proctors for Cross-libellants.

THE "JANE GRAY"

I.

On the 19th of May, 1898, a schooner left Seattle on the long voyage to Kotzebue Sound. Even in the Straits, it is said without denial, her behavior was cranky (Citing testimony from Crockett and Carlson). Be this as it may, it is admitted that no sooner was the ocean itself reached and Cape Flattery passed, than two things of moment occurred. First, the captain endeavored to put back, and second, he could not do it when he tried. Yet the weather, he admits, was not beyond what was to be then expected in that quarter of the earth, a moderate gale with cross-seas (Witnesses for both sides agree: Crockett, Hanson, Carlson, and Lessey).

Why, then, did he endeavor to put back and why did he not succeed? His passengers, he says, were sea-sick! This is his principal reason. His other reason was that he wanted to stop the hawser hole. (Crockett: his explanation that the passengers were sea-sick seems preposterous. Did he not expect this? How long was he to wait inside? Would they not get sick again? Turn back on this account with several thousand miles to go! As to the hauser holes, there is no attempt to explain why these could not have been plugged at sea. But why did he not get back when he desired? He says the ship would not beat windward, she was tender-sided, cranky, he at length conceded, in fact a better boat would have beaten back (The Captain so admits).

Unable to return this boat went on. She went on ninety miles in all and then went down. This was at two o'clock of the first night at sea, say fourteen hours after her attempt to put back, which occurred in the morning; only ninety miles on an open ocean voyage of several thousand. Had the weather become terrible? No, it was about the same as before (Carlson and Crockett agree on this). Not one green sea had been shipped. A squall of no unusual violence, (Carlson's testimony) a squall with a little rain struck her foresail, which was all the canvas then spread, (Carlson and Lessey presented the same testimony) and in fifteen minutes she went down.

The owners of this boat simply say she must have gone down from some secret defect in her hull. The survivors and the widows of the dead say she went down from above, that she capsized from defects that were obvious. A whaler, built crank as whalers always are, had been made dangerous and her whole purpose as a ship been changed by deckload, by superstructure, by elevated booms, and by a cargo of passengers. Then they add that not a single life preserver or life raft was furnished by the owners, and only two boats that could carry in all less than twenty (The captain admits these boats could carry even fewer than this, four or five each in that sea, about eight each in calm waters) of the sixty-three souls aboard, unless two launches unfitted with row-locks, oars, sail, or motive power, could be called provision for saving life. (The launches were carried for future coast service at Kotzebue.)

The theory of the owners that she sprung a leak is admittedly only a guess. They do not assert that there is any actual testimony to it, but contend that it is the only remaining explanation of the calamity, because the theory of the libellants, though indeed supported by testimony is untenable. But, while they maintain that she must have sprung a leak, it is they themselves that prove and insist that she left port only two days before with a sound and well inspected hull. At the time of her sinking she had been less than one day on open sea.

Now, there was some cause or other for this vessel's going down. That a ship should capsize from deck-load, superstructure, and passengers when she was never built to carry any one of them, and certainly not all at once, is, to say the least, as probable as that she should spring a leak just forty-five miles from the coast in seas only moderately rough, and after having been examined and found staunch just two days before. Of two contentions equally plausible is the Court to reject that which has testimony to support it, and adopt that which is not only without actual testimony, but is at war with the very testimony of those who advance it?

These owners, moreover, have not only shown that the hull was sound, but they have shown that there were pumps, which, in the event of a leak, could have proved the presence of water. Now, were these pumps in good condition? They were shown to be so before the boat left Seattle. Nay, they were actually in such condition at the time of the wreck, for at twelve o'clock (Hanson, the mate, applied the pumps at twelve o'clock before going below and got only a few buckets) and at one o'clock and just before the squall (testimony of Carlson) they were applied (Three mariners have testified that were in the wreck, Crockett, the captain, and Hanson, the mate, for the owners, and Carlson, a seaman on watch at the time, for the libellants. There is not one circumstance of the slightest moment in which they disagree). That they were in working condition is shown by the fact that they did bring up a little water, that there was no leak is shown by the fact that they brought up no more. These things are undisputed.

Thus the owners' theory, as we have said, is a guess. The other theory, though, rests on many facts and much testimony (Livingood. There was not spot to step in between cabins: Carlson and Blackwell). The boat, to begin with, was a whaler only 82 feet long, round bottomed and tender sided or crank, as such vessels are designed to be. She had a deck load varying, according to estimates, between ten and thirty-five tons, sufficient at any rate to fill her decks as high as the bulwarks from the forward to the after house (Hanson testimony). This forward house, as broad as the ship itself, and eighteen feet in length, was a new superstructure on the little whaler. Yet upon this, too, and upon the after house fresh load was placed, so that even the booms had to be raised two or three feet on both masts. The result was that, as she stood even in the quiet bay, ready to sail, a sheathing on her bow, carried to protect her as a whaler from floating ice and intended to project above the water line, was submerged two or three inches below it (Field. Their own witness. To this I see no attempt at contradiction). Sixty-three persons were then added to the deck load.

This boat, the libellants contend, had to sink. Let her reach the open sea and she must soon capsize. She behaved queerly even in the Straits, just out of them the captain tried to put back, twelve hours or the like later there comes a little squall and she goes down—down in less than twenty minutes, when it is clearly proved that from a leak it would require from one hour to three hours to fill, (Burns - this is the uniform testimony) and that she went down on her beam, when from a leak she would have settled straight (Crockett).

This ship capsized. There is no other explanation consistent with the testimony.

II.

THE ISSUES.

Of the four petitioners three deny that they were owners or had anything to do with the boat. They nevertheless seek to get the benefit of two Federal limitation statutes, the first of which in the plainest language extends its benefits only to "owners." These two acts, are that of 1851, (Rev. Stats. 4283) and the "Harter Act" of 1893 (The Harter Act expressly refrains from any repeal of the Act of 1851).

The first of these acts applies to all sorts of claims against ships or their owners, the latter only to claims affecting cargo. (The Viola 59 Fed. 632, Botany Mills vs. Knott, 76 Fed. 582).

The cross-libellants have prayed for in personam remedy against the petitioners on account of personal injuries, deaths and loss of goods.

The petitioner, while denying the ownership, which would entitle them to any benefits under the Act of 1851, have enjoyed its provisions already so far as to stop all suits against them and gain that inestimable time which scatters witnesses and discouraged pursuit. The purposes of the cross-libellants is two fold—to hold them owners and owners in fault, or if not owners at all and so not entitled to enjoy the statute, then in person and for the whole liability. We believe it would be unconscionable that they should now slip out of admiralty entirely after having both invited its shield and in part enjoyed its stay.

III.

WHO WERE THE OWNERS.

Let us next examine who were owning or, at any rate, operating this craft. On this point we do not think it necessary to dwell. The petitioners' defense is that this boat was owned by a man named Pacey only. The business relations of Pacey, however, with all the petitioners were as intimate as can possibly be imagined. Of the petitioner McDougall & Southwick Company Pacey was a trustee and the secretary, and he participated actively in the councils of the corporation. When Pacey purchased the boat he consulted the company's president, McDougall, when the boat was paid for McDougall carried the check, the money which Pacey in part borrowed to pay for the boat obtained upon a note upon which McDougall became surety and of the operations of Pacey in connection with the boat McDougall was kept advised. (Pacey's inability to remember whose name was first upon this note of $3000.00 is one of the most significant little circumstances in this branch of the case. He is either testifying untruly or the venture was joint and no feeling of principal and surety existed to impress on his mind a favor like that. He did not pay the note until after he collected the Jane Gray's insurance which, being after a question of liability and ownership had been raised, ought to have impressed the thing on his memory. McDougall, testifying later than Pacey, says he was the surety. The note is not produced. Pacey says he does not know what he did with it.)""

(Fredrick Bausman's handwritten note at the bottom of the page reads: "McDougall says he himself destroyed it. They lost it, it may be, for lawsuits were impending. It seems hard to believe that a businessman would destroy this note, under such circumstances, if it was favorable to him on its face.")

"By their own story McDougall and Pacey with Southwick, he remaining trustee of the corporation, had a partnership in which another, named Shultze, was included, in the outfitting business. This outfitting business was carried on in the very basement of the store of the company. The company itself had part of the stock of outfitters' goods in the basement. The outfitting company paid no rent to the company, but paid the advertising as its share of expenses. Of this partnership there were no articles of agreement, they say, nor is a single book produced, and as McDougall, Southwick, and Pacey are all seeking to escape the liability here, it is noticeable that the disinterested testimony of the other partner, Shultze, is not produced or accounted for, so there is no other evidence whatever of this partnership than the testimony of these interested persons, unsupported by a scrap of paper of any kind (The existence of this partnership, or of their being a distinct business concern of some sort below stairs might have been incidentally proved by separate bill heads or separate advertisements in the name of the concern. But there appears nothing of the kind. It is hard not to believe that this was simply another department of a large store having many others)."

"Even the outfitting partnership, it is claimed by them, did not own the vessel. Pacey, however, is impecunious, not carrying his bank account in his own name, or owning any of the shares of stock in the Company which he served as trustee. That the petitioners now under peril of a heavy liability are today denying all connection with this boat is true. But it is abundantly proved that she was advertised in the name of McDougall & Southwick Company broadcast in newspapers and placards. (The Court will notice libellant's exhibit--, a large photograph of the vessel. At the top of this photograph may be discovered the lower margin of a large canvas sign spread across the ship and bearing the words "McDougall and Southwick Company.") This was done with the previous knowledge of every trustee of the Company, by previous arrangement, and of the express profit expected and realized from selling goods to those who were also to become passengers (Pacey, Southwick and McDougall agreed on advertising her in the Company's name some time before. Southwick afterwards in New York took the "P.I." regularly for the express purpose of watching the company's advertisements, and these he saw. It is also noticeable that the pecuniary benefits from advertising in the Company's name were not general and remote. They were immediate. Most of the voyagers bought their outfits there). It is noticeable that checks were made by persons outfitting and going on this voyage payable to the order of the McDougall and Southwick Company and that these checks bear their endorsement. Nor did the Company at first repudiate liability when the claimants presented themselves."

"Against the abundant proofs of intimacy, joint interest and profitable arrangement resulting from the blending of the business of the ship with the business of the house, we have nothing but the testimony of the three interested persons unsupported by many natural proofs, which we think would be in their possession, but which have not been produced. The Court in passing upon the credibility of these witnesses must judge how much credence to give to the witness Pacey, who has unblushingly admitted that in advertising to the public he gives his imagination free rein, and the witness Southwick, whose peculiarly cold-blooded view of the disaster and whose contemptuous and very impatient treatment of the forlorn and ragged band of survivors will undoubtedly impress the Court with the belief that in anything which affected his purse this man would feel himself practically at liberty to tell things as he pleased. Nor can the Court fail to estimate severely the capacity for truth of business men who coolly avow that their intimate relations with Pacey were formed for "working" these people "both ways" and getting a double "whack," at them. Many of them without hats, many without shoes, all half naked, the band of survivors returned to walk through the streets of a city perhaps most thriving in the world. They went to one of its most prosperous houses of trade. All that they had was the bottom of the sea together with many hopeful expectations, and what they had parted with to buy that little all was, in most instances, in the pockets of the well clothed, well fed, successful men whom they addressed and who had sent them out in the crowded bark without even a life preserver. They were will to accept a mere hundred dollars apiece and a suit of clothes. But the owner, though sure of the good insurance on the boat, soon repented of giving encouragement; found something to get angry about; talked of charity; pew rent saved, and wished them back in their overalls again (The occurrences on the return are substantially the same as reported by all. Blackwell's story of the contemptuous "pew rent" is admitted by Southwick. His story of the heartless acceptance from him them of $18.50 which he had the spirit to offer the company, when he refused its charity, is also admitted. We mention this because by mistake of counsel arising from confusion of the names of the two Livengoods he was accused of a direct profit at the expense of one of his partners. The true state of things is found in Silas Livengood. It was this same Blackwell who divided his clothing with his half frozen companions in that terrible shipwreck during a day and a half of the cold spring winds of the North Pacific. He little deserves the censure imposed).

One thing is to be particularly noticed. Even if the Court should find that nobody but Pacey owned the ship, it certainly must find under the same testimony that these people were at least operators. I call particular attention to this point. If the Court should find that they are liable as operators, and that, as they contend themselves, they are not owners, they cannot get the benefit, we think, of the Federal statute of limitations. On the other hand, they having come into a Court of Admiralty denying that they are the owners, and yet inviting a settlement of the controversy, the Court, should it find them liable at least as operators, can surely assess against them as respondents under the cross-libel, the full award. Thus, if the finding of the Court should be what the petitioners contend for, that they are not owners, we think they are involved in a great difficulty as ever.

IV.

IS THE NEGLIGENCE CHARGEABLE TO THE OWNERS?

That the ship went out in an unseaworthy condition, that is to say, overloaded, or was so changed in her character as to be unfit for a voyage of several thousand miles with passengers, is to us abundantly clear from the testimony. Supposing this to be so, is the owner to be held liable for this, or is it a condition of things which he can charge to those by him employed?"

(Bausman's handwritten note at the bottom of the page: "McDougall voluntarily called themselves 'operators' of the craft. Then he withdrew it on apparently perceiving how well it supported libellants constructions of the facts.")

"In settling this question we do not think it necessary to go into a nice discussion as to the exact number of tons aboard a boat, or as to the exact distribution of the cargo. These technical points may or may not be important. We regard them as superfluous. A certain condition of things existed here beyond doubt; that the whole character of the ship was changed; her whole purpose diverted. Now, whether or not the owner may be liable for a nice distribution of cargo we need not discuss. One thing is certain, he is liable for a knowledge of the general capacity and nature of his ship. We believe it to be the law that an owner must know how many tons of freight his vessel will carry, while he may delegate to the captain the distribution of it. We do not, however, believe it to be the law that an owner may sit by and plead ignorance of the fact that he has changed a whaler into a passenger carrier; that he has put on her, in addition to the passengers, at least all she can hold in freight; that he has put a superstructure upon her, and that he has had her booms raised. Pacey admits that he knew the boat's character. The rest he must have known, even without going to the dock. But he admits more. He admits that as often as twice a day he would go to the dock so that he must have been cognizant of the way in which she was loaded. The law will presume him to have been acquainted with the changes made upon the vessel and with her general character to begin with; he admits, however, that he knew these things, and he admits also that he saw the loading and by his orders contributed to the placing of cargo upon her. The Court is accordingly called upon to decide:

FIRST, the broad proposition of whether an owner can under the statute, get a limitation of liability when he has diverted a boat from her original purpose, placed a deck load upon a boat never intended to carry one, placed a superstructure where there was none before, elevated her booms, and filled her, a comparatively small craft indeed, with sixty-three souls.

SECOND, if the first not be enough, whether he does not assume the risks of overloading a ship in her proper line of business and is to be held chargeable for an overload, even if he does not see it, on the theory of his always knowing the capacity of his ship.

THIRD, whether he does not assume liability for the manner and extent of the load when he personally frequents the dock, the statute being probably intended to protect those owners who act only through agents.

The first proposition, we think, will be found decisive, and the others will not require opinion.

May he do this and then may he leave behind life preservers and send her out without boats adequate for even half those on board? This question would seem to require a fatal negative.

Other briefs detailing both facts and citations will be filed in type-writing. It was thought useful to file with the court this printed summary.

FREDERICK BAUSMAN,

Of Proctors for Cross-libellants."

CHAPTER 37 - HANFORD ISSUES HIS OPINION

Frederick Bausman's analysis of the wreck may have rubbed Judge Hanford the wrong way. Particularly since Hanford considered himself to be of superior analytical thought. His favorite cases were those that required a mathematical or mechanical aptitude. In this he felt that his ability was unmatched. And he was not fond of anyone who might consider himself intelligent enough to challenge his rationale in such cases.

In addition, agreeing with Bausman's assessment of the sinking could have had a negative impact on Seattle's thriving shipping business. Then there was the huge public outcry for justice for the victims to consider. When Hanford issued his opinion, it seems clear that he believed that he had come to an equitable solution.

~~~

January 17, 1899:

"OPINION

HANFORD, District Judge:

Mr. John G. Pacey, as owner of the American schooner, Jane Gray, which foundered at sea on the morning of June 22, 1898, and certain of his business associates, commenced this proceeding in this court, pursuant to the provisions of the statutes limiting the liability of owners of vessels for damages resulting from marine disasters. In their petition they aver that the Jane Gray filled with water and sank in
~~~

the Pacific Ocean and became a total loss, and that thirty-four of the passengers and three of the crew on board were drowned and that "said accident happened, and the loss, damage, injury, and destruction above set forth, were occasioned, done, and incurred without fault or privity or knowledge of your petitioners, or any of them, and was due solely to the perils of the sea." The petition also avers as the reason for joining other persons with the owner of the schooner in the petition, that a number of actions to recover damages have been commenced, in which all the petitioners are charged as being joint owners of the Jane Gray, and jointly liable for damages alleged to have been sustained. The object of the petitioners in this proceeding, is to obtain an injunction to prevent the prosecution of the several damage suits which have been commenced as aforesaid, and to have a decree declaring the petitioners to be entirely exempt from all liability, or if the court shall determine, that any legal liability exists, to render compensation for losses or injuries on account of said disaster, that the petitioners and each of them, after paying into court for the benefit of persons entitled to such compensation the amount of pending freight, may be exempted from further liability. Pursuant to the rules governing such proceedings the court appointed an appraiser, who, after receiving the evidence, ascertained and reported to the court that the amount of pending freight for the voyage was the sum of $4,392.18, that being the gross amount of freight and passage money for the voyage, and in his report to the court said appraiser shows that he refused to make any deductions for expenditures in supplying and equipping the vessel for the voyage, and for wages paid to the captain and crew. The petitioners filed exceptions to said report, and without waiving the same, filed a stipulation by which they became bound to pay said amount into court whenever the court shall so order. Six of the surviving passengers and the widows and heirs of several whose lives were lost, have appeared in opposition to the petition, and have filed cross libels in which they charge that the disaster and consequent losses of life and property and personal injuries were occasioned by the wrongful conduct of the petitioners in knowingly sending the Jane Gray on said voyage when she was rotten, weak, and unseaworthy, and without boats or equipment necessary for the safety of her passengers, and very much overloaded, and each of said cross libellants prays for a decree against said petitioners jointly for full damages and costs. The court has heretofore overruled exceptions to the several cross libels, in which damages are demanded for lives lost, (see 95 Fed. Rep. 693,) and since said ruling, a large amount of testimony has been taken relative to the facts of the disaster, and the condition and appearance of the vessel, the nature and quantity of her cargo, and the manner in which it was stowed, and the case has been argued and submitted upon the questions raised by the pleadings, which are,

First, whether the petitioners, other than Mr. Pacey, are liable as owners.

Second, whether the loss of the vessel and the resulting injury happened in consequence of any fault in the vessel, or neglect of duty on the part of her owners, master or crew.

Third, whether the losses and injuries were occasioned or incurred without the privity or knowledge of the owner or owners, within the meaning of the terms used in Sec. 4283 U. S. R. S., which reads as follows:

"Sec. 4283. The liability of the owner of any vessel, for any embezzlement, loss, or destruction, by any person, of any property, goods, or merchandise, shipped or put on board of such vessel, or for any loss, damage, or injury by collision, or for any act, matter, or thing, lost, damage, or forfeiture, done, occasioned, or incurred without the privity or knowledge of such owner or owners, shall in no case exceed the amount or value of the interest of such owner in such vessel, and her freight then pending."

Fourth, whether the owner or owners exercised due diligence before the Jane Gray started on her voyage to make said vessel in all respects seaworthy, and properly manned, equipped and supplied within the meaning of the terms used in the third section of the act of congress, commonly called the Harter Act, 2 Supp. R. S. U. S. 81, which reads as follows:

"Sec. 3. That if the owner of any vessel transporting merchandise or property to or from any port in the United States of America shall exercise due diligence to make the said vessel in all respects seaworthy and properly manned, equipped, and supplied, neither the vessel, her owner or owners, agent, or charterers shall become or be held responsible for damage or loss resulting from faults or errors in navigation or in the management of said vessel nor shall the vessel, her owner or owners, charterers, agent, or master be held liable for losses arising from dangers of the sea or other navigable waters, acts of God, or public enemies, or the inherent defect, quality, or vice of the thing carried, or from insufficiency of package, or seizure under legal process, or for loss resulting form any act or omission of the shipper or owner of the goods, his agent or representative, or from saving or attempting to save life or property at sea, or from any deviation in rendering such service."

Fifth, if there is any legal liability, and if the owner or owners are entitled to benefit of the limitations prescribed by the statutes, whether any deductions shall be made form the gross amount of freight and passage money for the voyage on account of the expense of the voyage.

1. It is certainly established by a fair preponderance of the evidence, that Mr. Pacey was, in law and in fact, the sole owner of the Jane Gray. Mr. Pacey was, however, a stock holder, trustee and one of the managing officers of a mercantile corporation, and with his knowledge and consent and the knowledge and consent of the other trustees and managing officers, said corporation advertised extensively through the daily newspapers and other mediums and by a sign conspicuously displayed on the rigging of the Jane Gray while she was at the dock receiving her cargo, at and before the time of the sale of passage tickets to the passengers who went upon her, that said corporation was operating said vessel, and would dispatch her as a carrier of freight and passengers from Seattle to Kotzebue Sound. The evidence is direct and positive that the corporation did not in fact control the operation of the vessel and was not interested in the venture, and that the representations made to the public by means of said advertisements were merely intended to attract public attention to the corporation as a dealer handling large stocks of general merchandise. The advertisements certainly were calculated to influence people to take passage on the Jane Gray, in preference to other vessels bound from Kotzebue Sound, and it may be presumed that all of her passengers were to some extent influenced, as they would naturally be, upon being

solicited by or on behalf of a large and flourishing business house, and it is therefore too late, after sending the vessel upon the very voyage which she was advertised to make, with a large company of passengers who were thus influenced too go upon her, for the advertiser to change to a more favorable position with respect to its liability, by offering true information at variance with representations previously made. I hold therefore, that the corporation is estopped and it cannot be permitted to dispute liability as an owner of he vessel for the voyage. There is no evidence upon which to base a finding that the other petitioners were as individuals, interested in the venture, nor that any of the passengers were induced to go on the Jane Gray by any representations from which it might have been inferred that said petitioners were individually responsible in any way for the operation of the vessel, therefore, Mr. MacDougall and Mr. Southwick are entitled to have a decree exempting them from personal liability."

~~~

In Bausman's analysis of the wreck, he stated, in regards to ownership of the vessel, "on this point we do not think it is necessary to dwell." However, for Hanford to state that MacDougall and Southwick had no control of the operation, nor had any interest in the venture, contradicted the testimony of all who had any dealings with John Pacey, MacDougall, or Southwick. Pacey never made a move without playing "good cop, bad cop" with MacDougall. And voluminous evidence demonstrated that the MacDougall and Southwick Company controlled the purse strings - without their bank accounts, Pacey couldn't even write a check in his own name. While Hanford held the corporation liable as owners, he contended that John MacDougall and Henry Southwick were not personally
~~~

involved in the operation of the Jane Gray, nor did they profit from it personally.

Bausman's primary objective was to have the limitation plea dismissed by reasoning that operators and charterer's are not eligible for the rights of limitation afforded vessel owners. His second objective was to prove that the ship was knowingly sent out to sea overloaded, making ownership a moot point.

~~~

Hanford's opinion continued:

"2. The cause of the loss of the Jane Gray cannot be determined with certainty, probably the truth as to the cause of the disaster will never be known until the great ocean shall reveal the secrets buried in its depths. The vessel was comparatively new, and yet she had made long voyages from the Atlantic to the Pacific ocean, had crossed the Pacific, and had navigated the Arctic seas in the business of whaling, for which she was built, so that by actual service she had proved to be staunch, strong and seaworthy. In the month of March 1898, she was docked at San Francisco and was newly calked and painted, and at the same time she was inspected by two competent marine surveyors representing different insurance companies who found her to be sound and in good condition, and each made a report upon her to that effect. Upon her arrival at Seattle, she was examined by a ship builder employed for that purpose by Mr. Pacey, who relied upon his report that she was sound and in good condition, in completing his purchase of her. Just previous to being dispatched on her last voyage, she was overhauled generally and equipped for the voyage under the direction of a captain who was reputed to be a man of experience and good judgment, and
~~~

who according to the undisputed testimony was allowed to have everything done to fit her for her contemplated voyage, that he deemed necessary. According to the undisputed evidence the cargo which consisted of coal, flour, lumber, miners' implements, provisions, and miners' outfits and some machinery, was carefully stowed under the captain's directions, by the mate and crew, who were competent for that work. Besides her freight, there was placed in the bottom of her hold, 40 to 50 tons of rock ballast, which was planked over and made secure. The cargo placed on top of this flooring was sufficient to fill the space to her deck beams; there was also in the hold two large water tanks resting upon the bottom, which contained 1200 gallons of water. The vessel had capacity to carry 160 tons of freight, but on this voyage her whole burden, including passengers, crew, stores, water, cargo, ballast, and a new house built for the accommodation of passengers on the forward part of her main deck, did not exceed 140 tons less than 20 tons of which was above her deck. She was also inspected by two experienced mariners at the instance of passengers who must have been encouraged by the reports made to them, for they trusted their lives and property to her seaworthiness by going upon the voyage in her."

~~~

The holes in Hanford's statements were huge. None of his figures matched the testimony of numerous witnesses. While it was true that multiple individuals surveyed the Jane Gray, all did so prior to completion of the forward deckhouse, the raising of the main mast boom, and the loading of freight, passengers, and baggage. And even if the judge added the enclosed space of the new forward cabin to her net registered tonnage of 107.07, (which would
~~~

have violated the rules of measurement being defined by enclosed spaces within her hull) her total tonnage would have been approximately 130, not 160. Other erroneous factors appeared as the judge moved on through the case:

~~~

"The Jane Gray was designed for a whaler. Her model was medium sharp below the water line, but she was tender sided, that is, intended to roll easily to facilitate the work of hoisting on board whale blubber from the sea; her natural crankiness was increased by her deck load and the new house, but she was not top heavy. The deck load consisted of two steam launches placed upon her quarter-deck, the weight of which, with the machinery therein, amounted in aggregate to a little less than one-half tons; one ton of coal and a boiler weighing about one-half ton; and one crate of cabbage weighing 100 lbs., all of which were place on the main deck amidship, or nearly so; one ship's boat hung on the davits at the stern; and on top of the forward house one ship's boat, a dory and lumber and materials for four other boats, weighing in aggregate of less than half a ton; two cases of coal oil weighing about 100 lbs., 600 lbs. of fresh beef, a circular saw, and odd pieces of machinery and gas pipe, all of which was only of trifling consequence as regards its effect either as to weight or bulk. The bulwarks were built up about 3-1/2 feet high above the deck, and the forward cabin was extended about 3-1/2 feet above the top of he bulwarks. The after cabin was the usual construction, that is to say, the floor was below the level of the main deck and the roof formed a poop deck. Considering all the testimony as to the construction of the vessel and the manner in which she was ballasted and stowed, it is clear that while she would roll easily, she ought not to have capsized. If she was listed
~~~

over by pressure of the wind upon her sails, or by the force of the sea striking her, she ought to have righted up again easily, unless she was held down by the wind upon her sails, or her cargo shifted. If her cargo or ballast moved, the captain, mate and others of the survivors whose testimony has been taken, failed to hear any sound or feel any jar indicating such an occurrence. The evidence is equally convincing that the Jane Gray was staunch and sound, her pump was in good working order and was tried regularly every hour during the night before she foundered, without showing any indication that she was leaking. In an open sea, without any injury to her hull, a vessel in her condition ought not to have suddenly opened her seams and become water-logged, and if she did, she would naturally sink straight down, instead of laying over on her side."

~~~

Almost unbelievably, Judge Hanford glossed over Frederick Bausman's contention, in regards to the owner's knowledge, that "He is liable for the general capacity and nature of his ship. We believe it to be the law that an owner must know how many tons of freight his vessel will carry, while he may delegate to the captain the distribution of it." And Pacey had already admitted that he knew the boat's character and that she would roll easily.

In his report, Bausman missed an opportunity to call other factors to light. The new deckhouse, spanning the full width of the ship, eighteen feet in length – fore to aft, and seven feet high, would have acted as a new, unmanageable sail. In addition, on the night before the wreck, all of the men in the forward cabin had abandoned the lower berths. Their gear and forty-some bodies, now placed high off the deck against the outboard walls, changed the entire center
~~~

of gravity of the Jane Gray. All of the soaking wet coal and merchandise on deck likely complicated matters. One stiff breeze and the schooner's "tender-sided" nature would have made her resemble one of those drinking birds, her masts bouncing toward the waves like beaks in search of water.

And when Hanford stated that the cargo couldn't have shifted, that no one was reported "to hear any sound or feel any jar indicating such an occurrence," he blew off William Weaver's testimony that stated: "About ten o'clock Saturday night I was so sick that I could not sit in my chair and was thrown across the cabin several times by the violent lurching of the vessel." Charles Chard had to help him into his bunk and corroborated his story. While Hanford's assessment that she did not spring a leak from below was correct, he went on with more contradictory findings.

~~~

"As to what did actually happen, the testimony shows that, after being towed from Seattle to Port Townsend, the Jane Gray sailed down the straits of Fuca and out to sea, passing Cape Flattery on the morning of Saturday, May 21st, with a stiff sailing breeze or moderate gale drawing out of the straits, and encountered a heavy sea rolling in. With the wind and sea coming from opposite directions she labored heavily, but proved her seaworthiness by riding the waves successfully. The waves did not break over her, as only a dead swell was rolling, but a great deal of water came upon her deck through the hawse pipes, scuppers and seams of her bulwarks, flooding the passenger cabin situated on the forward part of her main deck. Finding that the lower bunks in that cabin were flooded, the captain put the vessel on a course before the
~~~

wind, so that she would come up level, and then stopped her hawse pipes, but as the water still came in through the bulwarks he attempted to beat his way back to Neah Bay, intending to wait for better weather and caulk the bulwarks but the vessel was unable to make headway towards Neah Bay because the wind was averse, and on account of crankiness, the vessel would not lay up when close hauled, so as to sail windward. After several hours of fruitless efforts, the attempt to run back to Neah Bay was abandoned and the vessel was again turned upon her course, steering west—southwest, and she continued on that course until 8 o'clock in the evening; at that time as the vessel was laboring heavily and most of the passengers were sick, the captain decided to heave to, all sails were taken in except her foresail and she was headed to the wind. Leaving the vessel in that position the captain went to bed at 9 o'clock and did not come on deck again until a few minutes before the vessel went down, about 2 o'clock the next morning. The mate was on watch from 8 o'clock until 12 o'clock, when he also retired, leaving only two seamen on deck. The conditions as to the wind and sea, and the action of the vessel continued about the same until about 1:30 o'clock on the morning of the 22nd, at which time, according to the testimony of seaman Carlson, the only man on deck who has survived to tell of the occurrence, the vessel was heading south—southwest, when a squall came from the southeast which caused her to list over on her starboard side; Carlson strapped the wheel to keep it steady and went forward and lowered the peak of the foresail, but instead of righting herself, the vessel lay dead in the water. According to the mate's testimony, he was awakened about this time by the cook who informed him that water was coming in the door of the after cabin, and the first thing he did was get up and shut the door, then he seemed to realize that something was wrong and he went on deck and ordered one of the seamen to "hard up his helm," and then he called the captain. According to the captain's testimony, when he came on deck the vessel was laying over with her lee rail under water; he at once called all hands on deck and ordered the foresail lowered, and it was lowered very quickly; he next ordered the men to set the forestaysail and that was done, still the vessel did not lift nor respond to her helm, but gradually settled in the water. The captain then ordered the men to set the jib, and in attempting to obey this order the halyard parted; by this time the captain realized that the vessel was lost and he ordered the boats cut loose and made what efforts he could to save the lives of the people on board. The vessel never straightened up, but continued listing more and more starboard, settling gradually so that when last observed by the witnesses, her topmasts were bobbing up and down in the water. She went out of sight in about ten minutes after the captain gave the order to cut the boats loose. Twenty-seven of those on board saved themselves by getting into one of the steam launches, which was not provided with oars, row-locks or other means of propulsion, but by means of paddles which they made out of pieces of lumber which they picked up, and an improvised sail made out of a piece of canvas found in the boat, they finally made their way to the shore of Vancouver Island."

~~~

When Hanford cited Crockett's testimony, it was not that of the captain of the ship, but the word of John Pacey. All who were on board, and survived, told the same story – water was washing over the bulwarks, flooding the decks and the forward cabin from the moment they left the
~~~

Straits. When the captain attempted to turn back to Neah Bay, not a single witness mentioned that he was "intending to wait for better weather and caulk the bulwarks." The Judge had clearly already made a decision and continued:

~~~

"The argument made on behalf of the petitioners is based upon the theory that the heavy cross seas which the Jane Gray encountered, strained her timbers so as to cause a large opening to be made in her planking below deck, so that she filled with water rapidly, and that her loss is due to that cause. This theory is inconsistent with the testimony showing that the vessel was staunch, sound and newly calked, and also inconsistent with the fact that she did not go straight down, but laid over on her side which a vessel loaded and ballasted as she was, would not have done if she had become waterlogged through and opening below her deck. The theory of the cross libellants is that the vessel was capsized by reason of having insufficient ballast, and being loaded on deck so as to make her top-heavy. Against this theory we have convincing evidence that the vessel was well ballasted, she was not over-loaded on deck, and she successfully buffeted with wind and sea for nearly twenty-four hours without being capsized, and in the end she did not capsize, nor behave like a top-heavy vessel, but merely listed over when the squall struck her, then gradually settled down as a vessel would if she were knocked over and pressed down until she filled with water through the openings in the deck. The theory which seems to me to be best supported by evidence, is that the Jane Gray was lost because of negligence and bad seamanship of her captain and crew. When she was hove to, instead of taking in her large foresail, and setting her forestaysail,
~~~

sheeted on one side and her jib the opposite way, so as to hold her steadily with her head to the wind, all the head sails and the mainsail were taken in and she was left drifting without steerage way and with only one sail—the foresail. If the testimony of the seaman Carlson is accepted as true—and there is nothing against it, except that in other respects his testimony is not accurate, the vessel was struck by a squall from the southeast when she was heading south—southwest with her foresail close hauled. With a vessel in that position, the wind coming abeam would naturally do what was done to the Jane Gray, that is, lay her over on her starboard side and hold her down. The wind would not be so directly abeam as to give her any headway, on the contrary, it would set her back so that her helm would not be of any assistance in righting her. It certainly was not vigilance on the part of the captain for him to go to bed at 9 o'clock the first night at sea in heavy weather, trusting the vessel so entirely to the care of his mate and seamen; and he was unreasonably slow in getting out of the cabin after the squall struck. It is probable that before his first order to lower the foresail could be executed, the vessel was down so that the sea rushed into her after cabin door and that the weight of the water flowing in held her down after she had been relieved from the pressure of the wind on her foresail; This supposition is supported by the testimony of Mr. Livingood, a passenger who had a bunk in the after cabin, who testifies that before he came out of the cabin he was standing in water up above his knees considerably, and that the water was rushing in. In giving his testimony on cross examination, the captain at first stated that the vessel filled through her cabin, but immediately afterwards in answer to a leading question he stated that it is now his opinion that she filled from below and that he always thought so. It is not unlikely that this captain would assent to any theory which would relieve him from responsibility for losing the vessel by bad seamanship."

"According to all the testimony, there was only a moderate gale of wind, and although the waves were rolling high, they were not breaking, and the sea did not at any time break over the vessel, so her loss cannot be attributed to extreme severity of a storm, which a vessel in seaworthy condition and handled by her officers and crew with ordinary good seamanship, should not have overcome, therefore, whether we adopt the theory that the vessel was lost by reason of a defect in the planking or timbers which caused an opening and let the sea in below her deck, or the theory that she rolled over because she did not have sufficient ballast, and was loaded on deck so as to make her top-heavy, or the most plausible one of all, that is, that the disaster is due to want of vigilance, or blundering on the part of the captain and crew, we are lead to the same conclusion, and that is, that there was some fault in the vessel, or on the part of those in charge of her, and by reason of that fault, whatever it may be, the injured passengers who have survived, and the wives and children of those who are lost, have a legal claim for compensation."

~~~

While there was an undeniable question as to the vigilance of the captain and crew, stating that the Jane Gray "was well ballasted, she was not over-loaded on deck" seems absurd. From deck to keel, the ship drafted just over nine feet. In addition to the new seven-foot high cabin, her forward bulwarks had been raised three and a half feet. And on top of her all manner of iron, lumber, boats and goods were stacked. Anything that might have been fouled
~~~

by salt water, as in the tons of flour, dry goods, and bacon, was stored below deck. And, Judge Hanford based most of his conclusions about the captain on the testimony of John Pacey, who certainly had the most to gain by the ruling that the captain and crew were incompetent, thereby relieving him of all responsibility.

~~~

"3. The evidence is direct and positive to the effect that neither Mr. Pacey, nor any of the managing officers of the MacDougall & Southwick Co. knew or had reason to suspect that the vessel was not as she appeared to be, that is, sound and seaworthy throughout, properly ballasted, stowed, equipped and manned for the voyage; they do not know what caused the disaster, and they cannot be blamed for not knowing, because after studying the voluminous testimony, and giving due heed to the arguments of counsel, and considering all the facts brought to my attention, I do not know what caused the disaster, and the witnesses do not pretend to know. In the argument, the owners are censured for neglecting to provide life boats, rafts and life preservers. I find from the evidence that it would have been nearly if not quite impossible for the Jane Gray to have carried a better supply of boats. It is true that the two launches were owned by passengers, but the objection to their being considered part of the equipment of the vessel for the voyage, is a mere quibble, as a matter of fact the survivors who were actually rescued by the use of one of these steam launches, did not at the time of extreme peril, stop to inquire who owned the boat, nor refuse to seek safety in her because she had not been provided by the owners of the Jane Gray, specifically for use as a life boat. The seaman Carlson testifies that the ship's boats were in such a bad condition as to be unfit for
~~~

use, but he is contradicted in this regard by other witnesses, and his testimony in other respects is certainly inaccurate, for instance, he fixes the day of departure of the Jane Gray from Seattle on Tuesday, and says that she sailed out of the straits the following Saturday night, and that she went down on Monday morning, whilst the truth is, she left Seattle Thursday, sailed out of the straits Saturday morning and went down on Sunday morning; and again, he testifies that the captain was on deck one hour before the vessel began to sink, while it is proved by all the other testimony bearing on the point, including the captain's own admissions, that he went to bed at nine o'clock and did not again come out of the cabin until the vessel was in a helpless condition. I therefore reject the testimony of Mr. Carlson as to the condition of the boats. If there was any neglect to furnish boats with oars and row locks, that is a mere matter of detail in the manner of the use of the equipments which were furnished by the owners; the testimony shows that there was plenty of oars on board the schooner, and row locks, if they were not placed convenient for use in and emergency, the captain and crew alone are to blame for such neglect. With the boards and materials for boat construction which was loose on top of the forward house, and which afloat, was just as useful as life rafts, any additional floating structures would have been a useless encumbrance. An act of congress requires all steam vessels employed in carrying passengers, to keep on board and accessible a supply of life preservers, just why this should be required of steam vessels and not be applicable to sailing vessels engaged in carrying passengers, I do not know, but congress has discriminated and has failed to enact a law requiring sailing vessels to carry life preservers. The testimony shows also that it is not customary for sailing vessels to carry life preservers. In view of these facts, it would be unfair and contrary to the spirit of the law to deprive the owners of the benefit of the statute for failure to supply the vessel with life preservers. Knowledge of a defect in the equipment of the vessel in this respect cannot be imputed to them, when neither the statute nor custom requires sailing vessels to carry life preservers as a part of the equipment necessary to fit them for service as carriers of passengers. I consider that for the safety of her passengers the vessel ought to have carried sufficient number of life preservers and her captain should have made a requisition for them, although there is no statutory requirement, but as the owners depended upon the captain to see that the equipment of the vessel for the voyage was complete in every particular, they are exempt from personal liability for his neglect in this regard the same as they are exempt from liability for his conduct in permitting the vessel to go adrift on a stormy night with only two sailors on watch."

"It is my conclusion that, the loss of the vessel occurred without privity or knowledge of her owner or of the managing officers of said corporation, and having stipulated to pay the amount of pending freight, according to the report of the appraiser appointed by this court, they are entitled to the benefit of Sec. 4283 R. S., which exempts them from liability for any greater amount."

"1. Having employed men of experience and skill in such work, to overhaul the vessel, make what repairs were found to be needed, and supply and equip her for the voyage and stow the cargo, and there being no evidence of neglect or mistake in these particulars on the part of the owners or their employees I must find that they did exercise due diligence to make the vessel seaworthy and properly manned, equipped and supplied, therefore, there is no liability for loss of property. The Harter Act exempts the vessel, her owners, agents and charterers from all liability."

"2. All that is available for distribution to compensate the sufferers by loss of the Jane Gray, is the amount of pending freight, the vessel herself being a total loss. The phrase "freight then pending: as used in the statute, has been construed to include, freight pre-paid for the carriage of merchandise, and passage money, and it has been decided by the highest authority that the phrase should not be taken in a narrow sense as meaning only the freight to be earned by a successful conclusion of the voyage. Main v. Williams, 152 U. S. 122-133. The petitioners, however, by filing exceptions to the report of the appraisers appointed to ascertain the amount of the value of the vessel and her freight then pending, have raised the question as to their right to subtract from the freight then pending, the amount of their expenditures in sending the vessel on her voyage. Their bill of items includes wages advanced to the captain and crew, a bill for towing the vessel from Seattle to Port Townsend, money paid to stevedores for stowing the cargo, and the price of stores and dishes supplied for the voyage; also money which they have disbursed since the loss of the vessel, including the fees of a notary public for protest respecting the loss of the ship, the cost of telegrams conveying information of the loss, and various sums which they paid for the comfort or benefit of the survivors. It seems to me that they might with equal propriety subtract all their other expenses connected with the purchase and fitting out of the vessel, and commissions paid to soliciting agents for inducing passengers to purchase tickets; if they can subtract the cost of supplies and dishes furnished for the voyage, they might as well include the value of the sails, rigging, anchors, cable, and hull of the ship."

"In the case above cited, the Supreme Court of the United States has declared that the real object of the act limiting liability of ship owners "was to limit the liability of vessel owners to their interest in the adventure; hence in assessing the value of the ship, the custom has been to include all that belongs to the ship, and may be presumed to be the property of the owner, not merely the hull, together with the boats, tackle, apparel, and furniture, but all the appurtenances, comprising whatever is on board for the object of the voyage, belonging to the owners, whether such object be warfare, the conveyance of passengers, good, or the fisheries.""

"The owner is required to suffer the entire loss of all that he has invested in the ship, and on account of the voyage, and all that he has received for freight and passage money, and all the ship would have earned by completing the voyage, and upon condition of his yielding whatever may be saved out of the wreck and freight pending for the benefit of the shippers and passengers, he is exempted from personal liability to them for "any loss, damage, or injury by collision, or for any act, matter, or thing, lost, damage or forfeiture done, occasioned, or incurred, without the privity, or knowledge of such owner or owners.""

"Except for the statute the liability of the owner to passengers and shippers for damages in consequence of the negligence of the captain or misbehavior of the crew, would be limited only by the amount of loss and by his ability to respond."

"As a basis for making a pro rata distribution of the fund, I fix the amount of damages awarded to each of the cross libellants who are survivors of the wreck at the sum of $1,000, and to the cross libellants who are suing as widows and heirs of passengers who were lost with the vessel, the sum of $5,000 for each life so lost. The fund will be distributed pro rata and on this basis will pay 12-2/10 % of the damages awarded. The usual taxable costs will be awarded the cross libellants.

C. H. Hanford

Judge."

CHAPTER 38 – THE SETTLEMENT

DECISION IN THE FAMOUS JANE GRAY CASE

Widows and Orphans of Those Lost in the Wreck Awarded Damages Against the McDougall-Southwick Company.

Image courtesy of the Tacoma Public Library.

Judge Hanford's ruling, while giving the survivors and widows a small amount of compensation, allowed Pacey, MacDougall, and Southwick to escape relatively unscathed.

Based on Hoyt's appraised value of the Jane Gray at $4392.18—which the Judge limited the award not to exceed, the settlement for the victims of the wreck was a pittance. In spite of John Pacey's plea to reduce the award by "expenditures in supplying and equipping said vessel for said voyage and for wages, or any other account," Judge Hanford ruled that the appraiser's valuation would stand.

In his final "Findings of Fact and Conclusions of Law and Decree," he stated:

"1. That the above named petitioner John G. Pacey was the sole owner of said vessel at the time of her said loss; that the above named petitioners Southwick and MacDougall had no interest in said vessel nor her pending voyage at the time of her loss; that the said corporation, MacDougall & Southwick Company, had no interest in the said vessel nor in her pending voyage at the time of her said loss, but that said corporation having a long time prior to the voyage upon which said vessel was lost held out to the world by means of numerous advertisements that it was interested in and an operator of said vessel upon her said voyage; and that the said MacDougall & Southwick Company by reason of said representations is estopped to deny its interest in said vessel and said voyage."

"2. That all persons owning and apparently interested in said vessel prior to her said voyage had no reason to know of any defect existing in the manning, equipment, or preparation of said vessel for said voyage; and that said vessel was well manned, well equipped, staunch and seaworthy at the inception of said voyage."

"3. That the loss of said Jane Grey as aforesaid was occasioned by the negligent conduct of her master and crew after the beginning of said voyage and immediately preceding her wreck."

"4. That all the above petitioners were without any privity or knowledge of the cause of the loss of said vessel."

"5. That each of the above named death claimants is entitled to have the sum of Five Thousand Dollars fixed as a basis of ascertaining the proportion due to each out of the fund hereinafter distributed."

"6. That each of the above named survivors is entitled to have the sum of One Thousand Dollars fixed as a basis of ascertaining the proportion to which each is entitled out of the fund hereinafter distributed."

"7. For further and more specific findings of fact with regard to the issues raised herein reference is hereby made to the opinion of this court, heretofore referred to."

~~~

After deducting legal fees and applying Judge Hanford's 12.2% to the sum available, each of the survivors received $122.00, the approximate amount they would have been given if Southwick and the outfitting firm had made good on their promise to reimburse the $100.00 baggage claim and provide one suit of clothing. A full eighteen months later, after a protracted legal battle, they got what they originally requested, while MacDougall and Southwick went about business as usual.

Each widow received $610.00, regardless of the number of minor children they were now supporting on their own.

Those who did not join the litigation received nothing, as provided by the monition that ordered any persons having a claim for damages make proof to Commissioner Bowman no later than May 4, 1899. Failure to do so barred any future claims.

If Judge Hanford had ruled that the vessel was overloaded, full liability would have fallen on the owners of the vessel for failing to make her seaworthy. If he had ruled that they were "operators," as seemed obvious from the evidence, they would have been ineligible for the limitation of liability and responsible for the full value of any claims awarded. That would likely have set a precedent for future cases against outfitting firms at a time when Seattle's burgeoning economy was due in large part to prospectors dropping their life savings on the way to the Klondike and
~~~

Alaska. By limiting Pacey's liability to the greater sum of the appraisement, while rendering MacDougall and Southwick blameless, Judge Hanford was able to somewhat placate all parties without further jeopardizing the economic well being of his cronies within the business community.

Knowing Hanford's power within the state of Washington, the *Seattle Daily Times* issued a column congratulating his ruling while condemning MacDougall and Southwick - and the legal loophole that the judge allowed them to escape through:

"The decision of Judge Hanford of the United States Court, handed down from the bench on Wednesday last, probably made an end of the famous 'Jane Grey' marine case, which has been before the public for a greater or less extent for much more than a year and a half. In order that the public may appreciate the judgment of the Court a slight historical review will be necessary:

In the great Klondike rush of 1898, the public will remember that The Times took advanced grounds with reference to the condition in which steamboat property condition should be put before departing for Alaskan ports--for there was a decided disposition on the part of ship owners and charterers to fit out any old hulk which could be kept afloat in Elliott Bay, load her to the guards with both freight and passengers, and take the chances of the cargo of property and human freight reaching its destination, two or three thousand miles to the North, where the gold prospectors hoped to find 'millions of the shining dust,' and out of the voyage the ship charterer and outfitter expected to reap a thousand per cent profit!

Among others who went into this business of fitting up 'old hulks' was the McDougall & Southwick Company, doing business for some time in Seattle, and who hit upon a vessel called the 'Jane Grey,' which left this port on her fateful journey, for Kotzebue Sound, 3000 miles to the North, in the month of May, 1898.

The 'Jane Grey' was not only an old and unseaworthy ship, but was loaded down to her guards with freight, something like fifty tons over her capacity being shipped, but sixty-one people, of whom many were passengers--and after being out upon the ocean a few days, in the darkness of night, without warning and at a time when no storm or high wind prevailed, suddenly capsized and went to the bottom of the ocean!

Of her passengers and crew thirty-four were drowned--only twenty-seven escaping in a small launch, and after being exposed to the perils and hardships of the ocean for many days, reached land in safety. These, however, had lost their baggage and suffered in health from the exposure to an extent which will never be repaired.

Suits were brought against the mercantile house of McDougall & Southwick by the 'orphans and widows' of those who had lost their lives, thereby seeking to obtain some compensation for the results of the awful disaster. Naturally enough McDougall & Southwick resisted, taking the position that they were not the owners of the vessel, and therefore not responsible.

Judge Hanford, however, found from the testimony that McDougall & Southwick, though not the 'original' owners, yet by their representations to the public, became liable as owners, as their conduct amounted to 'a deceit and fraud' on the public.

To show how indifferent some men were during those days of 'outfitting,' we cite the fact that McDougall, the local manager of the company, testified in court that McDougall & Southwick did advertise that they were the owners of the boat, and were the 'outfitters'--but that they did this simply to 'advertise their mercantile house' and to 'induce the public' to take passage on the 'Jane Grey,' instead of others which were offered at the time.

It may not be out of place to say that if the charterer and outfitter of the 'Jane Grey' had been unknown persons in Seattle, probably not a half dozen of the sixty-one people who took passage would ever have dreamed of so doing. It was the influence of alleged reputable and honest merchants which decoyed these people into the awful ambush that ultimately sent more than half of their numbers to a watery grave, without the slightest notice or opportunity of preservation, as if they had been a lot of old junk!

The testimony before the court shew that while technically the 'floor manager' of McDougall & Southwick--one Pacey--was the owner of the 'Jane Grey,' nevertheless the outfitting was done in the mercantile house of McDougall & Southwick, and that firm repeatedly advertised both in a newspaper and upon the streets that they were the 'owners and outfitters.'

Judge Hanford, therefore, very properly found as a matter of law that it would be a 'fraud' upon the plaintiffs--orphans and widows of those who were lost by the sinking of the 'Jane Grey'--for McDougall & Southwick to escape liability, and decided that the 'orphans and widows' were entitled to recover--and the court fixed the award at five thousand dollars for each person whose life was lost, and one thousand dollars damages for each of the survivors.

It takes but little figuring to demonstrate that the judgment thus rendered by the Court aggregated a total liability of almost $200,000--and that if equity and justice could have had their way the McDougall & Southwick Mercantile Company would have been wiped out of existence by this eminently fair decision on the part of the Court.

But McDougall & Southwick were able to shield themselves from the legal consequences of their awful acts by pleading a peculiar statute of the shipping act, which provides in cases of this kind, that the damages shall be 'limited to the extent of the value of the vessel and the money paid for the carrying of freight.'

As the ship went to the bottom of the ocean, nothing could be recovered on her account, and the money paid for freight was proven to be but $4300--and this amount, together with all costs of Court, the McDougall & Southwick Company are compelled to pay.

While this firm are thus able to escape the righteous judgment which aggregates $200,000, and get off by paying something like $6000, nevertheless the 'moral judgment' of the Court practically amounted to a declaration that this company was willing to enter into a scheme involving the lives of sixty-one persons, and take the chances of losing $6000 when put against the other 'chance' of making $50,000, as they undoubtedly would have done had the old 'hulk' named 'Jane Grey' not foundered and thus been able to weather the ocean, and arrived safely at her destination."

~~~

Finally, those involved in the court proceedings could move on with their lives.
~~~

CHAPTER 39 - OH JOHNNIE BOY

When the first University of Washington yearbook was published in 1900, several pages commemorated the legendary life of Jack Lindsay. From 1889, the first year the sport was played at the University, through 2009, only eleven men have held the title of two-time team captain. One of the team's first heroes, Lindsay earned the undying respect of everyone who knew him. And to this day, his valor and determination are still remembered.

The following is a memorial to Jack and the man he might have become.

"Washington Wins City Championship

Ralph Nichols was again the coach for the season. Jack Lindsay was the captain. The team opened with a loss to the Seattle Athletic Club (4-6), followed by two more losses to Port Townsend Athletic club (18-0), and the Multnomah Athletic Club (10-0). Three days later, on Dec. 15, they beat the Seattle YMCA, 4-0. On Dec. 19, their third game in a week, Washington again played the Seattle Athletic Club. The game was characterized as the greatest university athletic event ever, up to that point. With only ten seconds remaining, the score was tied at 6-6. Washington was three yards from victory. A newspaper account describes the action: "...in the lurking gloom of the YMCA grounds at the close of the game which those that witnessed it will never forget...On the one hand, desperate determination to check the awful onslaught of bone and muscle and seek consolation in a tie rather than suffer the sting of defeat; on the other hand an overwhelming irresistible force of impending victory which sweeps all before it. The ball was passed to Captain Lindsay. The heavy U backs thundered against the exhausted line of the athletic club, staggered a few feet, then with one herculean effort plunged over the line and the game was won and the university boys became the local champions.

~~~

""Husky Legend

Jack Lindsay

In describing early football greats, writers reserved the phrase "above all the great and only one" for Jack Lindsay. He scored every Washington touchdown during the 1896 and 1897 seasons and was a two-time captain. He was Washington's track captain in 1897. He set the Western Washington Intercollegiate Athletic Association record in the 50-yard dash in 1896 (5.75 seconds). A poem paid tribute to this outstanding young man.

Hurrah for Lindsay! The pride of our college.

The terror of foes, the wonder of all,

Cheer for his deeds in the wildest of carnage,

Crown him with laurel, the king of football.

Hurrah for Lindsay, the hero, the splendor,

The boast, the delight of our Washington,

Oh write his name on the bright scroll of glory

And honor, Oh College, thy peerless son.

Hurrah for Lindsay! Hurrah for Lindsay!

He covers our college with endless fame,

We'll deck him with honors, we'll drown him with praises,
~~~

Hurrah for Lindsay -once more—and again!

Lindsay was selected to the All-Time Washington football team covering the years 1892-1930. In the spring of 1898, Lindsay and two teammates, Victor and Conrad Schmidt, drowned on an Alaskan expedition outfitted by Prince Luigi of Italy. On an old wooden schooner, 15 men headed for the rich Kotzebue Sound country. The boat's seams opened; and it sank with 11 of the 15 going down with her."

~~~

From The Delta Sigma Nu Fraternity, Volume 16:

"IN MEMORIAM

John James Lindsay—Lost at Sea May 31st.

Far out into the stormy Pacific, 100 miles due west of Cape Flattery, sailed a frail bark heavily ladened with Alaska gold-seekers on the night of May 31st, and now, beneath the surface of those dark, restless waters, lies the body of one who was as loyal a Sigma Nu as ever took the vows of our beloved Order. Loyal, enthusiastic, ever moving, powerful Johnny Lindsay! The star of his class from the time he entered college, he rests peacefully beneath the waves, and well may the fraternity mourn the loss of this brother, who was a shining example of college and fraternal loyalty.

As an athlete, Brother Lindsay won the most honors for his alma mater. For two years he was captain of the track team, which won the championship of the State in 1896, and was counted on as the surest man in the short distances. For three years he was captain of the foot ball team, and the University's star half-back during this
~~~

period. The Seattle Daily Post-Intelligencer, in commenting upon his death says:

"Lindsay had been captain of the Varsity team for three years, and did more, his friends say, to make the University a factor in Washington foot ball matters than any other man in the University. Every fall for three years past he has been the hero of the Varsity girls and pride of the college men. At the various positions of left half-back and full-back, he played aggressive ball, never giving up, even in the face of sure defeat. He was noted for the manner in which he made ground in running with the ball after he had been apparently downed by the opposing team. One could never tell in a game when Lindsay would stop. His idea in going to Alaska was to secure funds with which to complete his college education. It was his intention to enter Stanford or some Eastern college on his return. His playing on the gridiron improved every year, and great things in an athletic way were expected of him by those who watched his career at the head of the University of Washington team."

Brother Lindsay was not born in opulence, to bask in the smiles of fortune without an effort on his part to attain that end. His brawn and muscle won for him the sinews with which it was possible for him to begin his college course. A few months later he secured a newspaper route in Seattle, and for two years the early dawn of that northern sky would find him busily at work, at the same time laying wires for his many successful encounters in college politics, as well as planning those brilliant coups, the execution of which on the foot ball arena classed him as one of the star half-backs of the Pacific Coast. Through a change of management he lost the paper route, but was selected by the student body as business manager of the

"Pacific Wave," the college publication, at the opening of his Junior year. But it was a hard struggle, these three long years, as only those know who have attempted to work for their education, play foot-ball, "do politics," and still maintain a high standard of scholarship.

Through indomitable energy he had been successful thus far, and now a greater ambition seized him—to take his degree at Stanford or one of the large Eastern Universities. To prepare himself financially for this undertaking, he resolved to chance a year in the gold fields of Alaska, whence so many of his fellow athletes and classmates had preceded him, including Brothers Abrams and Calhoun. Those who saw him last, waiving his farewell on the crowded deck of the ill-fated craft as she moved slowly away from the wharf on that beautiful Memorial Day, will ever remember the smile on his honest face, and his hopeful words of parting—they will be able to remember him as he really was.

As a "find" of Brother Clemans, Jack Lindsay was secured for the fraternity, and pledged himself to the establishment of Gamma Chi Chapter at the University of Washington. Why was he selected? I could not tell just why, though I know so well. Because of his attributes of integrity and manliness which marked his companionship with all, and made him the undergraduate ruler of his college; because of certain enviable qualities so evident in those who possess them, yet hard to explain; because—I will say—of the close affinity in character and disposition which he bore to the man who selected him. As one who knew them both so intimately, I will pay this my highest tribute. SCOTT CALHOUN.

The following telegram we clipped from the Louisville, Ky., Post:

Victoria, B. C., June 25.—The schooner Jane Gray is reported to be ashore near Kyuquat, about one hundred miles from the place where she was wrecked, causing the loss of thirty-six lives. The survivors of this marine disaster asserted that the vessel foundered at sea, but it is evident that such was not the case. The Indians who found the wreck state that there were no bodies in the cabin.

Lindsay.

Among the passengers on the "Jane Gray," an ex-sealer, bound for Alaska, which foundered off Cape Flattery May 22nd, was Bro. John J. Lindsay, of Everett, Washington, a member of Major Ingraham's gold seeking expedition. Bro. Lindsay was one of the charter members of Gamma Chi, and in his death the chapter and the fraternity loses on of its best members and most enthusiastic workers. He was ever alive to every interest of the fraternity and never lost an opportunity to do his part toward its welfare. As captain of the University foot ball team for two years and manager of the Pacific Wave, he was one of the best known members of Gamma Chi. He also gained the reputation of being one of the greatest halfbacks on the coast.

Entering the University in '95, he attended until Christmas '97 when his proposed trip to the Klondyke demanded his attention. On May 18th the ill-fated Jane Gray left Seattle and about two o'clock on the morning of the 22d, with only ten minutes warning, she sank off Cape Flattery with thirty-six of her passengers and crew. Twenty-seven of those on board escaped in a launch and reached Vancouver, one hundred miles distant. It is reported that Bro. Lindsay and several others suffered greatly from seasickness on the night in question, and when the alarm was given were either asleep or too weak to save themselves, and this is probably true; for had he been awake and well he surely would have take care of himself—or others, for he was made of that kind of stuff which would have developed the hero in such an emergency.

Bro. Lindsay was a young man of splendid character, and was destined to be a useful, honored citizen. His work in the chapter and for the fraternity, as in other lines, was only begun, but will always be remembered. When we gather in Seattle again that vacant chair will bring a touch of sadness to our hearts such as is now felt in the hearts of a wide circle of sincere friends.

The tributes to our esteemed brother are many, but among them I would repeat one paid by Miss Emma S. Yule, as principal of the Everett High School during his three years of study, was brought in touch with his sterling qualities as no one perhaps save his family. As a friend and classmate of Bro. Lindsay, I, too, remember him as one of the truest type of our American manhood, physically, mentally and morally, and these words of Miss Yule will be cherished by all who knew him:

"One voice the cruel waves has stilled forever. The shock of this horrible disaster is so benumbing that we can not fully realize our great loss."

"In the passing of this strong young life the city, the State and the Nation lost one who gave promise of one day being an honored son. Few young men are so rich in the possession of the best qualities of manhood as he was. Honesty, uprightness, integrity, loyalty to duty, devotion to purpose, physical and moral courage, and a mind which his persevering determination would have won him an enviable place among his fellow men, was his wealth of endowment."

"This promising life so cruelly sacrificed, was lived so fully, so dutifully, so loyally, so earnestly, so bravely, that it will be an inspiration to all who knew him to live better, truer and more useful lives."

S. A. FOWLER"

CHAPTER 40 – THE AFTER WORDS

Since many of the lives of those impacted by the sinking of the Jane Gray could easily warrant their own biography, the following is a brief snapshot of subsequent events:

As an example of what the futures of the young men lost may have looked like, had they survived, one need look no further than the footprints left by their friends and family. Scott Calhoun, who had himself worked in the gold fields and wrote so eloquently about his friend, Jack Lindsay, graduated from Stanford, where Herbert Hoover was one of his classmates. He went on to become the City of Seattle's corporate attorney. Carl Morford, who accompanied Ingraham and Prince Luigi on the ascent of Mount St. Elias and played football with Jack and the Schmid brothers, became a civil engineer, for a time employed by the City of Seattle. Theresa Schmid, Jack Lindsay's classmate and the sister of Victor and Conrad, graduated from the University of Washington in 1898, received her Ph. D. in Sociology and Economics at the University of Wisconsin, and returned to the University of Washington as a teacher. Under her married name, Theresa McMahon, she later became the outspoken author of publications such as "Women and Economic Evolution or the Effects of Industrial Changes on the Status of Women."

~~~

Before the trial was over, Ollie, the widow of Seattle contractor William Gleason, found employment as an insurance agent at the Bailey Building - where Dr. Luther
~~~

Lessey, Major Ingraham, and Frederick Bausman all held offices. For the next twenty years, she enjoyed a successful career in real estate and insurance sales, supporting herself into retirement.

~~~

Of those who are known to have returned to Alaska, Major Ingraham departed for the North before the court proceedings had begun. However, he did his best to help all whom had suffered the consequences of the ill-fated journey on a vessel that he had personally selected. Dr. Lessey, Clayton Packard, George Pennington, Charles Chard, and Coney Weston accompanied him. By June 28th of 1899, word reached Seattle of Ingraham's success and was printed in the *New York Times*:

"NEW ALASKA GOLDFIELDS.

The Expedition Fitted Out by Prince Luigi Opened a New District—Many Claims Already Located.

SEATTLE, Washington, June 27.—The latest advices from the newly discovered goldfields at Cape Nome, Alaska, are contained in a letter from Major E. S. Ingraham of Seattle, who writes under date of Feb. 2, 1899. Major Ingraham is the leader of a party of fourteen men who were fitted out by Prince Luigi of Italy and local business men. He went first to Kotzebue Sound, but finding nothing there, crossed overland to Cape Nome, with a portion of the party, enduring considerable hardships. Part of the time the men had but two pancakes a day. Major Ingraham writes:

'On Sept. 25 six men went to work to test their claims, some on Snow Creek, and the rest on Anvil Creek. The best pan was obtained on Snow Creek, and amounted to $8.52. The aggregate of four days' work was $4 less than $1,800. The gold was of good quality, and sold at St.
~~~

Michael without assay for $16.85 per ounce. On account of the lateness of the season and lack of supplies no attempt to reach bedrock was made. The news soon spread, and there had been a constant arrival of prospectors from Unalaska, St. Michael, and as far south as Kuskoquim. Fully 500 locations have been made to date. Two other districts have been organized, one at Lime Creek, beyond Cape Rodney, and the other with Bonanza Creek as a centre.'

'The rich finds at Cape Nome and on the Ne-Uck-Luck, a tributary of Fish River, prove beyond doubt that the rich mineral belt of the Yukon crosses to Siberia. Pay dirt is reported to have been struck on a river flowing into the chain of lakes having outlet at Port Clarence. Before starting from Kotzebue Sound, Dec. 15, 1898, prospectors had come in from Noatak reporting the discovery of a rich and extensive mineral belt north of the river. In November, 1898, there was a stampede from among the prospectors wintering on Kowak, who reported rich diggings on the Alashuck, a tributary of the Kynkuk. There is no doubt that next Summer will witness remarkable developments in the vicinity of Golvin Bay.'"

While in Nome during the winter of 1898-99, Ingraham remained devoted to the principals of education, inviting the natives into his cabin, where he taught reading and geography. After staying in his underground bungalow all winter, he took his launch around the Cape of Prince Wales to Nome, where he sent for his wife and two sons to join him. The family lived in Nome, actively engaged in the community and mining until the fall of 1901. Before his return to Seattle, the Major organized the rescue of a group of miners dying of Scurvy. With three of his own party; Ralph Sheafe, Gus Shaser, Bud Whitney, and Robert

Samms, a missionary, they trekked one hundred-seventy miles overland with supplies for the deathly ill prospectors. Although five of the miners had already perished, they were able to bring the remaining five back to Cape Blossom Mission by July 7th of that year.

Ingraham returned to Seattle with Myra and their sons, Kenneth and Norman, in 1901. He continued to write, print, teach, and scale mountains. With his friend, Edmond Meany, he actively helped in the establishment of boy scout and girl scout clubs, passing on his love of nature throughout the rest of his days.

~~~

Charles E. Chard, a survivor of the Jane Gray disaster from the Blackwell party, was enlisted to assist Ingraham in the Alaska expedition. By the fall of 1898, he had applied to Dr. Sheldon Jackson for permission to live in the cabins at the Teller reindeer station. That permission was granted with the provision that he would care for all of the government buildings at the station and that he would not allow any alcohol to be sold or given away on the premises. While acting as the property caretaker, he continued to mine with Ingraham. His report was printed in The *Record Union* of Sacramento, California on June 20, 1899:

"Seattle, June 19.—From advices received here it would seem that a mining expedition in which Prince Luigi of Italy is interested has struck it rich near Port Clarence, Alaska, a government reindeer station. A letter from Charles E. Chard of this city, one of the party, says he and two others took out $20 from Discovery claim with a rocker. He says a man could have worked out $100 a day by sluicing."
~~~

~~~

Clayton Packard, the expert miner and journalist from Snohomish, returned to Kotzebue Sound with Ingraham, and by July of 1899, wrote that the entire output of the Kotzebue region, "can be safely estimated at less than $1" and that during the year of 1900, the amount "will not exceed this." He was convinced that the crew of the steamship Grace Dollar had perpetuated the frenzy by purchasing $10,000 in gold dust "to be used in booming the Kotzebue Sound Country and making business for (their) boat the next year." With his usual biting candor, a disgusted Packard said, "should they come up here again next season with another invoice bunkoed 'suckers,' a large majority of their last year's victims will be in Kotzebue to entertain them with a warm Arctic soiree."

Packard was done with Alaska, and on December 5, 1900, the Oregon paper, the *Sumpter Miner*, reported on Clayton's colorful past and his latest venture:

"C. H. Packard and his Experience.

C. H. Packard arrived in Sumpter Friday of last week from Seattle, and left on the stage that day to take charge of the Prairie City Miner for its owners. Mr. Packard has had some interesting experiences during the past few years. Five years ago he owned the Snohomish (Washington) Eye, the most widely circulated and influential paper in the county. He became interested in mining and neglected his paper. He acquired valuable properties in the Monte Cristo district. A flood washed out the railroad into that section and Monte Cristo became a deserted camp. In the meantime The Eye had suspended publication. Mr. Packard started to Alaska with the expedition fitted out by an Italian prince, nephew of the king of Italy, first cousin of
~~~

the present monarch. The vessel on which the party sailed was wrecked and Mr. Packard was one of the first who were saved. He returned to Alaska and started again for the frozen north. For a year he didn't find a color. He got in on the first rush to Nome two years ago and staked some claims, returning to the states a year ago. He went back last spring and worked there all season, but bad luck followed him. He landed in Seattle a month ago. He is now in a country where his ability and experience will be rewarded."

~~~

And on board the steamer Grace Dollar when she reached Kotzebue Sound on August 17, 1898, was A. G. Kingsbury, with his still-bandaged shoulder. From there, he headed toward the Kobuk River on the stern-wheeler Arctic Bird, which had a barge in tow. When asked to stow his gear on the barge, he declined, packing most of it into a boat that he had brought along, which was also in tow. While crossing the Hathan Inlet, the barge went to the bottom with all of its cargo, forcing the entire group of passengers to return to Kotzebue.

After a few more trying incidents, Kingsbury finally made his destination, about five-hundred miles inland, and built himself a small log cabin. In camping there for the winter, he would be ready to begin gold prospecting by the spring thaw. However, on November 8th, his entire cabin burned to the ground with all of his equipment. He escaped in his bed clothing with only a thermometer and a hand sled. The next day, he started out alone for the Yukon River, a trip of another sixteen hundred miles.

Ever resourceful, this engineer who had worked on irrigation, electrical, and civil projects all over the United
~~~

States and Mexico, scavenged five-gallon oil cans from which he made tin stoves. With these, he was able to trade with the natives, secure a sled, and pick up an entire new outfit - valued at approximately $500.

Kingsbury eventually made enough money in the gold fields to return to Boston, where he was instrumental in forming the Corwin Trading Company. He and some other investors purchased the ship Corwin, fresh from revenue cutter service, in February 1900, with the purpose of transporting, coal, cargo, and passengers to Nome. While on board serving as an unofficial crewmember, he was simultaneously a miner and a correspondent for *National Magazine*, publishing several articles over the course of the next few years. Some of his later literary works can be found in *New England Magazine* and the *Bay State Monthly*.

~~~

Job Johnson, the Long Island man who stayed alive floating on an overturned boat, also returned to Alaska. In spite of the "aweful windup" that resulted in the death of his eighteen year-old friend, Wilbur Doxsey, he continued on their quest for gold, and on December 5, 1899, The *Brooklyn Eagle* told of Job's return to Long Island:

"HOME FROM THE KLONDIKE

Springfield, L. I., December 5—Job Johnson, brother of Mrs. Elva Rice of Springfield, who went to the Klondike with William Doxsey of Lynbrook, two years ago, returned home Sunday. On their way to the Klondike the ship was wrecked. Johnson was saved, but Doxsey has never been heard from since. Johnson expects to return to the Klondike in the spring, as he has several claims there."

~~~

Hanford had already enjoyed a long and successful judicial career by the conclusion of the Jane Gray case. However, his personal life was slowly beginning to unravel. While his wife, Clara, remained a patient at Eastern Washington Hospital for the Insane, he wrote to Edmond Meany in 1901, requesting that the professor assist with his biography. Meany declined, in essence stating that not a personal word had been mentioned in his long list of self-aggrandized accomplishments. In February of 1902, Cornelius and Clara's twenty-three year old daughter, Jessie, fell ill with typhoid fever and passed away at Seattle General Hospital. Alone at Deaconess Home in Spokane, where she had been moved, Clara died quietly in 1904 at the age of forty-seven. The cause of death was listed as tuberculosis. An article of not more than ten lines was published in the local paper. While marking her passing, it merely stated that: "she has been an invalid for years." Nothing more seems to have ever been written about this mother of eight. Around 1906, the grand mansion that Cornelius and Clara built at the corner of Boren and Madison was demolished to make way for the Perry Apartments. Not long after, Judge Hanford's star began to spiral from the heavens. Accused of "high crimes and misdemeanors" and of being a "habitual drunkard," impeachment proceedings were initiated. Testimony accused him of being "drunk in the bars, drunk in the streets, drunk in the streetcars, drunk (and asleep) in the courtroom." In addition, he was accused of favoring his wealthy buddies in court rulings. Other cases spurred public outcry and with the threat of condemning evidence forever tarnishing his image, Cornelius Holgate Hanford sent his letter of resignation to President William Howard Taft on July 22, 1912. Two weeks later, it was accepted.

Cornelius Holgate Hanford, although his days in the field of law were over, went on to become a modestly successful author. And, somewhat ironically, his three-volume set, "Seattle and Environs," was occasionally referred to for background information in this narrative.

~~~

In September of 1900, things seemed to be going well for John Pacey. A friend from Kansas who came out to Seattle and sailed on the Nellie G. Thurston, reported in the *Wichita Daily Eagle*: "Pacey was slim when he left Wichita ten years ago. He is big and robust now and looks, Mr. Hays says, like an aristocrat. He owns a big store in Nome and another in a mining district fifty miles away, and owns three vessels that make the trip from Seattle several times a year. Pacey is getting rich. The captain of one of his vessels grounded one of his ships early this season and deserted her. The cargo was damaged $10,000 and it took $1200 to fix up the ship. Pacey stood this loss without any inconvenience. He has been in Seattle for eight years and does all his business from this point. It cost $75 fare from Seattle up in May, but fare were as low as $30 when Mr. Hays left on his return."

It should have been a joyous time at the little Pacey home on Olympic Place. Just a month after the report from Kansas, on October 23, 1900, Annie Pacey gave birth to their first child, John George Pacey, Junior. However, the situation at MacDougall and Southwick was not as it seemed to the outside world. Between March of 1900 and May of 1901, John Pacey accepted the delivery of merchandise from Goodyear Rubber Company. $1779.79 worth of rubber boots, shoes, and other rubber goods were invoiced in his name and never paid for.
~~~

By 1902, John's life took another turn: he was no longer employed by MacDougall and Southwick and did not reside in Seattle. Perhaps Annie had fallen ill, for he had taken up temporary residence at 2828 H Street in San Diego, California.

In November of 1902, John Pacey transferred $5,000 to MacDougall and Southwick. While it seems likely that his intent was to cover any merchandise or debts that he owed through transactions at the outfitting firm, the bills were never paid. In addition to Goodyear, eleven other creditors were looking for him.

Unable to locate John, Goodyear Rubber Company, with their attorney, Frederick Bausman, attempted to force John G. Pacey into bankruptcy in absentia. In their filing, they claimed that John did: "On the 1st day of November 1902, and while insolvent, as aforesaid, transfer and pay to J. B. MacDougall and to The MacDougall & Southwick Co., a corporation, the sum of five thousand ($5000) Dollars, and that said transfer and payment was made to said J. B. MacDougall and to the MacDougall & Southwick Co. with the intent and for the purpose of hindering, delaying and defrauding the creditors of said John G. Pacey, and particularly this petitioner. That said transfer and payment aforesaid was made by said John G. Pacey with intent to prefer said J. B. MacDougall and The MacDougall & Southwick Co. over the other creditors of said Pacey and particularly over this petitioner; and that said J. B. MacDougall and The MacDougall & Southwick Co. accepted said payment well knowing said Pacey to be insolvent."

Although John did not immediately return to Seattle, he learned of the proceedings against him and, through an attorney, contested the bankruptcy proceedings and the claims that he was insolvent, stating that he had not "been with the State of Washington."

When Pacey finally came back to Seattle in 1904, it was without Annie. His ties with MacDougall and Southwick severed, he took a bookkeeping job at a lighting company and with the help of his sister, Annie Pacey Draper, raised his son. John never remarried.

~~~

The MacDougall and Southwick outfitting store continued to be embroiled in various litigations and by 1910, the president and vice president sold out their interests in the Seattle operation. Before doing so, John MacDougall began a corporation dealing in property and irrigation projects along the Columbia River. These too became embroiled in various legal proceedings. As for Southwick, he continued much as he always had, dealing in merchandise on the East Coast, while spending his summers on Long Island.

~~~

Vene Gambell's brother, Dr. Frances Gambell, who had accepted a post as the physician at the reindeer station at St. Michael, delivered the news of the family's death to the villagers on St. Lawrence Island. At his suggestion, the natives who had grown to love Nellie, Vene, and baby Margaret, renamed the town Gambell in their honor.

And when the new Presbyterian Church in Winfield, Iowa was dedicated in December of 1900, it boasted two soaring stained glass windows. One depicted the sun rising over the ocean with the caption "when the sea gives up the dead." These gifts from the communities of Winfield and Wapello, both dedicated to the memory of the Gambell family, cast colorful light across the halls of that church to this day.

~~~

Erminio Sella had perhaps the most remarkable change of fortune of all of the survivors. After his soul-searching trek through national parks of the United States, he returned to Italy in October of 1898.

The following year marked a new beginning. Erminio sailed from Marseilles with his brother, Vittorio, on August 10, 1899 to join Dr. Douglas William Freshfield as photographers on an expedition around the highest Himalayan peaks. Dr. Freshfield later detailed their expedition in "Round Kangchenjunga: A Narrative of Mountain Travel and Exploration."

Some time during that same year, Erminio went on a hunting trip to the island of Sardinia with his cousin, Edoardo Mosca. There, they stumbled on a large piece of land in Alghero, purchased it, and began what would become one of the largest private vineyards in all of Italy. Although now owned by Campari, the Sella & Mosca label continues to produce some of the world's finest wines even today.
~~~

CHAPTER 41 - THE CAST OF CHARACTERS

This brief summary is organized alphabetically by last name, with the age of each person at the time the Jane Gray went down, in parentheses, if known.

~~~

Aiken, Charles C. (Age unknown): Sacramento, California, LOST. According to the boarding manifest, Aiken was traveling with Claudius Brown, Captain Crockett's father-in-law from Seattle, who was also LOST. Charlie worked as a gang foreman in the railroad car repair department at the Southern Pacific Company under Victor Lemay. He was one of the first to buy a ticket on the Jane Gray and the last to board her before she sailed.

~~~

Ausprung/Arnsprung, Leon (Age unknown): Residence unknown, LOST. He was a crewmember, likely the third seaman.

~~~

Bausman, Frederick (Age 37): Seattle, Washington. Attorney for the plaintiffs who become cross-libellants in Admiralty, Frederick was with the firm Bausman, Kelleher (Daniel) & Emory (George M.). His residence in 1897 was 128 Roy, telephone: Union 8. The office was located at 626-628 Bailey Bldg., telephone: Main 323.

Frederick Bausman wrote a scathing examination of the accident that placed the blame squarely on the shoulders of the owner(s). He also made a valiant case for proving
~~~

that MacDougall & Southwick, if not named on the title of the Jane Gray, were most certainly "interested" parties.

Much later, he represented the Goodyear Rubber Company in a bankruptcy action against John Pacey when he skipped town on his debts in 1902.

For more on Frederick Bausman, see: http://templeofjustice.org/justice/frederick-bausman/

~~~

Bianchetto, Secondo (Age unknown): Biella, Italy, SURVIVOR. He was a member of the Italian team organized under Erminio Sella and Edoardo Gaia and an employee at the family textile mill. His name is reported in several variations: Beachetto, Bianchett, Bianchitts, and Biancaetto. His cousin, Secondo Bissetta, was lost in the sinking.

~~~

Bissetta, Secondo (Age 30): Biella, Italy, LOST. His surname was also reported as Bessatte. He was a cousin of Bianchetto and an employee of Sella and Gaia.

~~~

Blackwell, James Eustace (age 43): Seattle, Washington, SURVIVOR. Blackwell was the leader of his own prospecting party, which originally consisted of twelve people, eleven of whom sailed on the Jane Gray for Port Clarence, not Kotzebue Sound. The rest of his official party included, William S. Weaver, Silas Livengood, William F. Deterling, and William Otter. Both Deterling and Otten were among the missing.

Blackwell, Weaver, Livengood, accompanied by Chard and Boak survived the sinking. Otten and Deterling
~~~

(whose names are also reported as Otter and Levering) did not. James Blackwell reportedly gave members of his group any clothing he can spare while on the return to Victoria and Seattle.

Back in Seattle, he became the leader of the "committee" who decide to recover damages from MacDougall & Southwick. Initially seeking only $100 and a suit of clothes for the survivors, James hired prominent attorneys once the Southwick gang got nasty.

Named in Admiralty case 1398, filed action number 25632 in King County Superior Court, Blackwell asked for a sum between $6155.57 and $6218.04. James was awarded $122.00 at the closing of the Admiralty case.

From the Washington State Department of Archaeology and Historic Preservation:

Seattle architect James Eustace Blackwell was born in Fauquier County, Virginia on September 9, 1855. His father, Moore Carter Blackwell, was a captain in the confederate army. James was trained in civil engineering at the Bethel Military Academy in Warrenton, VA, and graduated as a 1st Lieutenant. His skills in civil engineering prepared him well for an initial career in surveying.

Upon graduation he reportedly worked on the James River and Kanawha Canal in Virginia. In 1879, he married his first wife, Lucretia "Lula" (McLean), who was the daughter of Major McLean, the owner of the house at Appomattox in which General Lee surrendered to General Grant. She died in 1886 at the age of thirty, leaving him with two small children.

In 1888 he took a job in Washington, D.C. working in the office of Federal Supervising Architect, leaving Fannie and Wilmer in the care of his parents.

When he moved out to Washington around 1891, the thirty-four year old Blackwell had recently married his second wife, Eleanor. He and Eleanor had a daughter, Lenore, in January of 1892. His other children, Fannie and Wilmer, remained in Virginia, where they were raised by their grandparents.

Blackwell likely came to Washington State to work on a design for the first drydock at the Puget Sound Naval Ship Yard in Bremerton. While working on the project he lived in Charleston (a suburb of Bremerton). Active in social and political circles, Blackwell sat on the town council and eventually became mayor.

During this same time period he also entered into a partnership with architect Robert L. Robertson. The firm Robertson & Blackwell first had offices in Tacoma (1891-1893), but then moved to Portland, Oregon for a short time (1894-1897) before opening up an office in Seattle (1897-c.1906). Known projects by the firm include the Louderback Building (1890) in Tacoma; Vorhees' Grain Elevator (1891) also in Tacoma; the Puyallup Opera House (1891); and a rear addition to the Yesler Building (c.1904) in Seattle.

For a few year, Blackwell had his own firm (c.1907 - 1910). Porject during this time include the M.F. Backus Warehouse (1907); the E.O. Graves Warehouse Building (1908); and Colsky Building (c.1909), all in Seattle.

In 1911, Blackwell formed a new partnership with Frank L. Baker (1911-1922). Together the firm of Blackwell & Baker designed the Grand Trunk Dock (1911); the James A. Kerr

House (1911); the Bellingham Armory (1912); Wenatchee Library (1911); Boardman Building (1912) in Olympia. Projects during the later part of his career include the Carnegie Libraries in Olympia (1914) and Burlington (1916); and a proposed housing tract of over 100 homes for the Vancouver Home Company (1918), a subsidiary of the shipbuilder Arcadia.

In 1917, for reasons unknown, the partnership was dissolved and Blackwell continued an independent practice for another 10+ years. During the early 1920s Blackwell served as the City Superintendent of Buildings (1920-22) for the City of Seattle.

Later projects, many of which have a Late Gothic Revival style, include the Fairfax Apartments (1923) on Capitol Hill; Shafer Building (1924) in downtown Seattle; and the Evans' Building (1930) in Renton. His last known project was a large women's ward building (Ward L-M) for Northern State Hospital (1933) in Sedro Wooley.

Throughout his career, Blackwell was involved in a variety of social and civic organizations. He served as resident engineer for the United States Shipping Board (1918-1920). He was a member of the Board of Public Works, the Rainier Club, the Municipal League of Seattle, the Chamber of Commerce, the Seattle Zoning Commission, and was the director of the Commercial Club. Blackwell as also an active member of the Washington State Chapter of the AIA, serving as Seattle AIA President in 1905 and was a member of the Pacific Northwest Society of Engineers.

Blackwell died in Seattle on April 5, 1939 at the age of 83.

(Portions written by Michael Houser, State Architectural Historian - July 2012)

~~~
~~~

Boak, George Rupley (age 22 - Born November 8, 1875): Hughesville, Pennsylvania, SURVIVOR. He was a passenger named in Admiralty case 1398, and filed action number 25635 in King County Superior Court – asking for a sum between $6155.57 and 6378.57. He was one of the "committee" who decided to recover damages from MacDougall & Southwick – of which he was awarded $122.

In 1897, George was listed in the Sigma Chi Fraternity directory as a Manufacturer's Agent at Hughesville, Pennsylvania.

~~~

Brown, Claudius (age 47): Seattle, Washington, LOST. Brown was traveling with Aikens, Charles C., also LOST. He was last seen entering the aft companionway in an attempt to help the Reverend Gambell, his wife, and child escape the sinking ship. He was Captain Ezekial Crockett's father-in-law. At the time of the publication of the 1898 Seattle Directory, Claude V. Brown listed his occupation as "vegetable peddler" and resided at 332 Denny Way.

~~~

Carlson, Andrew (age unknown): Seattle, Washington, LOST. Seaman, perhaps the second mate. He received an advance on his wages of $52.50 when the Jane Gray departed the Yesler dock. At the time of the publication of the Seattle guide in 1898, Andrew Carlson was a deckhand on the steamer City of Champaign.

~~~

Carlson, Charles (age unknown): Seattle, Washington, SURVIVOR. He received an advance on his wages of $39.90 when the ship left port. Carlson was a member of
~~~

the crew and the seaman who was at the helm of the Jane Gray on the night of her sinking. In the 1898 he listed his occupation as longshoreman with a residence at 7th Avenue South and 4 North Norman.

According to Judge Hanford, his testimony was inconsistent.

~~~

Ceria, Abele (age unknown): Biella, Italy, SURVIVOR. A member of Erminio Sella's team, he was accompanied by the rest of the Italians and Hans Wachter.

~~~

Chard, Charles E. (age 45): Seattle, Washington, SURVIVOR. He was named in Admiralty case 1398, and filed action number 25636 in King County Superior Court. In his claim he asked for a sum between $5834.98 and $5894.98. He was one of the "committee" who decide to recover damages from MacDougall & Southwick.

When Charles left on this trip, he listed his occupation as clerk in the Seattle directory, residing at 802 Third Avenue.

After his return to Seattle on June 2nd, he and the rest of the gang of penniless survivors worked to secure copies of the receipts for all of their purchases.

During the winter of 1899-1900, Chard occupied a cabin at Teller, Alaska - near St. Michaels, where he was assisting Major Ingraham in another venture backed by Prince Luigi.

A Canadian immigrant, Judge Hanford granted Charles E. Chard U. S. Citizenship on May 5, 1905.

~~~
~~~

Coutoure/Coutre/Conture, J. H. (age unknown): Hartford, Connecticut, SURVIVOR. He was traveling with C. J. Reilly, but did not participate in the lawsuit against Pacey, MacDougall and Southwick.

~~~

Crockett, Ezekial E.: (age 30 - Born in July of 1867) Seattle, Washington, SURVIVOR. Crockett was the captain of the Jane Gray. Upon departure from Seattle, Pacey advanced him $147.50 in wages.

At the time of the publication of the 1898 Seattle Guide, Ezekial E. Crockett was the president of Yukon Rapid Transit Company at 434 Pioneer Building with a residence at 105 Fifth Avenue North.

Crockett, at the time captain of the schooner Willard Ainsworth, was one of the first to sight the wreck of the General Siglin in 1897. Before being hired by MacDougall and Southwick, he was the captain of the steamer Townsend.

His performance as the master of the vessel was called into question by Judge Hanford, regardless of the high praise the survivors had for his performance during the sinking.

By the time the case went to court in 1899, Crockett was living in Rampart City, Alaska, engaged in the business of reindeer management.

He was married to Emma Cora Brown on May 3, 1896. His father-in-law was Claudius Brown, who drowned in the sinking.

~~~

Davenport, Percy J. (age 26): Harrisburg, Pennsylvania, SURVIVOR. He was traveling with a fellow postal clerk,

Frank W. Ginther, one of the lost, and George Hiller. Percy and George survived. Ginther's widow, Emma, joined the other litigants in the suit against MacDougall and Southwick, however, neither Davenport nor Hiller is named in Admiralty case number 1398.

~~~

Deterling, William F. (age unknown): Pennsylvania, LOST. Some newspapers reported his name as "Levering." Handwritten notes and other documents confirm this was indeed William F. Deterling.

Deterling was a member of the James. E. Blackwell party, William Otten was also lost, while Blackwell, Weaver, Livengood, Chard, and Boak survived.

~~~

Doxsey, Wilbur P. (age 18): Lynbrook, Long Island, New York, LOST. His partner was Job Johnson of Long Island, New York.

~~~

Dunlap, Archibald Bard (age 28): Dwight, Illinois, LOST. The son of Ingraham's cousin, Eliza Ingraham Dunlap, Bard was a member of the Major's team.

~~~

Frost, Bert S. (age 30): Springfield, Massachusetts, LOST.

~~~

Gaia Genessa, Edoardo (age 29): Biella, Italy, LOST. Gaia accompanied the Mount St. Elias expedition in 1897. A lawyer and friend of the Sella family, he married Vittorio and Erminio's sister, Giuseppina, in 1896. At the time of his death, he had a one year old son.
~~~

~~~

Gambell, Sylvenes "Vene" C. (age 35): LOST. He was a missionary for three years on St. Lawrence Island in the Bering Sea and drowned with his wife and child. Vene's brothers are Mr. Herbert F. Gambell of Tacoma, a post office employee, and Dr. Francis H. Gambell of Winfield, Iowa. Their father was J. C. Gambell, also of Winfield, Iowa.

Christian work on St. Lawrence Island began about 1887 when the Episcopal Church of America first built a mission church at a site called Chibuchack or Sivuqaq, Sevuokok, later renamed Gambell. No missionary could be found to take up the work.

Sheldon Jackson acquired the building in 1890 and approached the Gambells. Having been recruited from his post at Wapello, Iowa, the Rev. Mr. Gambell and his wife Nellie proceeded to St. Lawrence Island under the auspices of the education effort of the federal government. While Gambell was hired as a public schoolteacher, he also had to assure the Rev. Jackson of the soundness of his Christian faith.

The Gambells arrived on the island in August of 1894, just before the onset of winter.

The Gambell's daughter Margaret was born in April of 1897 in the village. In November of that year, the Gambells went to the States where Mrs. Gambell was hospitalized all winter.

In the summer of 1898, Vene Gambell's brother, Dr. Francis Gambell, government physician in Alaska, visited the Island with Dr. Jackson. They told the people of the death of the three Gambells and asked if they would like to change the name of the village to "Gambell" in memory of
~~~

the missionary-teachers and their infant daughter. The people said they would, and the name was changed.

From the Winfield, Iowa Historical Society:

There is a memorial monument in Scott Township Cemetery stating these dates:

Vene Gambell 1863 - 1898 (age 35) Nellie Gambell 1874 - 1898 (age 24) Margaret Gambell April 1897 - May 1898 (age 13 months and 9 days).

There is a stained glass window in the north end of the First Presbyterian Church, Winfield, Iowa, which was a gift of memoriam donated by local friends and relatives, citizens of both Wapello and Winfield. The plaque merely reads: "In memory of Rev. Vene Gambell, Nellie Gambell and their daughter, Margaret." There is a second window on the east and is a scene of the sun rising over the ocean waves with the inscription: "When the sea gives up its dead," Rev. 20:13, In memory of Vene, Nellie and Margaret.

~~~

Gambell, Nellie (age 24): LOST. She was the wife of Vene C. Gambell. Her maiden name was Nellie Webster, born in Iowa.

~~~

Gambell, Margaret (age 13 months): LOST. She was the one year-old child of Vene C. and Nellie Gambell. The passengers and crew quickly became fond of the little girl and dubbed her their "mascot."

~~~

Ginther, Frank W. (age 42): Harrisburg, Pennsylvania, LOST. He was born on September 20, 1855 in the United
~~~

States to German parents. He married Emma C. Abbot on August 3, 1882 in Harrisburg, Pennsylvania, but had no children. Emma stated that her husband was a good man, healthy and hearty, who earned $95.00 per month as a postal clerk. She last saw her husband on the first Monday in April 1898, when he left Harrisburg in the company of Percy Davenport and George Hiller, both of whom survived.

~~~

Ginther, Emma C. (age 37): Harrisburg, Pennsylvania. Emma was born Emma Abbott on December 7, 1860 in Harrisburg, Pennsylvania and was the widow of Frank W. Ginther. She was represented by her proctor, J. M. Weistling, in case number 1398 against Pacey, MacDougall and Southwick and sued them for $30,000.00. Her claim and deposition were filed from Harrisburg, Pennsylvania.

~~~

Gleason, William H. (age 47): Seattle, Washington, LOST. Gleason was a member of the Ingraham party who the Major had chosen to head one of his teams. He earned an average of $2,000.00 per year, was forty-seven years old and the time of his death, and was survived by his wife, Ollie Gleason, and a twelve year-old daughter, Bessie.

In the 1897 Seattle directory, William listed his occupation as carpenter residing at 820 Washington. The 1898 director listed him as a contractor living at the same address.

Ollie and W. H. Gleason were married in Sheridan, Oregon on April 4, 1882. Ollie Gleason sued for $5,000.00.

~~~

Gleason, Ollie (age 38): Seattle, Washington. Ollie was the widow of William H. Gleason and mother of Bessie
~~~

Gleason who resided in Washington State. She is sued for $5,000.00.

When the 1900 Seattle directory was published, Ollie Gleason was listed as the widow of W. H. Gleason, engaged in the insurance business at 223 Bailey Bldg (Dr. Lessey and Frederick Bausman had offices in this building.) and a residence (bds) at 112 7th Avenue South.

By 1902, Ollie was a real estate and insurance agent doing business from the same office at 223 Bailey Building. She continued in this business, earning a living for herself for nearly thirty more years.

~~~

Gleason, Bessie (age 11): Seattle, Washington. She was the daughter of William H. and Ollie Gleason.

~~~

Hamilton, Uehl (age 24): Ashland, Illinios. Possibly a member of Ingraham's team.

~~~

Hanford, Cornelius Holgate (age 49): Seattle, Washington. Hanford was the judge presiding over case 1398. In the 1897 Seattle directory, Cornelius was listed as a U. S. District Judge, 4th Avenue - N.E. corner of Marion; residence at 1021 E. Madison. Ada L. and Elaine E. Hanford both resided with him.

Judge Hanford's brother, Clarence Hanford, owned a large business in Seattle that includes outfitting, shipping, and printing.

Lowman and Hanford Stationary and Printing Company was located at 616 First Avenue. James D. Lowman, Henry Yesler's cousin, was the president; Bernard Pelly, secretary;
~~~

Clarence Hanford, manager of the printing department; John N. Jackson, manager of the stationery department. They were wholesale and retail stationers, booksellers, printers and binders. In additions, they vended cameras, photographic supplies, maps and charts.

Lowman and Pelly were also agents and managers of estates, financial brokers and insurance, operating out of the same building where Lowman and Hanford Lithographic Company was another of Clarence's business entities.

One of Judge Hanford's other brothers, Frank, was a partner in Hanford and Stewart, general insurance agents at 207 Pioneer Building, with a secondary company, Western Marine Insurance, operating out of the same offices. Frank Hanford resided at 820 Spring with his daughter Jessie, who was a student at the U of W, and his widowed mother, Abbie.

Another Hanford brother, Arthur (who sometimes went by his middle name, Ellwood), was a lawyer. In 1898, he resided with Frank and the family at 820 Spring Street. Arthur remained single his entire life.

For more on Hanford, search for articles at Historylink.org.

~~~

Hanson, John (age 37): Ballard, Washington, SURVIVOR. As the mate, John was paid $104.45 when the Jane Gray departed from Seattle. The 1898 directory listed him as a sailor residing at n s Baker between 1st and 2nd Avenues in Ballard with his wife, Katrina.

Many of the survivors commended his bravery during the sinking.

~~~

Hawco, John (age unknown): Residence unknown, LOST. A last-minute hire on the Jane Gray, he was reportedly a waiter.

~~~

Hederlund/Hedelund, Nick (age unknown): Residence unknown, LOST. Although Nick checked 1054 pounds of goods into the holds of the schooner on the day of her sailing, nothing else about him was recorded or remembered by any of the survivors or by John Pacey.

~~~

Hiller, George (age unknown): Harrisburg, Pennsylvania, SURVIVOR. On the first Monday of April 1898, George Hiller, Percy J. Davenport, and Frank W. Ginther departed Harrisburg, Pennsylvania for Seattle. Both George and Percy survive. F. W. Ginther does not. Neither Hiller nor Davenport was named in Admiralty case 1398, nor do they participate in the trial.

~~~

Hoyt (Esquire), John P. (age unknown): Mr. Hoyt was appointed by Judge C. H. Hanford to appraise the value of the Jane Grey immediately after the wreck. The value, including freight pending was established at $4392.18. In the 1897 Seattle directory, John R. Hoyt, was listed as Judge, Supreme Court, State of Washington, with rooms at the Hotel Butler. In 1898, he was also listed as being on the U of W Board of Regents.

~~~

Ingraham, Edward Sturgis (age 46): Seattle, Washington, SURVIVOR. Commonly known as the "Major," Ingraham was the leader of the expedition funded by Prince Luigi of

Italy. Ingraham accompanied Prince Luigi on his ascent of Mount St. Alias in the summer of 1897.

The 1897 Seattle directory listed Edward S. Ingraham as the president of the Calvert Company and publisher of the Seattle Guide at the northwest corner of 1st Avenue and Marion, with a residence at 2109 2nd Avenue. In 1898, the Seattle Guide, now the Seattle Pocket Guide, was published monthly at a subscription price of $1.00 per year. The Calvert Company was in the business of books and stationary.

In 1887, Ingraham, with a party from Seattle, climbed the northeast side of Mount Rainier to the 13,800 foot level

In 1888, Edward S. Ingraham, John Muir, Daniel W. Bass, Norman O. Booth, William Keith, N. Loomis, Charles Vancouver Piper, Philemon B. Van Trump and Arthur Churchill Warner were packed in to the Camp of the Clouds at Paradise (Mount Rainier) by John Hays and Joe Stampfler. The party, except Hays, Keith and Stampfler, climbed to the top.

In 1889, Edward S. Ingraham, Roger S. Green, Dr. H. E. Kelsey, L. M. Lessey, Rev. E. C. Smith, J. Van Smith and Grant Vaughn climbed from Paradise to the summit of Mount Rainier.

In 1894, Major Ingraham's Seattle party of 14 included 3 women, Dr. L. M. Lessey and H. E. Holmes. All reached the top of Mount Rainier.

Again in 1894, Major Ingraham summited Mount Rainier. This trip was sponsored by the Seattle Post-Intelligencer. He was accompanied by Dr. L. M. Lessey, George Russell and W. N. Sheffield (P. I. Photographer). Guided by E. Coke Hill and R. H. Boyd, the team checks on a report of an eruption on Mount Rainier.

In 1897, Major E. S. Ingraham and his party, including Frank A. Fredericks and F. W. Hawkins, took homing pigeons up the slopes of Mount Rainier.

Of his team of seventeen, only three others survived: G. H. Pennington, C. H. Packard, and L. M. Lessey. None of the survivors or deceased of the Ingraham team were involved in Admiralty case 1398.

Ingraham wasted no time in finding another ship to continue with his Alaskan expedition. In fact, he has already made Kotzebue Sound by the time litigation against Pacey, MacDougall and Southwick heated up. Prince Luigi of Italy funded the second trip as well.

From the Haller Lake Community Club Historian, Greg Dziekonski:

Ingraham High School is named after an adventurous gentleman who engaged in many careers but is remembered for being the first superintendent of Seattle Schools. Born in Maine in 1852, he was educated at a teachers' college where he claimed that incessant reading injured his eyes, giving him an excuse to go west to visit his brother. Ten days after arriving on Yesler's wharf on August 26, 1875, he was hired as a teacher at Central School, which was on 3rd and Madison. A certain Miss Chatham was the only other teacher in the building. At the time, there were two other schools in Seattle, each with two teachers: North School at 3rd and Pine, and South School at 6th and Main. Both were on the edge of virgin forest. The Belltown School at 3rd and Vine opened one year later. Total enrollment was about 150. Schools were heated by stoves, water was available at a pump, and janitors, electric lights, and telephones were nowhere to be found. Ingraham mostly taught art and history, requiring his students to recite the United States Constitution verbatim.

A grading system was first introduced by Ingraham in 1876, and the first trappings of high school courses commenced shortly thereafter. He was named superintendent of Seattle Schools in 1883, a position he had held in everything but name until that time. He presided over the graduation of Seattle's first high school class in 1886, which numbered twelve. When the Central School burned in 1888, Ingraham took the initiative to arrange its students' accommodation in the other facilities until Central School was replaced.

Ingraham resigned the superintendency shortly thereafter and went into the printing business, a vocation in which he had apprenticed before embarking on his teaching career. He also found time to serve on the state board of education following Washington's admittance into the union, and was elected to the city council.

He caught gold rush fever in 1898, and he and his party of 16 embarked on the schooner Jane Grey. The ship foundered 100 miles off Cape Flattery, and 34 of the 61 aboard drowned. Ingraham's tenacity revealed itself as he managed to cut a launch loose, reach Vancouver Island with 26 others, and swiftly organize a second party which reached Kotzebue Sound. While in Alaska, he led a rescue mission 175 miles up the Selawik River in order to save some miners who were dying of scurvy.

After mining and prospecting in Nome, he returned to Seattle with his family in 1901. He was an avid mountain climber, Ingraham Glacier on Mount Rainier being named for him, and was later instrumental in establishing Seattle's first Boy Scout chapter. He continued to teach part time, and passed away in 1926.

~~~

Johnson, Albert (age unkown): Seattle, Washington, SURVIVOR. He was a crewmember and assistant cook/waiter on the Jane Gray. When the vessel left port, Pacey advanced him $29.00 in wages. The 1898 directory listed him as a seaman on the steamer Fairhaven.

~~~

Johnson, Job (age unknown): Long Island, New York, SURVIVOR. The Seattle Post-Intelligencer reports him as being a seaman from Long Island, New York. Along with C. J. Reilly, he was found floating on debris from the wreckage in the early dawn hours and pulled into the launch by the other survivors. He was traveling with Wilbur P. Doxsey, who drowned.

~~~

Johnston, W. Arnot (age 22): Seattle, Washington, LOST. Before leaving on the Jane Gray, Arnot worked as a collector at the Seattle Post-Intelligencer and lived with his mother, Anna J. (widow of Nathan M.), at 823 Seneca. He was a member of Ingraham's team.

~~~

Kingsbury, Albert G. (age unknown): Boston, Massachusetts, SURVIVOR. Kingsbury was traveling with Bernard D. Ranney of Mexico City and Kalamazoo, Michigan. His partner did not survive.

Kingsbury was a noted author and mining expert in the eastern United States.

In 1900 Ellsworth Luce West, a whaling captain from Martha's Vinyard, and some Boston investors formed a company to develop the coal deposits near Cape Lisburne to supply the Nome market. Needing a suitable ship, they entered the winning bid for the Corwin and organized as the Corwin Trading Company. The project increased in scope when one investor (veteran prospector, engineer, and writer A.G. Kingsbury) pledged Nome gold claims for his shares. Although Kingsbury described them as "conservative Boston capitalists" the investors appear to have been as much enthusiasts as any Nome prospectors; all insisted on joining the expedition. To create cargo space in the Corwin, West had the entire wardroom torn out. The lost accommodations were replaced with a cabin constructed from the stern to the engine room, creating a raised poop deck. This modification is shown clearly in a 1902 photograph. West describes the Corwin as brig-rigged in this period, but photos from 1900 continue to show a gaff on the foremast and no yards crossed on the mainmast, so this is more a difference of terminology than a change of sail-plan.

A few of the literary works of A. G. Kingsbury published in National Magazine include: In the Canal Country, Seattle and the Nome Rush, A Summer in the Arctic Circle, Through Unknown Regions of Alaska, Winter and Spring in the Arctic Eldorado.

~~~

Lessey, Dr. Luther M. (age 32): Seattle, Washington, SURVIVOR. The 1897 Seattle directory listed Luther M. Lessey, Dentist, at 310 Bailey Bldg. (Bausman, Kelleher & Emory conducted business here, as well as did Major Ingraham.) Luther's resided at 2221 5th Avenue with his wife, Lulu.
~~~

In addition to Major Ingraham, G. H. Pennington, and C. H. Packard, Lessey was one of four surviving members of the Ingraham Expedition.

On at least three occasions, Dr. L. M. Lessey was known to have climbed Mount Ranier with Ingraham: once in 1889 and twice in 1894.

The doctor returned to Alaska with Ingraham after the sinking of the Jane Gray.

~~~

Lindsay, John James "Jack" (age 21): Everett, Washington, LOST. Jack was a member of the Ingraham expedition. The son of Kezia Collins Wright and Hugh Lindsay, he was a two-time University of Washington football team captain (1896-1897), 1897 Washington track team captain, business manager of the "Pacific Wave," and a charter member of the Sigma Nu – Gamma Chi Chapter fraternity.

In the 1897 Seattle directory, John J. Lindsay was listed as a student at the U of W with rooms at E Hall, old U of W while the 1898 directory showed his room at north hall of the old university.

The University of Washington records reflect that John attended from September 3, 1895 through the end of 1897. When he enrolled, he declared his major as pursuing a Ph. D. in Pharmacy, but at some point changed it to a Bachelor of Science in Chemistry. At the time of his death he had accumulated 50 credits in Political & Social Science, History, English, German, Chemistry, Military Science & Tactics, and Geology.

~~~

Little, Philip C. (age 26): Seattle, Washington, LOST. A member of the Ingraham party, Phil was the son of Frank

N. Little, a member of the board of public works and superintendent of streets, sewers and parks with an office at city hall, residing at 532 Bellevue Avenue North in 1898. His sister, Etta, lived there as well and was employed as an operator at Sunset Telephone and Telegraph Company. At one time Phil was employed as a janitor at city hall.

~~~

Livengood, Silas (age 66): Seattle, Washington, SURVIVOR. Livengood bought his outfit with the other members of the Blackwell party: Blackwell, Weaver, Otten (drowned), Deterling (drowned), Chard and Boak. Once back in Seattle, he became a member of the "committee" named in Admiralty case 1398. Prior to that action, he filed action number 25633 in King County Superior Court suing Pacey, MacDougall and Southwick for $5871.32 or $5949.00 in damages.

During his testimony, he stated that he had a berth in the after cabin and that water was above his knees at the time that he woke to make his escape.

His brother, James K. Livengood, was originally scheduled to depart on the Jane Gray, however, for reasons unknown, he did not.

~~~

Livengood, James K. (age 46): After meeting in Seattle in the fore part of May 1898, James Livengood, a brother of Silas, purchased his outfit with the James Blackwell party, but did not purchase a ticket or embark on the Jane Gray even though they had negotiated the ticket price together.

Livengood testified from his home in Lincoln, Nebraska on May 12, 1899. By 1908, James was living in Hutchinson,

Kansas, where another Livengood brother, George, resided.

~~~

MacDougall, John B. (age 43): John was the President of MacDougall & Southwick Company. Incorporated in 1891with partners Henry C. Southwick and John A. Fraser, the company started with capital stock of $200,000 divided into 2000 shares at $100 each. Other silent partners joined later, one by the name of Shultz, who signed John Pacey's immigration papers.

An immigrant from Scotland, he served as the Seattle School Board Director from 1890 to 1895. The 1897 Seattle directory listed John B. MacDougall, President of MacDougall and Southwick Company, with a residence at 1100 Terry Avenue, telephone number Buff 521.

With his wife Minnie, who he married in 1897, they had one son and one daughter. John later formed The Grand Dalles Land and Irrigation Company, which he was president of, purchasing property along the Columbia River and in various locations around Douglas County, Washington.

~~~

McKelvey, Patrick (age 43): Eau Claire, Wisconsin, LOST. Patrick was the last man to purchase passage on the Jane Gray, arriving so late that his freight was never entered into Pacey's ledger.

~~~

Meany, Edmond Stephen (age 35): Seattle, Washington. Meany is mentioned here because of his close association with the University of Washington, Mountaineering, and conservation. He was one of the University's faculty
~~~

representatives at the Sigma Nu Gamma Chi fraternity where Jack Lindsay was a charter member. The 1897 Seattle directory listed him as the secretary for the Board of Regents and Registrar at the U of W. His residence was at Cambridge Avenue and Federal, Brooklyn.

By 1898, Meany was a faculty member at the U: Edmond Stephen Meany, B.S., Professor of American History and Lecturer on Forestry.

For more on Edmond Meany, see his files at the University of Washington.

~~~

Millay, William David (age 30): Inaccurately reported as being from La Conner, Skagit County, Washington, LOST. Millay was from South Thomaston, Maine, and knew Ingraham from the Major's early days teaching school there. He was one of Ingraham's first choices to accompany the expedition and shared his bunk with Clayton Packard when the water got too deep in the forward cabin.

~~~

Oleson/Olsen/Olson, Charles A. (age unknown): Seattle, Washington, SURVIVOR. He is a crewmember and the cook on board the Jane Gray. Pacey advanced Charles $77.25 before leaving Seattle. He was the first person to alert seaman Charles Carlson that water was entering the aft cabin.

At the time of publication of the 1898 Seattle directory, Charles Olsen was a cook on the steamer Greyhound with a residence at n s Mercer, corner of 4th.

~~~
~~~

Otten, William (age unknown): Inaccurately reported as being from Pennsylvania, he was from Minnesota, LOST. On the list of missing, he was most often referred to as "Otter." Along with Deterling, Otten was one of two members of the J. E. Blackwell party to parish in the sinking.

~~~

Pacey, John G. (age 33): Seattle, Washington. Owner of the Jane Gray and secretary at MacDougall & Southwick Company, he appears to have been the company fall guy - an individual who assumes all liabilities and claims neither assets nor the ability to pay any debts.

The 1897 Seattle directory listed John G. Pacey, secretary at MacDougall and Southwick, 717-723 1st Avenue, residing (bds) at 904 5th Avenue. This same year, he married Annie McGinnis, a teacher in the Seattle public schools.

July of 1898 found Pacey escaping the Seattle controversy in Providence Wells, Kansas. The Wichita Daily Eagle got wind of it and reported his stay in the local paper: "John Pacey was spending a few days at Providence Wells. Pacey is now at Seattle, and owned the big steamer which went down in the Pacific the other day."

Pacey was later declared bankrupt, in absentia, by Goodyear Rubber Company. Perhaps because his wife, Annie, was ill, John lived in San Diego at the time. However, it is apparent from this investigation that he hid his assets well.

~~~

Packard, Clayton Hall (age 39): Snohomish, Washington, SURVIVOR. Along with Ingraham, Pennington, and

Lessey, he was a surviving member of the Ingraham Expedition.

In the 1892 Seattle directory, Clayton H. Packard was listed as a journalist residing at 2618 Front. By 1900, when he can be found in Seattle again, he lists his occupation as miner. At the time, there also seems to have been a business called "Packard Mining Engineering."

SNOHOMISH, SNOHOMISH COUNTY, The Snohomish Eye, established on January 11, 1882, by H. F. Jackson and Clayton H. Packard, the latter being editor and manager throughout the paper's existence. One main reason for the publication and a chief source of its revenue was the legal necessity for publishing timber land claim notices. It was started as a four-column, four-page weekly. Mr. Jackson retired on January 17,1883, and about that time C. A. Missimer joined the firm. The paper was increased to five columns and lengthened. In 1884, Mr. Missimer retired and Clayton H. Packard became sole proprietor. A brother, Charles F. Packard, was part owner for a year. The paper suspended publication in 1897. (History of Skagit and Snohomish Counties, page 435.) Charles Prosch wrote this compliment: "It was spritely and newsy and paid its way from the outset, according its enterprising proprietor something more than a living. The fact of its being quite frequently quoted abroad is evidence that the Eye is not unknown beyond the borders of the town and county in which it is published." (In Washington Press Association Proceedings, 1887-1890, page 37.)

Clayton Packard's father, Myron W. Packard, was a Civil War Veteran from the Wisconsin 30th Infantry who lived in Snohomish from 1871 to 1879. When his father returned to Wisconsin, Clayton remained in Washington.

Packard was later employed with the Zoology department at the University of Washington - in 1906, the year that William Rufus Lindsay, Jack Lindsay's brother, graduated with a degree in mining engineering.

Clayton H. Packard was a noted Snohomish City editor himself, having published the Snohomish Eye from 1882-97. Born in 1859, Clayton came to Snohomish in 1871 when his father, Myron W. Packard, moved his family to Snohomish. After eight years here, his parents moved back to Wisconsin and then lived in Skagit valley but Clayton founded the Eye, switching roles with Eldridge Morse; Morse employed him before at the Northern Star. An outdoorsman, Clayton was also an ardent hunter, a Free-Thinker, and issued physical challenges to the competing publishers. From 1891-93 he took on a partner, George E. MacDonald, a famous editor of Free-Thinker journals. In MacDonald's 1931 autobiography, he wrote that Packard shut down the Eye after suffering financially through the Depression that started in 1893. Packard nearly lost his life on a windjammer that was blown ashore, leaving him a castaway among the Indians. Finding no gold in paying quantities, he returned to Puget Sound country and then moved back East to work for The Truth Seeker journal. After returning again to Washington – possibly around the time he wrote this eulogy (in 1914), he was in an accident that permanently paralyzed one of his legs and his right arm. By 1931 he was an inmate at the Home for Union Printers in Colorado Springs. In March, we will share many of the Packard stories from the Eye days when he explored Skagit and surrounding counties as Morse did in the 1870s and '80s.

~~~
~~~

Palmer, Horace (age 36): Lebanon, Ohio, LOST. Horace was a member of the Ingraham party and left behind his thirty year-old wife, Belle, an eight year-old daughter, Edith, and a four year-old son, Clayton. He had formerly worked at Mansfield Buggy Company.

Two years after Horace's death, Belle died, leaving the children in the care of his mother, Margaret. Horace and Belle share a common headstone at the cemetery in Lebanon, Warren County, Ohio.

~~~

Pennington, George H. (age 48): Snohomish, Washington, SURVIVOR. Along with Ingraham, Packard and Lessey, he was a surviving member of the Ingraham expedition and returned to Alaska with the Major after the Jane Gray went down.

By mid-1900, George and his wife Emma, along with five of their seven children, operated a boarding house in Excelsior, Whatcom County, Washington.

~~~

Prince Luigi of Italy (age 25): Prince Luigi Amedeo, Duke of the Abruzzi, funded the Ingraham Expedition with $10,000.00.

Born on January 29, 1873 in Madrid during his father's brief reign as King Amedeo of Spain, Luigi was a grandson of King Vittorioa Emanuale II of Italy. He was the youngest of three sons born to Amadeo and his consort, Maria Vittoria dal Pozzo. King Humbert, or Umberto, was Luigi's uncle.

Although a nobleman with the extensive title of "Prince Luigi Amedeo Giuseppe Maria Ferdinando Francesco di

Savoi di Aosta," he chafed at the title and excelled at his true passion – exploration and adventure.

~~~

Ranney, Bernard David (age 44): LOST. Born in Stockbridge, Madison County, New York on July 5, 1853, he was once a farmer in Comstock, Michigan and was at some point engaged in the real estate business in Kansas. Newspaper articles state that at the time of his death, he was either from Mexico City or Kalamazoo, Michigan. A. G. Kingsbury (a survivor), the writer and mining expert, was his partner on the expedition to Alaska and was known to have worked hydroelectric projects though out Mexico and the United States. It is likely that they shared the same occupation.

Ranney was at one time the proprietor of the Princess Restaurant in Wichita, Kansas. John G. Pacey worked at the First National Bank in this same town and visited friends and family there after Bernard was lost in the sinking of the Jane Gray.

~~~

Reilly, C. J. (age unknown): Hartford, Connecticut, SURVIVOR. Reilly was pulled aboard the launch after spending several hours floating on lumber from the wreck and provides a vivid account of that night and the following day. He witnessed William Gleason's death. His traveling partner was Conture (or Contre or Contoure) who also survived. At some point, C. J. had been involved in the theatrical business.

~~~

Ritter, Edward F. (age 35): Poughkeepsie, New York, LOST. Ritter was traveling with Coney Weston, who
~~~

survived. His brother, George, visited Edmond Meany's friend, Jim Bushnell, in Poughkeepsie, looking for answers as to the cause of the sinking.

~~~

Roberts, Manuel F. (age unknown): Seattle, Washington, SURVIVOR. Manuel Roberts was traveling with Ben E. Snipes, Jr. In the 1898 directory, Manuel was listed as the janitor at the Rainier Hotel at 5th Avenue and Columbia where he also lived. Ben E. Snipes was a resident of the hotel, as was his son Ben Jr., who was a bookkeeper at Oceanic Packaging Company. The manager of the Rainier Hotel was Frederick Sawyer.

Prior to sailing, Manuel F. Roberts received a check in the amount $100.00 drawn on the Boston National Bank of Seattle and endorsed by Nellie Cale-Sawyer, presumably to cover his passage on the Jane Gray. Nellie later wrote another check in the amount of $6.50 to MacDougall and Southwick Company that said: "account paid in full."

After the sinking, Manuel befriends Erminio Sella.

~~~

Saulsberry/Saulsbury/Salisbury, Frank G. (age unknown): Minnesota, LOST. Frank was one of the Ingraham party. M. H. Salisbury of Amboy, Minnesota represented him at the meeting for friends of the lost on June 8, 1898.

~~~

Schmid, Conrad George (age 21): Mercer Island, Washington, LOST. Conrad was a member of the Ingraham expedition and a classmate of Jack Lindsay at the University of Washington, football player, engineering major, and brother of Victor J. Schmidt. His father was Vitus Schmid, a Seattle pioneer.
~~~

The University of Washington records, some admittedly missing, reflect that Conrad Schmid attended from December 1896 to March 1897 and had not declared a major by the time he left.

~~~

Schmid, Victor Joseph (age 23): Mercer Island, Washington, LOST. Victor was a member of the Ingraham expedition, a classmate of Jack Lindsay at the University of Washington, junior year football player, and brother of Conrad G. Schmidt. His father was Vitus Schmid.

Victor was one of the University of Washington students who served as a pack mule for Prince Luigi's Mount St. Elias expedition in 1897.

The 1897 Seattle directory listed Victor J. Schmidt as a student at the U of W, but no residence was listed. The name above his is Teresa Schmidt, his sister, who was also a student at the U, residing at (bds) J. S. Krape, Brooklyn.

The University of Washington records reflect that Victor attended from September 1895 to February 1897 and was majoring in Mathematics and Astronomy.

~~~

Sella, Erminio (age 32): Biella, Italy, SURVIVOR. Erminio was a brother of famed photographer Vittorio Sella, His brother-in-law, Edoardo Gaia, died in the sinking of the Jane Gray.

Born on July 20, 1865, Erminio was a son of the pioneer of Italian photography Giuseppe Venanzio and Clementina Mosca Riatel. Sella graduated from the university at Turin in 1887. A civil and mechanical engineering major, he later specialized in meteorological science in Berlin.

To learn the use of photographic equipment and gain mountaineering experience, Erminio accompanied his brother, Vittorio, and Prince Luigi on the 1888 winter crossing of Mont Blanc and the 1889 ascent of Monte Rosa.

After returning to Italy, Erminio toured India, photographing Hindu and Muslim sites in 1899. Over the next several years, he continued his photographic exploration, traveling to Sri Lanka, Trinidad and Tobago, Colubia, Venezuela, and Panama, eventually returning to the vineyards of his homeland, where the family operated the Sella and Mosca Winery in Biella.

To this day, the Sella Foundation of Italy maintains the photographic collections of the entire Sella family.

~~~

Snipes, Ben E., Jr. (age 23): Seattle, Washington, LOST. Ben was a young man about town in Seattle, belonging to the Agayne Club, a local society organization. He took a position within the city, then gave it up to pursue riches and adventure in Alaska.

At the time of the publication of the 1898 Seattle Directory, Ben was employed as a bookkeeper at Oceanic Packaging Company. He lived at the Rainier Hotel, as did his father. His traveling partner was Manuel F. Roberts, the hotel janitor and night watchman.

In 1890, Ben's father started the branch house known as the Roslyn Bank of Ben E. Snipes & Co. to accommodate the mining interests of that locality. He also owned extensive landed interests in Klickitat and Kittitass counties, and purchased the Hill tract of 100 acres within the city limits of Seattle, which he had platted and subdivided before placing it on the market. Mr. Snipes was married in Columbus, Klickitat County, in 1864, to Miss Mary A.
~~~

Parrett, a native of Oregon, and they had one son, Ben E., Jr. In July of 1890, Mr. Snipes moved his family to Seattle, and purchased a handsome residence on the corner of Eleventh and Madison streets.

~~~

Southwick, Henry C. (age 41): Although Henry was merely the vice president and treasurer of the MacDougall & Southwick Company, he was a controlling factor in the organization. Born in New York on January 2, 1857 to Henry Clay and Elsa (Eames) Southwick, he acquired a great deal of wealth at a young age. He continued to reside in New York, making frequent trips out west to oversea his business interests. The 1897 Seattle directory listed him as the vice President and treasurer of MacDougall and Southwick, residing in New Rochelle, New York.

He admitted to making the notorious statement about "paying pew rent."

~~~

Spencer, Burrey S. (age unknown): San Francisco, California, LOST. Burrey worked for the Union Paper Company of San Francisco as an attorney at law. He was a single man, survived by his brother, George Spencer. He was traveling with Charles Wilkinson, Ed and Fred Taylor.

~~~

Stutzman, John M. (age unknown): Westfield, New Jersey, LOST. John appears to have been traveling on the Jane Gray alone. He was survived by Mrs. John Stutzman and three children in Westfield, New Jersey. He was a florist, well known as an expert on African violets.

~~~

Taylor, Edwin Mastick (age 39): San Francisco, California, LOST. Nearly 40 years old at the time of his death, he was survived by his wife, Nellie M. Taylor. He was the son of Samual P. Taylor, a wealthy paper manufacturer in San Francisco, and the brother of Frederick Taylor, who also died on this voyage of the Jane Gray. At the meeting for friends of the lost on June 8th, Frank Olsen, secretary of the board of works, and H. W. Carrol represent both of the Taylor brothers.

He last saw his wife, Nellie, when he departed from San Francisco on May 4th, 1898.

From the Hotel Seattle, Edwin paid one cent to mail a letter to his wife on May 18th, 1898. Addressed to 308 Buchanan Street, San Francisco, this letter made the 3:00 p.m. post. The following day, Edwin sent his last communication to Nellie from the Hotel Seattle. As it was stamped with the 6:00 p.m. post, it seems likely that he dropped it at the desk on his way to the ship.

~~~

Taylor, Nellie (age 37): California. Nellie Noble (Martel) was the widow of Edwin Taylor. They were married on March 13, 1883. At the time of her deposition on May 3, 1899, she was 38 years old, lived at the Hotel Bella Vista in San Francisco and had no other income than "what my brother gives me." She last saw Edwin on May 4, 1898 when he was still 39 years old. She last heard from him on May 19, 1898. She stated that he was an honorable husband who was 40 years old and earned about $4000.00 per year in the "wholesale paper business and special agent." Nellie sued Pacey, MacDougall, and Southwick for $6000.00.

Additional notes about the Taylors:
~~~

Samuel P. Taylor is well-known in the annals of Marin County history, and the county has a state park which bears his name. Members of his family were prominent residents of San Anselmo for many years after his death and during the town's formative years. Five Taylor homes were built in town in the 1890s, and four still stand today.

Samuel Penfield Taylor was born in Saugerties, New York, on the Hudson River, in 1827. The Gold Rush lured him to California from Boston in 1849, and the search for lumber for his San Francisco lumber yard brought him to Marin in 1853. Samuel was likely familiar with the operation of paper mills along the Hudson River and in Connecticut, and he saw the potential in the area along Daniels Creek, later called Papermill Creek, for the West Coast's first paper mill. He purchased property and started construction of the mill the following year. The venture was highly successful.

In January 1886, Samuel P. Taylor died at the age of 58 leaving his wife, Sarah Washington Irving Taylor, and seven sons and one daughter. In 1888, the family began to purchase lots in San Anselmo. Sarah borrowed money using the mill business and property in Taylorville as collateral to keep S. P. Taylor & Company going, but in the economic depression of 1893, she was unable to make the mortgage payments. The Taylor family lost the business and property and was forced to move. Sarah, four of her seven sons, and her daughter relocated to San Anselmo.

The four still-standing Taylor homes provide a lovely visual reminder of earlier days in San Anselmo.

101 Ross Avenue:

In February 1888, Ella I. M. Taylor, the wife of Sarah and Samuel's fourth son William Penfield Taylor, purchased lots in the Sunnyside subdivision along Ross Avenue. The Taylor's simplified Stick Style Victorian house at 101 Ross Avenue was constructed about 1893.

While all the Taylor's sons worked in some capacity for the S.P. Taylor Company, only Will Taylor was educated and trained in the manufacture of paper, eventually becoming the superintendent of the mill in Taylorville. In San Anselmo, Will was one of the three first elected trustees of the San Anselmo School District when it was formed in 1893. He was appointed San Anselmo postmaster in January 1898. When Will was elected Marin County Sheriff the following year, he, Ella, and their two sons moved to San Rafael. Will's brother George McCullen Taylor took over the duties of postmaster and was officially appointed to that job on April 7, 1905. George Taylor continued to serve as San Anselmo's postmaster until February 1907.

The house on Ross Avenue was rented until it was sold by the Taylors in 1904 to Laura Daniel. It is owned today by the San Francisco Theological Seminary.

102 Ross Avenue:

Frederick Sproul Taylor, the youngest son of Samuel and Sarah Taylor, and his wife, Kate R. Eagleson, purchased the lot directly across the street on Ross Avenue from James Foss in October 1892. Based on the photographic evidence and the 1928 Marin County Assessor's records, the house was built about 1896. Today, it sits behind St. Nicholas Russian Orthodox Church and serves as the parish hall.

In contrast to the house at 101 Ross Avenue, this house projects a spacious and sprawling sense of the Shingle Style even though it deviates from the classic Shingle Style in that the exterior walls are clad in narrow clapboard.

Many Shingle Style homes include polygonal towers and dormers of varying shapes, including the low arched eyebrow seen here.

Frederick and his brother Edwin Mastick Taylor were salesmen for the S.P. Taylor Company. Like their father before them, they caught the gold rush fever, and they left in the spring of 1898 for the Klondike gold fields of Alaska. Both men perished when the schooner Jane Grey sank off Cape Flattery, Washington. Frederick's widow moved east with her two daughters to live with her mother and brothers.

206 Saunders Avenue:

In 1891, William Penfield Taylor purchased an 8.76 acre parcel in San Anselmo from Camille Grosjean. The property was transferred to James Irving Taylor, eldest son of Samuel and Sarah, and his wife Jean Wooster in 1899. The James I. Taylor family is enumerated here in the 1900 census. The house was constructed on San Anselmo Creek about 1895 at 206 Saunders at the corner of Taylor. The Bungalow Style house with its roof design and decorative detailing radiates a unique Eastern sensibility.

Jim Taylor worked as a salesman for his father's business in San Francisco. Later, he took over management of the hotel at Camp Taylor and established the Irving Fur Tannery on the Taylor property. Both enterprises closed when the Taylors lost the property to foreclosure.

Jim Taylor was one of five men elected to the Board of Trustees when San Anselmo was incorporated in 1907. He served one year before being elected to the State Assembly on the Republican ticket, representing Marin County in the 30th Legislative Session. Three of the four sons of Jim and Jean Taylor had careers in the paper industry and a fourth son, a career in journalism. In addition to their own children, the Taylors raised a young orphan, George Anderson Martin (1875-1945). George Martin, one of the best known San Anselmo pioneers, served as the first town marshal and pound master, and ran the local express company.

Jim Taylor died in 1916, Jean in 1921, and the house was sold in 1922. Ownership has been in the Reardon family since then.

The land north of San Francisco that was once known as Camp Taylor is now a California State Park.

~~~

Taylor, Frederick Sproul (age 31): San Francisco, California, LOST. He was also a son of Samuel P. Taylor, a wealthy paper manufacturer in San Francisco and the brother of Edwin Taylor, who went down with the Jane Gray. He was 31 years old and earned $2400 per year at the time of his death. Fred was survived by his wife, Kate E. Taylor, and their minor children, Edna M. and Frances M. Taylor.

At the meeting for friends of the lost on June 8, 1898, Frank Olsen, secretary of the board of works, and H. W. Carrol represented both Taylor brothers.

~~~

Taylor, Kate E. (age unknown): California. Kate (Eagleson) was the widow of Frederick Taylor. They were married on September 2, 1890 in San Francisco. On May 3, 1899, she filed a claim for $6000.00 against John Pacey and the MacDougall and Southwick outfitting firm. In June of 1899, Kate and the children had moved to Mount Vernon, New York, to live with other family members.

~~~

Taylor, Edna (age 6): At the time of Nellie Taylor's deposition, Edna was the seven years old. She was the daughter of Frederick and Kate Taylor.

~~~

Taylor, Frances (age 3): At the time of Nellie Taylor's deposition Frances was four. She was the youngest daughter of Frederick and Kate Taylor.

~~~

Taylor, James I. (age 42): San Anselmo, Marin County, California. James was a brother of Fred and Ed Taylor who testified with Nellie in June of 1899. He was also and agent in the paper manufacturing business. He last saw his brothers on May 4, 1898 in San Francisco.

~~~

Wachter/Waechter/Wachker, Hans (age unknown): Biella, Italy or Tyrol, SURVIVOR. Hazarding an educated guess, he was from the northern alpine border of Italy, and likely an Austrian. Some evidence indicates he was a well-known mountaineer in that area or possibly the artist Hans Wacker.

~~~

Weaver, William S. (age 35): Muncy, Pennsylvania, SURVIVOR. Named in Admiralty case 1398, Weaver filed action number 25634 in King County Superior Court. His suit was varied between the amounts of $6831.72 and $6858.82. Weaver was a member of the Blackwell party and the "committee" who banded together in pursuit of damages from Pacey, MacDougall and Southwick.

~~~

Weston, Coney (age 31): Skowhegan, Maine, SURVIVOR. Coney left his wife, Annie, and eight month-old baby, Irene, back in Long Island when he embarked on the gold prospecting trip. At some point, Weston met up with Edward Ritter who drowned on the Jane Grey.

Coney became a member of the second Ingraham party to go to Kotzebue Sound.

~~~

Wilkinson, Charles W. (age unknown): San Francisco, California, SURVIVOR. Wilkinson was the only surviving member of the Taylor Brothers' party of four. He was the foreman at Valeau and Peterson's Press Rooms in San Francisco. In addition to Edwin and Frederick Taylor, Wilkinson was traveling with Burrey S. Spencer. As the lone survivor of his party, Charles joined the "committee" and sued Pacey, MacDougal and Southwick for $6276.72. Like the other survivors who participated in the legal action, he was awarded $122.00.

~~~

Williams, Charles (age 56): Olympia, Washington, LOST. A native of England, he had resided in Washington State for a very short time and was survived by wife of one year, Mary Williams.

~~~

Williams, Mary (age unknown): Olympia, Washington. Mary was the widow of Charles Williams who got her claim in past the filing date set by Judge Hanford.

~~~

Young, Spencer W. (age 62): Seattle, Washington, LOST. Spencer was survived by his wife, Cordelia A. Young, and a minor daughter, Effie Young. The 1897 Seattle directory listed Spencer as a miner residing at 811 Pike. His sons, George W. Spencer, a clerk, and Preston W. Spencer, a seaman, lived there as well.

Before moving to Seattle, he was a successful log dealer in Packwood, Snohomish County, Washington.

~~~

Young, Cordelia A. (age unknown): Seattle, Washington. Spencer Young and Cordelia were married on April 10, 1869 in Rostock County, Maine. She stated that he earned $2500.00 per year and sued for $5000. Like the other widows, she was awarded $610.00.

~~~

Young, Effie (age 17): She was the daughter of Spencer and Cordelia A. Young who worked at the Western Union office. Effie was one of the first to learn of the sinking of the Jane Gray.

SELECTED REFERENCES

"$200.00 REWARD." Victoria Daily Columnist, June 8, 1898: 6. Online. http://www.britishcolonist.ca

Action 24632, Blackwell, James E. v. Pacey, John G.; MacDougall, John B.; Southwick, Henry C.; and the MacDougall & Southwick Company, a corporation, June 22, 189; Superior Court for the State of Washington for the county of King; Records of the Superior Courts of the Washington States, Microfilm; Washington State Archives-Puget Sound Regional Branch (Bellevue).

Action 24633, Livengood, Silas v. Pacey, John G.; MacDougall, John B.; Southwick, Henry C.; and the MacDougall & Southwick Company, a corporation, June 22, 189; Superior Court for the State of Washington for the county of King; Records of the Superior Courts of the Washington States, Microfilm; Washington State Archives-Puget Sound Regional Branch (Bellevue).

Action 24634, Weaver, William S. v. Pacey, John G.; MacDougall, John B.; Southwick, Henry C.; and the MacDougall & Southwick Company, a corporation, June 22, 189; Superior Court for the State of Washington for the county of King; Records of the Superior Courts of the Washington States, Microfilm; Washington State Archives-Puget Sound Regional Branch (Bellevue).

Action 24635, Boak, George R. v. Pacey, John G.; MacDougall, John B.; Southwick, Henry C.; and the MacDougall & Southwick Company, a corporation, June 22, 189; Superior Court for the State of Washington for the county of King; Records of the Superior Courts of the

Washington States, Microfilm; Washington State Archives-Puget Sound Regional Branch (Bellevue).

Action 24636, Chard, Charles E. v. Pacey, John G.; MacDougall, John B.; Southwick, Henry C.; and the MacDougall & Southwick Company, a corporation, June 22, 189; Superior Court for the State of Washington for the county of King; Records of the Superior Courts of the Washington States, Microfilm; Washington State Archives-Puget Sound Regional Branch (Bellevue).

Admiralty file 1398, (Limitation of Liability), Pacey, John G.; MacDougall, John B.; Southwick, Henry C.; and the MacDougall & Southwick Company, a corporation, January 3, 1899; U. S. District Court for the Northern Division of the State of Washington; Records of the District Courts of the United States, Record Group 82; National Archives and Records Administration-Northwest Region (Seattle).

Admiralty file 1452, Pacey, John G. v. the schooner Una, August 14, 1899; U. S. District Court for the Northern Division of the State of Washington; Records of the District Courts of the United States, Record Group 91; National Archives and Records Administration-Northwest Region (Seattle).

"Alaska Schooner Lost." New York Times, June 3, 1898. Online. http://query.nytimes.com/search/sitesearch/

Ancestry.com: http://www.ancestry.com/

"Ashland Boy Drowned." Daily Illinois State Journal, June 4, 1898: 4. Online. GenealogyBank.com.

Author Unknown. An Illustrated History of Skagit and Snohomish Counties: Their People, Their Commerce and Their Resources, Interstate Publishing, 1909. Online.

http://www.archive.org/stream/illustratedhisto00inte#page/n3/mode/2up

Bagley, Clarence. The History of Seattle From the Earliest Settlement to the Present Time, Three Volumes, The S. J. Clarke Publishing Company, 1916. Google eBook.

Bankruptcy file 2426, Pacey, John G., February 4, 1903; U. S. District Court for the Northern Division of the State of Washington; Records of the District Courts of the United States, Record Group 12; National Archives and Records Administration-Northwest Region (Seattle).

"Brevities of the Day." Morning Olympian, May 26, 1898: 3. Online. Genealogybank.com.

"Brevities of the Day." Morning Olympian, June 3, 1898: 3. Online. Genealogybank.com.

Caldbick, John. Federal District Judge Cornelius H. Hanford resigns during impeachment investigation on July 22, 1912, Essay, Historylink.org, 2010. Online. http://www.historylink.org/index.cfm?DisplayPage=output.cfm&file_id=9547

Caller, James Moore, and Ober, Maria A. Geneology of the Descendents of Lawrence and Cassandra Southwick of Salem, Mass: The Original Emigrants and the Ancestors of the Families Who Have Since Borne His Name, New England Historic Geneological Soc., 1881: pp 380, 381, 496, 498. Google eBook.

Canada, Department of Fisheries. Annual Report, Volume 28-31: pp 408. Google eBook.

"C. H. Packard and his Experience." Sumpter Miner, December 5, 1900: pp 14. Online. http://chroniclingamerica.loc.gov/lccn/sn96088466/1900-12-05/ed-1/

Daves, Jim, and Porter, W. Thomas. The Glory of Washington: The People and Events That Shaped the Husky Athletic Tradition, Sports Publishing Inc., 2001.

"Decision in the Famous Jane Gray Case." Seattle Daily Times, January 17, 1900: 3. Online. Genealogybank.com.

"Drawn to Death Beneath the Waves of the Pacific." Seattle Post-Intelligencer, June 2, 1898: 1, 6. Microfilm, Seattle Public Library.

"Faced Death Locked in a Last Embrace." Seattle Post-Intelligencer, June 3, 1898: 12. Microfilm, Seattle Public Library.

Filippi, Filipo di. The Ascent of Mount St. Elias, 1900. Google eBook.

Findlay, John, "Bricks, Brains, and Partisan Politics: Edmond S. Meany, the University of Washington, and State Government 1889-1939," Pacific Northwest Quarterly, Fall 2008, Volume 99 Number 4, pp 181-193.

"Flotsam From the Jane Gray." Boston Evening Transcript, June 7, 1898. Online. http://chroniclingamerica.loc.gov/newspapers/

"For Jane Grey Disaster. Judge Hanford Holds Schooner's Owners Blameless." Seattle Post-Intelligencer, January 18, 1900: 6. Microfilm, Seattle Public Library.

"Gold Fields Lured Away Many Seattle Athletes." Seattle Post-Intelligencer, June 5, 1898: 17. Microfilm, Seattle Public Library.

Haller Lake Community Club, http://hallerlake.info/about/history/

Hanford, Cornelius H. Seattle and Environs, The S. J. Clarke Publishing Co., 1929.

"Has Not Been Found." Victoria Daily Colonist, July 8, 1898: 8. Microfilm, Tacoma Public Library.

"Her Awful Deck Load." Seattle Daily Times, June 6, 1898: 5. Microfilm, Tacoma Public Library.

"History of the Jane Gray." Seattle Post-Intelligencer, June 1, 1898: 6. Microfilm, Seattle Public Library.

"History of the Lost Schooner Jane Gray." Seattle Post-Intelligencer, June 1, 1898, Fourth Edition: 1. Microfilm, Seattle Public Library.

Historylink.org, www.historylink.org

Houser, Michael. James Eustace Blackwell, 2012. Online. http://www.dahp.wa.gov/learn-and-research/architect-biographies/james-e-blackwell

Hunt, Herbert; Kaylor, Floyd C. Washington West of the Cascades: Historical Descriptive; the Explorers, the Indians, the Pioneers, the Modern, Volume 2, The S. J. Clarke publishing company, 1917: pp 455-456. Google eBook.

"I Will Never Forget That Scene." Seattle Post-Intelligencer, June 2, 1898: 6. Microfilm, Seattle Public Library.

"Ingraham's Story of the Disaster." Seattle Post-Intelligencer, June 1, 1898, Fourth Edition: 1. Microfilm, Seattle Public Library.

"Is Reward of Merit." Daily Register Gazette, January 30, 1899: 3. Online. GenealogyBank.com.

"It Was Wholesale Murder." Sacramento Daily Record, June 9, 1898. Online. http://chroniclingamerica.loc.gov/newspapers/

"Italian Expedition To Alaska." New York Times, March 26, 1898. Online. http://query.nytimes.com/search/sitesearch/

"The Jane Grey Case." Seattle Daily Times, January 20, 1900: 6. Microfilm, Tacoma Public Library.

"Jane Grey Comes Ashore." Seattle Daily Times, June 25, 1898: 2. Microfilm, Tacoma Public Library.

"Jane Grey Did Not Sink." Victoria Daily Columnist, June 25, 1898. Online. http://chroniclingamerica.loc.gov/newspapers/

"Jane Grey Survivors are Indignant at the MacDougall, Southwick Co." Seattle Daily Times, June 6, 1898: 5. Microfilm, Tacoma Public Library.

"Jane Grey Survivors Make Informal Demand on MacDougall, Southwick Co." Seattle Daily Times, June 4, 1898. Microfilm, Tacoma Public Library.

"Jane Grey. The Report of Finding Bodies False." Seattle Daily Times, June 9, 1898: 8. Microfilm, Tacoma Public Library.

"Jane Grey's Survivors." Seattle Daily Times, June 8, 1898. Microfilm, Tacoma Public Library.

"John Lindsay." Seattle Daily Times, June 7, 1898: Microfilm, Tacoma Public Library.

"Klondike Marine Disasters." New York Times, June 26, 1898. Online. http://query.nytimes.com/search/sitesearch/

"Latest Gold Find." Seattle Daily Times, June 10, 1898. Microfilm, Tacoma Public Library.

Levi, Steven C. Boom and Bust in the Alaska Goldfields: A Multicultural Adventure, Greenwood Publishing Group, 2008.

Lindsay, Ron. Personal Family Records.

"Lost at Sea." Mission Home Monthly, June 9, 1898. Online.

"Luigi Pays The Bills." Kansas City Journal, April 3, 1898: 17. Online. http://chroniclingamerica.loc.gov/newspapers/

"Luigi is Successful." San Juan Islander, August 27, 1897: 1. Online. http://chroniclingamerica.loc.gov/newspapers/

Macdonald, George Everett Hussey. Fifty Years of Free Thought, Arno Press, 1929. Online. Google eBooks.

Meany, Edmond Stephen. Mount Rainier: A Record of Exploration, The McMillan Company, 1916. Google eBook.

Meany, Edmond S., papers. Special Collections, University of Washington Libraries, Seattle, Washington.

Mine and Quarry News Bureau. The Mine, Quarry and Metallurgical Record of the United States, Canada and Mexico. The Bureau, 1897: pp 321, 648, 649. Online. Google eBook. http://books.google.com/books?id=cXMAAAAMAAJ&dq=%22c.+h.+packard%22+mines&source=gbs_navlinks_s

"A Missionary Drowned." New York Times, June 13, 1898. Online. http://query.nytimes.com/search/sitesearch/

"The Moonlight Wrecked." Butte Weekly Miner, August 4, 1898: 2. Online. GenealogyBank.com.

"New Alaska Goldfields." New York Times, June 28, 1899. Online. http://query.nytimes.com/search/sitesearch/

"No Bodies Were Found." Seattle Post-Intelligencer, June 9, 1898, Second Edition: 3. Microfilm, Seattle Public Library.

Norcross, Frank Wayland. A History of the New York Swamp, Chiswick Press, 1901: pp 36, 53, 87, 91. Google eBook.

"Penned Up Like Sheep Many Persons Drown." Daily Ledger, Tacoma, June 2, 1898. Microfilm, Tacoma Public Library.

"A Pleased Prince." Los Angeles Daily Herald, August 27, 1897. Online: http://chroniclingamerica.loc.gov/

"Prince Luigi..." Boston Herald, June 4, 1898: 6. Online. GenealogyBank.com.

"Prince Luigi's Big Party." Seattle Post-Intelligencer, May 18, 1898. Microfilm, Tacoma Public Library.

"Recovered a Judgment." Morning Olympian, February 2, 1900: 3. Online. Geneologybank.com.

"Relics of the Jane Gray." Seattle Post-Intelligencer, June 7, 1898: 10. Microfilm, Seattle Public Library.

"Sailed In Leaky Coffin." Daily Ledger, Tacoma, June 3, 1898: 2. Microfilm, Tacoma Public Library.

"Schooner Jane Gray Lost At Sea." Seattle Post-Intelligencer, June 1, 1898, Third Edition: 1. Microfilm, Seattle Public Library.

Seattle City Directory, R. L. Polk & Company, 1898. Google eBook.

The Sella Foundation, Biella, Italy.

"Seven Victims of the Jane Gray Disaster." Seattle Post-Intelligencer, June 7, 1898: 9. Microfilm, Seattle Public Library.

Sheldon, Charles H. The Washington High Bench: A Biographical History of the State Supreme Court, 1889-1991, Washington State University Press, 1992.

"Sons of Italy." Seattle Post-Intelligencer, June 1, 1898: 6. Microfilm, The Seattle Public Library.

"A Springfield Man Lost." Springfield Republican, June 3, 1898: 4. Online. Genealogybank.com.

"Suggest a Search For Missing." Daily Ledger, Tacoma, June 3, 1898: 2. Microfilm, Tacoma Public Library.

The Delta of Sigma Nu, Volume 16, 1898. Google eBook.

"The Ascent of Mout St. Elias." Overland Monthly and Out West Magazine, Volume 31, A. Roman and Company, 1898. Google eBook.

"The Ill-Fated Schooner." Eau Claire Leader, July 10, 1898. Online. http://chroniclingamerica.loc.gov/newspapers/

"The Jane Grey Goes Down Off of Cape Flattery." Seattle Daily Times, June 1, 1898: Microfilm, The Tacoma Public Library.

"There May Be Survivors." Seattle Post-Intelligencer, June 10, 1898: 5. Microfilm, Seattle Public Library.

"To Identify the Bodies." Seattle Post-Intelligencer, June 9, 1898: 9. Microfilm, Seattle Public Library.

"The Summit Reached." Los Angeles Daily Herald, August 27, 1897. Online: http://chroniclingamerica.loc.gov/

USRC *Thomas Corwin* (1876), Wikipedia. Online. http://en.wikipedia.org/wiki/USRC_Thomas_Corwin_(1876)

"Victim of the Jane Grey Wreck." New York Times, June 6, 1898. Online. http://query.nytimes.com/search/sitesearch/

"Was a Wichita Man." Wichita Daily Eagle, June 22, 1898. Online. http://chroniclingamerica.loc.gov/newspapers/

"Well Known Victims." Seattle Post-Intelligencer, June 2, 1898: 6. Microfilm, Seattle Public Library.

"Were to Dig Gold For Prince Luigi." Seattle Post-Intelligencer, June 1, 1898, Fourth Edition: 1. Microfilm, Seattle Public Library.

Winfield Historical Society. Online. http://www.winfieldhistoricalsociety.com/gambellstory.htm

"Wreck of the Jane Gray." Seattle Post-Intelligencer, June 10, 1898: 5. Microfilm, Seattle Public Library.

"Wrecked Off Cape Flattery." Pullman Herald, June 4, 1898. Online. http://chroniclingamerica.loc.gov/newspapers/

ABOUT THE AUTHOR

Michelle Merritt is a native of Washington State. Born at Seattle's Providence Hospital in 1964 to a Ballard family, she was raised on the East side of the Cascade Mountains. In 1982, Michelle returned to Seattle, where she attended the University of Washington for a short time. Dissatisfied and impatient with academic life, she joined the United States Air Force as a reservist and received a certificate in Aircraft Maintenance technology.

In the subsequent years, Ms. Merritt enjoyed a long career in the automotive industry, worked a brief stint as an insurance agent, owned a restaurant, and managed a non-profit. She holds a current merchant mariner's license and is working toward accumulating enough sea time to become a licensed captain on international vessels.

Since publication of her first book, *One Night in Rome: And the End of Life as I knew It,* Michelle has traveled by land, air, and sea to Italy, Monaco, France, England, Fiji, Turkey, Canada, Mexico, Costa Rica, Panama, and forty-five states within the United States of America.

She is the mother of two grown sons and a grandmother who now calls Tacoma, Washington her home.

Discover other titles by Michelle at MichelleMerritt.com

~~~
~~~

ONE NIGHT IN ROME SAMPLE CHAPTERS

Chapter 1 - Family First

"How did you meet him?" Is usually the first question I'm asked when people find out that I have an Italian boyfriend in Italy.

"Well it's a really long story, but I met him one night in Rome," I reply, blushing to be recounting the tale once again. To my ears, it sounds like a preposterous story. Sometimes I wonder if they'll think that I'm just a consummate liar or a charlatan snake oil salesman peddling the cure for a lovelorn heart with some secret potion. "My sister and I went on a three week vacation last year," I launch into the tale, "And it was my first time to Europe."

I suppose that my subconscious had worked on me for a while; allowing me to secretly believe that I could meet a man on that trip, however, on the morning I left Seattle, it wasn't the first thing on my mind. As I stood on the sidewalk under one of those perpetually drab Pacific Northwest skies, scanning the walls for the name of my airline, escape was the word that was burning in my brain. Escape from everything that I was torturing myself over.

Now, I know that I am not the first woman to have gone through the death of parents. Nor am I the first person to have grappled with that mid-life chasm of empty nest syndrome that shockingly opened beneath my feet once my sons were grown. But I was roasting myself over the fire of a now uncertain future. I wasn't even sure if I would have a job to come home to. The logical part of my mind knows that regret is a waste of time, so I focused on the positive. What I did have was three weeks of Italy and Spain spanning before me, a blank canvas waiting for the paint of possibilities.

In order to tell you how I ended up at the airport that morning, kicking my carry-on through the switchbacks to ticketing, I must first tell you about the death of my mother. No matter where I lived or what challenge I faced, she was never farther than a phone call away. She was my rock. I believed that she would live to be one hundred years old, so the day my oldest sister called me to say that Mom had driven herself to the hospital, I reacted with calm disbelief, "They think she might have had a heart attack?"

"Yes, but they aren't sure." Patty was with Mom in the local emergency room. "I guess she had a coughing fit this morning then drove herself here when she couldn't get it to stop. They want to transport her to the hospital in Olympia overnight for observation. Apparently, they don't have any room for her here."

Unlike me, my oldest sister is one of those solid people who has taught at the same school, lived in the same house and been married to the same man for over thirty years. Not much alarms her, so if something were direly wrong, she would have told me. She'd already enlisted her husband's help and went on to say, "I'm going to the hospital with Mom to make sure she gets settled. Keith is taking Dad to our house and I'll call you a little later to let you know how things are going."

At that point, I was certain that Mom was probably having a stress attack from taking care of Dad. (The fifteen-year age span between them had gone largely unnoticed for most of their marriage, but could no longer be ignored.) I'd been hounding her for months to hire someone to come to the house and help. Of course, she never did. Taking care of Dad until "death do us part" was what she signed up for when they got married. In her mind, hiring somebody to take the burden off would have been shirking her responsibilities. (This was a woman who recycled bread bags, saved the twist ties, and clipped coupons - a frugal child of the Great Depression. She even had a can full of saved chicken "wish bones" on the kitchen counter for that after dinner wish in the event you needed one.)

In telling this story, I realize that I never would have met Angelo on that night in Rome if the chips hadn't fallen the way they did. I imagine that's why I still have a few cobwebs of guilt lingering in the corners of my mind.

On the day that my mother entered the hospital, I had a clear mental picture of what the next twenty years would hold for me. My grandmother, my mom's mom, was still alive at the ripe old age of ninety-four. So it stood to reason that at seventy-three, my own mother would be around for quite some time. We were going to hang out together for the next couple of decades, shopping and traveling. My oldest sister and I even hatched a plan to build Mom's dream house someday.

Dad, on the other hand, was eighty-nine and legally blind. Although he still had most of his wits about him, things were starting to slip; little telltale signs that he didn't have a lot of time left on this earth. He was well aware of that and had everything planned for his own demise: all but a contingency for the worst-case scenario, Mom dying first.

Just as she said she would, Patty called me later that evening with a status report, "Mom's resting in her room now, but they want to take her into the cath-lab for tests in the morning."

For the uninitiated, the cath-lab is that place where they take you to check out your plumbing. After injecting your body with blood thinners and dye, technicians send a microscopic Roto-Rooter up through your groin to look for restrictions. That happened to me once with an old house I owned. When the boys were little, my oldest flushed a toy down the toilet just to see what would happen. It was one of those colorful, unsinkable, snap-together beads that float in the bathtub. I suppose he thought the toilet might do the trick. You know how little kids are. When the Roto-Rooter guy snaked out the ancient lines, a lecture ensued about the evils of unleashing feminine hygiene products into the root-infested waste stream of a nineteen-twelve era home. Apparently, I was equally responsible for the mess. This is pretty much what they were going to do to Mom that morning: go looking for unwanted debris and build-up then clear her plumbing if they had to.

Patty was busy the next day. "I have a class that I need to teach in the morning, otherwise I'd stay," she informed me. Mom and my sister worked out together three times a week, so she wasn't concerned either.

"No problem, I don't have any tests tomorrow and I can work from my phone." In a third attempt to finally finish college, I'd ditched my twenty-year career in the automotive industry, re-enrolled in school, and taken on a part-time job that barely made ends meet. The job was flexible and most of my work involved the phone, so I knew nobody would miss me at the office.

After arriving at the hospital at five the next day, I found Mom in her room. She was awake with a nurse prepping her for the procedure. "Hey Mom, how are you doing?" Smiling, I tossed my briefcase into the chair.

"Oh, honey. You didn't have to come." She downplayed the situation in typical Mom fashion. "I'm not feeling myself. I think I'm just tired. You have classes to study for and your new job is so important."

That was my mother. Everyone else's life was more important than hers.

As part of the preparation for this routine procedure, the nurses instructed me to remove all of Mom's valuables. Those consisted of simple gold earrings and the rings on her hands. Lathering her swollen fingers with lotion, I pulled off her wedding band and her diamond engagement ring. It wasn't really an engagement ring though. I'd been with her the day that she bought it. Her real engagement ring was a 1977 Datsun pickup truck. At the time, she thought diamonds were a senseless waste of money and opted for a practical vehicle instead. That truck didn't even have a radio. I'd been in my twenties when she and I went shopping for the ring. She saved up her pennies and coupon money until she finally thought she deserved one. It was the only diamond she'd ever had in her life. Pulling it off of her finger that day, I told her that I remembered the name of the store where we'd found it. "Remember, Mom? I lived in that old house on the South Hill in Spokane. The one with the bad plumbing and newspapers for insulation."

Remembering the day, she laughed with me, "Yes. I do, Honey."

The nurses wheeled Mom down to the lab while I staked out a spot in the hospital lobby. I had a busy day ahead of me. My oldest son, Chase (the one who had flushed the toy down the toilet), was stationed in Afghanistan and his young wife was landing at the airport around noon. She'd been lonely, by herself in an apartment in Boise, so she and I had planned for her to stay with me for a couple of weeks. I thought she could help me out at the office or maybe just hang around with my other son and me. Of course, this had been scheduled before the events of the past twenty-four hours and I didn't have any inkling as to what was about to happen.

Around eight o'clock, the doctor arrived in the waiting area with the test results. Unfolding a black and white photographic image of my Mom's heart, he said, "Everything looks good. We didn't find any blockages, but we inserted a stint here." He pointed to an area outside of her heart that they'd placed the little tube. "There is another area over here that we should keep an eye on, but it should be fine for now." The doctor circled an almost imperceptible narrowing in another artery. It was really nothing to worry about.

"Is she in her room now?" I wanted to check on her, to make sure she was doing as well as he said. If she was, I could get on with my work. I don't want that to sound callous or unfeeling because I'm not. It's just the way my parents raised me. Take care of your family, pull yourself up by your bootstraps, and get on with life.

"The nurses should be getting her settled in her room. Give them a few minutes then you can go up." He smiled and said he'd check in on us later, leaving me with the picture of her heart in my hands.

The first person I needed to call was my sister. "Everything went fine," I said, "The nurses are with her now. I'm going upstairs in a minute. How's Dad doing?"

"He woke up in the middle of the night looking for the bathroom. He was a little disoriented, but he's fine. Keith stayed home with him today and I'll try to get to the hospital before you leave for the airport." I'd reminded her that I needed to pick up my daughter-in-law, so Patty was going to take over the afternoon shift for me.

I entered Mom's room just as they were wheeling her in on a gurney. In spite of the fact that my mother was born in a Minnesota farmhouse in the fury of a December blizzard, weighing in at a paltry two pounds, she grew into a long-legged willowy blonde woman, towering over most of the family at five foot ten inches. The nurses must have been unprepared for her stature because while struggling to move her prone, groggy body from the gurney to the bed, they pulled the IV from her arm. Still, nothing seemed amiss. Those things happen, right? That's what I was thinking when one of the nurses made an excuse, then another one claimed responsibility for the incident. If that sort of thing had happened to one of my kids, I probably would have ripped somebody's head off. But there were a million reasons why the woman in that bed was invincible to me.

After they tidied her up and reinserted her IV, I went out to the hall. I should probably call other family members. The thought hadn't crossed my mind until that moment, seeing her barely conscious on the hospital gurney. My brothers should probably be told. Yes, I have brothers - three of them. I called everyone I could think of that morning. My aunts, cousins, and the two brothers that I had phone numbers for. In a calm, cheery voice I informed them of the facts, "I'm sure she'll be fine. It was a very minor procedure."

My other brother was missing somewhere in Alaska. I had an idea as to how to get a message to him because, the year before, I'd organized a family effort to wish him a happy birthday on his fiftieth. I found a bush pilot online who gave me the contact information for the radio station in Bethel. We all called in to the station, uncertain if it would work. Later we heard through the family grapevine that it had and, better yet, we now had a phone number where calls might actually reach him.

When Patty arrived, I'd leave that phone call to her.

As an afterthought, I called Suzanne. I know this may be confusing right now, but she is my stepsister. (We consider ourselves sisters today, even though we barely new each other at that time.) Reaching her voicemail, I left a message, "Hey Suzanne, I thought I should call you. Mom might have had a heart attack and she's in the hospital. Dad's fine and Mom seems to be doing ok, but I thought you should know." Click. I didn't know if it would matter to her, but I'd long ago promised Dad that I would try my best to make her feel like she was a part of the family.

To explain the dynamics of my family seems a bit premature here, but unbeknownst to me, Suzanne would become the reason that I went to Italy. She is the reason that we ended up in the hotel bar where I met Angelo at midnight on a Sunday in Rome.

(The Roulette table that we all unwittingly buy chips at every day of our lives is so unpredictable. Let the chips fall where they may, indeed.)

Most people might think that, as the youngest of five children, I would be the babied one or the little princess that everyone takes care of. I admit, I do suffer from a bit of the princess syndrome, but having three older brothers torture the crap out of me probably made me more of a warrior princess. I've often had visions of myself in full-on World War II uniform, back-to-back with my troops, battling the enemy until the bloody end. (Undoubtedly from all of those slingshot wars and B B Gun fights.) All that aside, when it gets down and dirty, I'm your man. That doesn't mean I won't cry a river of tears once in a while, it just means that I keep doing what Mom said I should: Pick yourself up and get on with it.

After I rallied the troops, my two brothers and my sister took over for me at the hospital. Things were starting to get a little weird by then. The nurses had to place a tourniquet on my mother's groin to stop the bleeding. (This tourniquet resembled the nylon cinch straps I use to secure my kayak to the roof of the car). During the move, the suture on her femoral artery had been torn. If you don't know this already, the femoral artery is the most accessible pathway for performing the aforementioned procedure, but located at the inner right groin, it also happens to be one of the easiest places to cause someone to bleed to death. Mom was nauseous from the painkillers and vomiting.

Flashing red lights were going off in my head, but I had to leave. My youngest son was waiting for me at my apartment and I needed to pick up my daughter-in-law at the airport. Kissing and hugging everyone, I said I'd be back in a few hours.

On my way up the freeway, I continued with the phone triage. Suzanne called me back, but like the rest of us, she was certain that everything would be all right and confirmed that by saying, "She probably just needs some rest."

"I'll keep you posted. Dad's still at Patty's house with Keith," I explained, "We didn't think the hospital was a good place for him to wait." At his age, we all knew that seeing Mom in a hospital bed might be too much for him to handle.

Not fifteen minutes passed before my phone rang again. It was Patty. "Michelle?"

"Yea, is everything ok?" I asked.

"No, it isn't. Things have taken a turn for the worse." She let out a deep sigh, "They can't stop the bleeding and Mom's blood pressure has dropped. They're taking her back to the cath-lab. We think we should try to find Tom now."

Cursing my needy eighteen year-old daughter-in-law, I drove north with tears pouring down my face. I wanted to run back to the hospital, but I couldn't. I had to go on, to get my son, to get her, and to get myself back to Mom as quickly as possible.

Those three hours on the road are a giant blur. I remember my sister calling again to say they had moved Mom to the Intensive Care Unit. I remember sobbing and calling Suzanne again. I remember the feeling of utter helplessness. And I remember the swarm of family members that were gathered in the hospital lobby once I returned. Dad was there with Keith, my brothers with their wives and children, nieces and nephews, fiancés and girlfriends: almost everyone was there waiting.

Immediately, I found my older sister. "What's happening?"

"The doctor says that a hole has developed in Mom's heart. They want to try to stabilize her, wait for the blood thinners to wear off and perform open heart surgery in the morning." I was sick to my stomach with shock and needed to know how this could have happened. Everything had been fine that morning. The doctor said they couldn't find anything wrong.

My oldest brother silently hovered at the edge of the conversation, waiting to jump in. I could tell he was eager to describe his interpretation of the events in technical terms. You see, Michael is a fabricator, welder, mechanic, and inventor. The two of us have a unique connection when it comes to the technical. I'd been his tool monkey when he was in high school. "Pass me the crescent wrench," he'd tell me as we both lay on our backs in the dirt under his '41 Ford Pickup. "Get up here. I need your little fingers to help me set this windshield." We'd both dust ourselves off and climb into the cab. His way of babysitting was showing me the way around a carburetor, how to replace a rear-main seal and how to drive tractor. He did all of this before I was eight. By the time I was nine he made me an aunt. (I suppose that made me both the youngest and the oldest.) So it made sense that he and I would be having this logical conversation about Mom's condition. Like a technician explaining the reason that a fuel pump fails in the heat of summer, he described what the doctor had shown him - where an unseen area had lost blood flow and the tissue had ruptured between the chambers in her heart.

The earlier events of that morning - the pulled IV and the tourniquet – kept telling me that something else had to have gone wrong. But, at that moment, all I could think of was Mom and Dad. Losing my mother would kill Dad. The thought of losing them both was killing me.

Finding him comfortably ensconced in a lobby chair surrounded by chattering grandchildren of all ages (my son, Bond, was there with him), I kissed my dad and asked, "How are you holding up?"

"As well as can be expected, Honey." Or maybe he said, "Not bad for an old guy." I don't recall the exact words, but I do know that he smiled at me with his usual optimism. I could tell that he was hiding his fear under that weathered Scottish exterior and for his sake I needed to be just as strong.

While I was on the road to the airport, Patty had launched the search for our missing brother. None of us had seen him for seven years, but she still had the number for one of our stepsisters in Alaska. She'd already left a message for Tom to contact us, call us collect, send up a smoke signal, or anything just to let us know that he was alive and understood the gravity of the situation. If that failed, we all agreed that we would call the radio station again.

(This is where the telling gets complicated and you might need to get a notepad to sketch out this family tree.)

At the end of his senior year in High School, enticed by promises of great wealth in Alaska, our brother had flown to the town of Bethel on the barren banks of the Kuskokwim River. I don't know why anyone would want to live in that desolate place, but our biological father had convinced Tom to move to there. I considered the man sitting in the hospital waiting room my dad, but to my older siblings, the man in Alaska had been their father. Biological is the way I refer to him because Larry abandoned my mom with five kids in Seattle when I was only a year old. I didn't even know his name until I was six.

Tom had embraced the life in an Eskimo village, living out decades with this other family. One of the last times I saw my brother was the year Larry died. At the very last minute, the other four of us flew up to join him for the funeral. We were bundled in snowmobile suits with the frozen wind howling across the tundra as we watched men in parkas use an auger to drill a hole for the grave. After we buried Larry, our stepsiblings wanted us to attend a traditional native ceremony. It seems that the Eskimos believe you must burn the item where the dying person held their last breath. By that, I mean whatever article of furniture they were sitting, sleeping, or otherwise indisposed on. In Larry's case, the sofa had to be sacrificed. The locals said that the fire would set his spirit free.

People in this town don't live in what most of us would consider houses because the remote location requires that they float all of their materials up from the Bering Sea during the months when the river isn't solid.

Not only that, they have to put whatever structure together before the next Arctic blast renders the whole place a frigid wasteland. Larry's home was a bit luxurious by Bethel standards: it was a doublewide shored up on blocks to keep it from sinking into the permafrost. Imagine this - we returned from the last rites only to find that my brother and stepbrother had taken a chainsaw to the couch. I guess they couldn't get it out of the mobile home door in one piece. Tom tossed the last chunk of upholstery into the bed of a pick-up truck right as we pulled into the driveway.

Now it was time to go to the Eskimo ceremony where we would release Larry's spirit at "fish camp."

What is "fish camp" and how do you get there? From what I understand, almost all Native Alaskan families have one. In the summer, they go there by boat to net all the fish they need for the year. In the winter, the task is much easier because there isn't just one choice, but three: you can get there by snowmobile, sled dog, or best of all, by driving up the frozen river.

I didn't know what I was in for when I got into the back seat of that Dodge Neon. It wasn't until we'd followed the truck down the boat ramp and my head was bouncing against the headliner that I understood what we were doing. About the time we launched over a massive frost heave in the ice, I was nearly blinded by the sun setting in my eyes and thought I must have been hallucinating when two sled-dog trains passed us on their way into town. I wasn't.

We had a bonfire that night with the remnants of the couch. Everyone drank a beer and took turns sitting in the sweat lodge. Then somebody passed a fifth of Jack Daniels around the fire as we watched the ashes of Larry's soul join the native spirits in the midnight sky.

Anyway, the experience was enough to convince me that no sane person could live where my brother chose to.

Over the years, Tom seldom returned to the southern tropics of Washington State. I think he might have found some kind of security in that isolation or maybe Bethel was his own private island – a place where he didn't need to justify his life. Regardless of the reasons, Mom always thought it was her fault, that somehow she'd failed him as a mother. That was the thing that made finding him so important. If her situation got any more dire than it already was, we wanted Mom to see Tom and for him to see her.

Patty already had a one-way plane ticket waiting for our brother at the airport. But first, we had to find him.

Leading Dad down the sterile corridor to the ICU with his arm locked in mine, I wasn't sure what we'd encounter when we got to Mom. He just wanted to see her. He needed to touch her, to kiss her, and to tell her that he loved her. Even after thirty years of marriage, Dad still called her his "Viking Princess." Sometimes I'd catch him patting her on the behind when he thought nobody was watching. He bought her little gifts. She laughed at the ribald stories from his seafaring days and cooked his favorite meals. I can think of a thousand other little things they did for each other. My parents had the kind of life-long love that I'd always wanted, yet never found.

Mom was sedated, but conscious. "Hi Honey," she said to Dad, her eyes full of concern, "I'm so sorry. Are you ok?" Flat on her back, attached to a grapevine of machines, she apologized for being in the hospital. Can you believe that?

"Oh, Babe. I'm fine, but I need you to get better." Dad kissed her while choking back tears. I felt like I was watching the end to a tragic movie. It was all I could do not to become a blubbering baby myself.

Standing in the hospital hall, it seemed impossible that any of this could be happening to her. She really was an amazing woman. When she was married to Larry, my mother endured the nomadic life of a military wife. For three years, she lived in Africa. I found photographs of her in Libya and Morocco when I was going through her things. You should have seen her - seven months pregnant, standing in the desert with two toddlers in tow. Mom even gave birth to Tom in a tiny aluminum trailer while they were stationed in there. I suppose it's small wonder that I thought she could survive anything.

Over the next few hours, our entire family paced the lobby waiting for news about what would come next. My poor daughter-in-law, who thought she was taking a vacation, found herself in the midst of an unanticipated family disaster. She was bored and wanted something to do. Bond put forth his best effort to entertain her, but there isn't a lot to do in a hospital lobby. I was beginning to despise her. (My lifetime around men really made me intolerant of this kind of behavior. Besides, Mom would have said if it's not broken or bleeding, get up and get over it.) I know that I should have had more sympathy. I just couldn't find any in my reserves.

While Dad and I were down the hall with Mom, Patty located Tom. He was on his way to the airport in Bethel and hoped he'd make that first plane in time. He didn't. Tom missed three flights before he caught the last one. Even then, we weren't certain he would make his connection in Anchorage.

My other brother, Matt sat with his wife at a laptop watching the flight status. The two of them even called the airline periodically to confirm that Tom was on his way.

Like fishermen bagging the big one, they gathered us to report that the wayward son had been captured as soon as he boarded his connection. They knew his arrival time and would take custody of him at the airport that night.

In the hospital waiting area, a long anticipated update came our way. The staff had called in a surgeon. They were unable to stabilize Mom and could no longer wait for the blood thinners to dissipate. The decision to operate on her that night had been made. Rounding us up, the nurses herded our family down the same ICU corridor to a private room where we could wait for the surgeon's prognosis. I did my best to comfort Dad as we packed the little room, filling every chair and parts of the floor.

What happened next, I would not wish on anyone's family. The surgeon had the bedside manner of Attila the Hun and couldn't have cared less about how we were feeling. He brushed my eighty-nine year old father away with the wipe of his hand.

"Are you the husband?" the surgeon barked.

"Yes, I am." Dad gripped my hand until I couldn't feel my fingertips.

"Well let me tell you all," oblivious to our distress, the doctor went on with his merciless tirade, "less than twenty percent of the people who experience this type of event ever make it this far." Collectively holding our breath, we were still hoping for a miracle. Hope was not what this doctor was there to deliver. "Of those people, only one in three survives this operation." Brutal and unforgiving, he threw the final punch, "Mrs. Lindsay will be lucky to make it out alive."

I didn't know if Dad could hold it together any longer.

"Grow up Lindsay! What in the hell are you crying for," Dad shouted to himself. All of those years living the military life must have made him feel the need to put on his armor. Even so, there wasn't a single person in that room who didn't know the depth of his pain right then.

Not a moment too soon, the doctor left, closing the door behind him. He was giving us a minute to talk before they wheeled Mom into surgery. Although Dad and I aren't religious in a church-going sense, the rest of my family is and we needed all of the help we could get at that moment. Forming a chain of interlocked fingers, every one of us bowed our heads in prayer. I didn't care if "Our Father" was God, or Allah, or Buddha, I wanted some higher power to intervene. Someone or something had to save my parents.

The prayer finished, I lifted Dad by his elbow. He wanted to see Mom before she went to this place that she only had a thirty percent chance of emerging from. She lay on another gurney, twenty feet down the hall, ready to be rolled to the only place that could save her – and into the hands of that merciless, angry surgeon.

Later we talked about him, wondering if that was just a side effect of the job, yet it didn't seem right to put the life of someone we loved into the hands of someone who seemed so brutal and uncaring. I had to think that reading the surgeon the riot act might be tantamount to cussing out the cook - you never know who's going to spit on your steak or stomp on your burger. Remaining silent seemed the prudent thing to do.

Dad and I huddled around Mom, but I wanted them to have a moment alone together; in case, God forbid, it was their last.

"Sweetheart, I love you." Mom squeezed his hand as I waited a few steps up the hall.

"I love you too. I can't bear the thought of living without you." The audience gone, Dad finally let his tears flow un-checked. By the time they started moving Mom toward surgery, I had to wrap my arms around his shaking body to keep him from falling.

I kissed my mother and told her, "I love you." As much as I didn't want to cry, it was impossible not to.

She raised her head as they wheeled her down the abyss of a hall to the last corner. "Don't worry! I love you both. I'll see you in a little while."

Dad collapsed in my arms, sobbing. I'm fairly certain that I am one of the few people he ever let see him that way.

I'm not sure how long we waited at the hospital, but I can vaguely remember stuffing some cash into my son's hands and telling him to take his sister-in-law home. "I'll call you as soon as we know something. I love you."

Sometime in the middle of it all, a hospital staff member suggested we take Dad to a room in the "Sunshine House" – a hotel sanctuary in the parking lot specifically for people like us, families in crisis - a place to rest.

Miraculously, Mom survived the surgery and Tom actually arrived at SeaTac Airport. I will never forget the way my Mother's face lit up, lying in her recovery room, when my brother walked through the door and announced, "Mom, I made it!"

Seven years with no phone number or no address to reach him, she often had that far away look of a parent whose child had been kidnapped. She wondered where he was, if he was ok. That day, the doctors had installed a patch in her torn heart. And her son had finally come home. The significance of those two events did not escape anyone in our family.

A few days into Mom's recovery, Patty and I came to the realization that neither of us could keep up the full-time care of our Dad. Mom couldn't handle it either. Once the doctors let her go home, she'd need help with the chores that she'd always done.

Putting my combat helmet on, I got to work finding a solution. Our salvation came in the form of a buxom little woman named Anna. The caregiver agency provided us with others, but she was the one that stayed with us the longest. For three month, sometimes six days a week or twenty-four hours a day, that wonderful little woman took care of all of the things that we couldn't.

Mom was moved to a rehabilitation facility a short time after her surgery. Every day, while the rest of us were at work, Anna drove Dad over to visit her. Often times they'd stop at a restaurant or a bar on the way. Dad really enjoyed those small glimpses of normalcy.

It was a Saturday afternoon, twenty days after Mom drove herself to the emergency room, the last time I spoke with her. On the phone she said, "You've missed so much school and work already, Dear. Don't worry about me, just come down when you can." The prospect of going home had her sounding like her normal self again.

"I'll be there first thing in the morning, I promise."

And I was in my car, on the way to her, when my phone rang. It was the nurse at the care center. "Ms. Merritt?"

"Yes?" I'd recognized the incoming number and thought maybe they were putting a call through from Mom.

"Your mother has had another cardiac event. We called 911 and the paramedics are working on her now. The ambulance is on the way to take her back to the hospital." Stunned, I listened to the nurse and tried to think of what to do next.

"I'm driving there now. I'll be there in less than thirty minutes." I called my sister. She'd just listened to her answering machine and would be on her way too. I called my brothers, but before I could finish explaining what was happening, our conversation was interrupted by another call.

It was the care center again. "Ms. Merritt? I'm sorry to tell you that your mother didn't make it."

"What do you mean, she didn't make it? What happened?" Barely able to see the road in front of me, I gasped for the air to speak. "I thought she was going home soon."

The distraught nurse went on, "I was with her in her room. She was getting ready for her morning physical therapy when she sneezed. She said something was wrong, but in the time it took to call the doctor, she was in full cardiac arrest. The paramedics did everything they could. I am very, very sorry."

My head was spinning in vertigo. Pictures of my mom's face flashed through my mind. She'd known what was happening - that her last minutes might be near. And I hadn't been with her.

Oh God, what about Dad? "You didn't call my father, did you?" I prayed they hadn't already told him.

"We did, but we only spoke with his care giver. We just told her there was a problem and that we would call you." At least the nurse had the presence of mind not to reveal the truth.

"Thank you. Where is my mom now?" I was clueless as to what we were supposed to do next. She explained that they would keep our mother in her room until we had time to make arrangements with a mortuary. I had never had to handle anything like this - never in my life.

Before I could collect my thoughts, Patty called crying as hard as I was. "Michelle, the care center just called me. Did they already reach you?"

"Yes they did," I sobbed, "How are we going to tell Dad?" We were both thinking the same thing.

Still driving, I was almost to the care center. My parent's place was only another twenty minutes further. "Listen, there isn't anything we can do for Mom now. I'm just going to keep driving and I'll meet you at Dad's."

I suppose that my battlefield mentality took over right then. That survival instinct must be a lot like what happens to a war casualty when they wrap a tourniquet around their own severed limb. Even so, I'd be giving myself too much credit if I didn't acknowledge the role that the rest of my family played. While my sister and I sped toward Dad, everyone else took on the phone duty. People that I hadn't seen for years offered to help in whatever way they could.

Telling him was easier than showing him. I can clearly remember every movement of that morning: closing my car door, counting the steps to the front door, turning the handle, Patty behind me stepping over the doorsill, and the two of us holding Dad while we all cried our eyes out. He wanted to see her, to say goodbye to his beloved girl.

The rest of the family was already waiting for Dad's arrival at the care facility. I think it was out of respect that they felt he should to go first. Since he was too weak to walk on his own, I pushed him down the hall in a wheelchair.

The sight of Mom's lifeless body was something neither of us was prepared for. I don't imagine that anyone ever is. The door to her room was open. The sheets were pulled up with her hands laid across her chest. A violet bruise spread on her pale brow. Her mouth was agape and her right hand was almost black from that final struggle. The long nails that she usually filed into graceful almonds had gone un-manicured. I promised her a visit to the salon that very week. Why had I waited? Why hadn't I taken care of it myself?

Dad leaned over her, kissing her open lips. "Oh Pat, I can't live without you. I already lost one wife. I can't lose you too."

The buckets of tears I cried that day could fill Puget Sound, but I knew I needed to be strong for my dad for as long as he could hold on. And now, there were burial arrangements to be made.

Remember what I said; "Take care of your family, pull yourself up by your bootstraps, and get on with it?" That is exactly what Mom would have done. That's what she always did.

There were so many things to deal with in the aftermath of her death, but much of it is relevant to the evolution of my relationship with my other sister, Suzanne. And then there is the big fat elephant in the living room, money. Ah, the will and money. You see, there was not a contingency plan for Mom to precede Dad in death. Dad was supposed to die first and everything would go to my mother. After that, she said she would respect his wishes, but in reality, it would have been up to her.

~~~

Chapter 2 - Enter Suzanne

I have to say that this trip to Europe was a huge leap of faith for Suzanne and me. Because although we consider ourselves sisters today, it took a long while for us to get where we are. We had only met each other once more than a decade prior to my Mom's death.

You might want to get that notepad out again while I explain this a little further. I am the youngest of five siblings, two girls and three boys. We are all the biological children of my Mother and Larry (the guy that left us in Seattle). When I was thirteen, Mom married the man that I call Dad.

Dad's first wife died of cancer when he was in his early thirties. In those days, cancer detection was in the dark ages and almost always a death sentence without the possibility of parole. I didn't really understand that part of his life until I found records that indicated he'd only been home from a trip to sea for twelve days when Dorothy died in 1952. After that, I could see why he'd sought his own escape from grief. He found that solace in his life at sea.

As a teenager, I used to harass Dad about all of the girlfriends he'd had during his life as a dashing Merchant Marine. (Of course, that was before he met and fell in love with my mom.) Surely he must have a child out there? He said that he didn't think so then made a remark as a sort of side note: "But there was this one time."

The "one time" turned out to be Suzanne. Long before she re-entered his life, Dad adopted me.

Needless to say, I wasn't that shocked the day Dad called me in 1992 to say, "Michelle, you have a sister and she's only a year younger than you are." I had a lot of questions, but he was pretty tight-lipped about it and only gave me the basic details.

Years before, he had a tumultuous affair with a married woman and she had gotten pregnant. Her husband's name was listed on the baby's birth certificate even though the baby wasn't his. At some point, she sent Dad a letter denouncing him as the father and, after consulting an attorney Dad had no further contact with the woman or the child. He just went back to sea and resumed his life as though nothing had happened.

Ultimately, it was Suzanne who found him.

Flash forward with me to Mom's death. Like a bank robber, suspicion was lurking in everyone's minds, waiving a loaded gun around the room. It was a whispered secret, a rumor spread at family gatherings, that Suzanne had been out to loot my parents. They lived a frugal life and weren't millionaires, but they had some money squirreled away.

Please don't be hasty in drawing a conclusion yet because Suzanne must have had her own suspicions. Who wouldn't? After Dad died, Mom could have changed the will and left her out in the cold, right? And a word about my father: he was a genuinely loving guy, but he could lead you around with the promised green carrot until your legs fell out from under you. Unless you told him to stuff it and keep his damn money like I had. I lost track of how many times he changed his will and frankly, I didn't care anymore.

Suzanne hadn't had the years to get wise to Dad's game, but she'd had enough time to build up a little resentment.

I'm sure he never meant it to sound like it did, but he sometimes joked about how he'd gotten the best parts of fatherhood: "No diapers, and no child support." Funny, huh? Not so much, if you're the kid on the non-receiving end. I know because I was one of the non-receiving biological children of Larry.

A woman who had seemingly documented and planned everything, our mother departed this earth without planning her own funeral. Not a note, not a plot, nothing. Not even a hint as to what she wanted. We found boxes of bank statement from the sixties and all of our grade school report cards, but not a word about her final wishes.

As gently as possible, we asked Dad if he knew what she wanted. But he'd descended into the murky quagmire of grief and was almost oblivious to what was happening around him. He sat on the couch, unable to eat. Patty and I had no choice but to wing it. Dad was leaving it up to us. All he could say was, "Whatever you girls want is fine with me, Honey."

Suzanne came for the funeral and to spend some time with Dad. Suspicion came along as a stow-away, hiding in her luggage, begging the questions: how could we, the stepchildren, have Dad's best interests in mind? What was our motive? What were we after?

On the day she arrived, tension crackled in the air with those unspoken questions while a never-ending stream of family that she'd rarely seen before visited Dad. All were eager to help with whatever they could. But there was no greed hidden in anyone's motivation, only concern. It didn't take long for Suzanne to see that.

I think it was on the second day of her visit when the iceberg between us began to thaw. Patty and I embarked on the dreadful journey through coffins and cemetery plots while Suzanne sat with Dad. During those days, the whole family took turns finding things that would bring him a little pleasure. One of us would run out for crab cakes and fried shrimp. Another would pick up his favorite wine. Suzanne dug through Dad's old photographs, coaxing out stories of happier times. I tackled the obituary and what to dress Mom in for her burial. As the executer, Patty dealt with all of the other issues.

Once, when Suzanne was helping me find pictures for Mom's remembrance collage, she stumbled across a racy one of Mom lying in bed, clearly disrobed beneath the covers with a satisfied smile on her face. Suzanne thought it was sweet and suggested we use that picture.

"Oh my God, no! Mom would roll over in her grave," I gasped.

She and I laughed, agreeing to hide the photo. That may have been the last patch of ice between. Suspicion went away to his dark little corner; leaving our new friend, trust, in his place.

Dressed in full Scottish regalia, Mom was laid to rest that May morning in 2007. The inspiration struck me one day when I was rummaging through her endless wardrobe. There was no other item of clothing that she was more proud of than her Clan Lindsay kilt. (Just as she did with everything else about Dad, Mom embraced the Scottish tradition when she married him. My parents had even been clan representatives at all of the regional highland festivals.) In burgundy and green plaid, the finely woven wool draped her from waist to ankle. Dad donned his kilt, too. Wearing his knee high socks, his dirk, and his sporran, the only thing missing was the bagpipes. In honor of our family, everyone wore a piece of tartan that day. At the last minute, my sister-in-law took care of the bagpipes with a C.D. I can't recall the exact tune, but I'm pretty sure that it's playing in your head right now.

My dear Angelo doesn't have the foggiest idea of what he's gotten himself into. Once I finish this story in English, I'll be translating it into Italian so that he can better understand my life. Shortly after I joined him in Calabria, Angelo divulged his family history to me. He told me that he is the only child of peasants – at least, that's how the word translated. He thought that revelation would be a deal-breaker for me. In a disbelieving tone, I asked him if he understood what America was like. Many of us are the descendants of peasants and proud of it. In America, we plate our bootstraps in gold then hang them on the wall, trophies for the world to admire. (Viva America – when life hands you lemons, make lemon meringue pie!) It has taken me a long time to grasp the Italian culture and the importance of a deep family history. I've yet to adequately explain America to him. Maybe this will give him a glimpse.

Four days after my Mom's funeral, my grandmother, the ninety-four year-old matriarch died too. When my Aunt called to tell me the news, it didn't even register on my grief Richter scale. I think I was numb or perhaps sorrow had become the whale and I was Jonah, trapped in the belly of the beast.

Even with a live-in aide, taking care of Dad was a second full-time job, so I put college on the back burner and dropped out of school again.

Beyond that, there were the mountains of stuff to sort through. By mountains, I mean all of those bank statements, report cards, family records, and every other thing my lovely mother had rat-holed for the past half of a century. To complicate matters, my parents had downsized to a smaller home a couple of years earlier. All Mom had managed to do in the time since was cram the contents of her six-bedroom house into the garage of a home half the size. Out of sight, out of mind, right?

With Dad, there was a tightrope to walk when it came to Mom's things. I didn't want him to feel like anyone was attempting to erase her memory any more than I wanted him to feel violated by a gang of people rummaging through his life like a mad horde at a foreclosure sale. So I left all of Mom's clothes in her closet, her makeup in the bathroom, her books on the shelves as though she hadn't gone. Every once in a while, the scent of her perfume would waft from the bedroom. I knew that Dad was spraying it just to feel like she was still there.

The grim statistics told us that our days with him were numbered. I have to tell you, making the decision to move Dad into a nursing home seemed like admitting defeat. Or worse yet - handing him his own death sentence. For a blind man of his age, there is no such thing as "assisted living." No matter what rosy name we put on it, a nursing home was the last place that he wanted to be. For a while, he'd ask, "When is the doctor going to let me out of this place?"

We'd lie and tell him, "Oh, as soon as you're better."

We got pretty creative in our attempts to make what remained of his life a little more pleasant. The doctor even gave us a prescription so Dad could medicate himself with a small glass of Kahlua in the evenings.

As I'm sure many have experienced, there were unexpected funny times too. A few weeks into Dad's stay at the nursing home, Patty called. "Michelle," she said with another patient sigh, "I feel like I've just been called into the principal's office."

"Why, what happened?" I asked.

"Well, the director of the care center just called me. And you know how Dad likes to sleep in the nude?" That may seem like more than you should know, but he was a ladies man to the very end. Both of us thought that as long as it didn't offend anyone, he could do what he wanted. For God's sake, he was almost ninety!

"Yeah." I waited for the other shoe to drop.

"Well, it seems that Dad got up in the middle of the night to go to the bathroom. When he came out, he got into bed with his roommate and slapped him on the butt. He must have thought that he was getting into bed with Mom." Patty was absolutely mortified.

I thought the whole incident was hilarious and couldn't control my own laughter. "Oh God, what happened next?"

"The guy knocked him out of bed and screamed for the nurse." I think my sister mustered a chuckle by then.

Other than a little bruise, Dad was ok. The next morning, he didn't remember anything that happened and the nursing staff had already moved him to another room. Patty and I thought we were probably lucky that the other guy's family didn't file a restraining order or sue us.

Eventually Dad realized he wasn't leaving that place. I knew that he'd given up when he asked me what day it was. From the look on his face, it seemed as though he was counting the months since Mom had died. That sudden cognizance was like watching someone wake from a long coma. At that very moment, he knew exactly how long he'd been there.

I called Suzanne and told her to come one last time. Dad's end of life orders left nothing to chance. No IVs, no feeding tubes, no extraordinary measures were to be taken. Period. A bright green sheet of paper stating, "DNR – Do Not Resuscitate" was tacked to the wall in his room.

On the last day of his journey, all of us said our goodbyes. A shell of his former self, he lay crumpled under his favorite fleece blanket. I stayed by his side and was the last one in his room that night when the nurse gave him a drop of morphine to ease the pain of starvation. His breathing barely perceptible, I kissed him and held him before I left.

Around five o'clock the next morning, Dad passed away. It was six months to the day after his beloved Patricia Belle.

We had a party for Dad instead of a funeral. This time we didn't ask anyone if we could serve wine. With her "rules are meant to be broken" rationale, Suzanne said, "What are they going to do - kick us out of the cemetery?" So we bought a dozen bottles of his favorite Gewürztraminer and lined them up on a tartan-covered table near his grave. Everyone made a toast to Mom and Dad that frosty November day.

"He always said as long as he could pronounce 'Gewürztraminer,' he could still have another," Suzanne reminded us, laughing through her tears.

The evening after we buried Dad, the entire clan gathered at my parents' favorite restaurant. Suzanne's family joined us, including the brothers and sisters who I'd never met until then. There were so many people at the restaurant that night that the din from our party nearly got us evicted from the place. It was a rowdy goodbye and the closing to an enormous chapter in my life.

Now it may be more understandable as to why escape was the word burning in my brain as I kicked my carry-on bag through ticketing on my way to Italy.

~~~

The rest of the story is available from Amazon.com and other retail outlets.

46324783R00250

Made in the USA
Middletown, DE
26 May 2019